W9-AVT-427

CRITICAL INSIGHTS

Thomas Jefferson

CRITICAL

INSIGHTS

Thomas Jefferson

Editor
Robert C. Evans
Auburn University at Montgomery

SALEM PRESS
A Division of EBSCO Information Services, Inc.
Ipswich, Massachusetts

GREY HOUSE PUBLISHING

SWOSU-Sayre / McMahan Library

Cover photo: Lithograph after the 1805 portrait by Rembrandt Peale. (Photo by Universal History Archive/Getty Images).

Copyright © 2020 by Grey House Publishing, Inc.

Critical Insights: Thomas Jefferson, published by Grey House Publishing, Inc., Amenia, NY, under exclusive license from EBSCO Information Services, Inc.

All rights reserved. No part of this work may be used or reproduced in any manner whatsoever or transmitted in any form or by any means, electronic or mechanical, including photocopy, recording, or any information storage and retrieval system, without written permission from the copyright owner. For information, contact Grey House Publishing/Salem Press, 4919 Route 22, PO Box 56, Amenia, NY 12501.

∞ The paper used in these volumes conforms to the American National Standard for Permanence of Paper for Printed Library Materials, Z39.48 1992 (R2009).

Publisher's Cataloging-In-Publication Data
(Prepared by The Donohue Group, Inc.)

Names: Evans, Robert C., 1955- editor.
Title: Thomas Jefferson / editor, Robert C. Evans, Auburn University at
        Montgomery.
Other Titles: Critical insights.
Description: [First edition]. | Ipswich, Massachusetts : Salem Press, a division
        of EBSCO Information Services, Inc. ; Amenia, NY : Grey
        House Publishing, [2020] | Includes bibliographical references
        and index.
Identifiers: ISBN 9781642653755 (hardcover)
Subjects: LCSH: Jefferson, Thomas, 1743-1826--Criticism and interpretation.
        | Jefferson, Thomas, 1743-1826--In literature. | Jefferson, Thomas,
        1743-1826--In motion pictures. | American literature--18th
        century--History and criticism. | American literature--19th century--
        History and criticism. | Presidents in literature. | Presidents in
        motion pictures.
Classification: LCC E332.2 .T41 2020 | DDC 973.46092--dc23

First Printing

PRINTED IN THE UNITED STATES OF AMERICA

Contents

Critical Contexts

Critical Readings

Resources

About This Volume

Robert C. Evans

This volume, like all the others in the Critical Insights series, is divided into several major sections. It begins with an introductory essay by a prominent scholar and then offers a brief biography of the volume's subject— in this case Thomas Jefferson. The "Critical Contexts" section includes four essays, each with a different focus. The first offers an historical perspective; the next explores relevant scholarship; the third adopts a particular "critical lens"; and the fourth takes a comparative approach. The "Critical Contexts" section is then followed by a series of deliberately diverse "Critical Readings." Finally, the volume concludes with a "Resources" section that offers a chronology of Jefferson's life, a list of works by him, and another list of works *about* him. These listings are followed by brief biographies of the editor and the contributors and by a comprehensive index.

The book begins with a lengthy and wide-ranging essay by John Ragosta, a leading Jefferson scholar. Ragosta examines the complex and sometimes controversial legacy of Jefferson, especially in recent years. Among the many issues he explores, Ragosta suggests that perhaps "we should embrace Jefferson's admonition that in a struggle between power and liberty, when in doubt, we should side with liberty. But," he continues, "one might well ask what are the limits to individual liberty in a modern society— a question and concern that are not evident in many of the popular Jefferson quotes about individual liberty and political violence." This is true "both because he could not begin to see our interdependent society and because he lived in a world that was truly challenged by fundamental economic, educational, political, and religious tyrannies." Ragosta's probing essay is then followed by a brief biography of Jefferson prepared by the volume's editor.

Critical Contexts

The four essays in the Critical Contexts section begin with a historical piece by Daniel Roeber that narrates "particular occurrences in which the Capitol . . . was used for religious services" and that considers "the rationale behind such events." He argues that "these events show that policies of religious liberty in the Constitution represented a response to a history of religious oppression and dissension in Europe, as well as an attempt to find unity amidst the colonies' diverse religious perspectives." He particularly comments on Jefferson's involvement in such services and suggests that while "a sense of the religiosity (and the cultural and political power of an assumed pan-Protestant identity) of the nation can be ascertained from these events, the services speak more to a civil religion that was a foundational part of the country's emerging national identity." He contends that the "civil religion manifest in the frequency and variety of religious services at the Capitol reinforced the republican ideal of government by broadcasting respect for different opinions and by educating attendees in the variety of theological views espoused by American citizens. These services," he concludes "provided a forum celebrating American religious freedom as a contribution to good government."

Brandon Schneeberger's essay on "Jefferson as Reader and Writer" opens by suggesting that in addition to his many accomplishments as a statesman, Jefferson "was also a very well-read man who once said that he could not live without books." Schneeberger notes that one "especially valuable book about Jefferson as a reader and writer remains Eleanor D. Berman's 1947 monograph entitled *Thomas Jefferson among the Arts: An Essay in Early American Esthetics*." Berman, he observes, "was less interested in Jefferson's reading of works in political philosophy or practical statesmanship than in his reading of works about matters he himself classified as the 'Fine Arts,' including painting, sculpture, architecture, gardening, music, rhetoric, and literature." Schneeberger argues that "Berman's interest in [Jefferson's] responses to these last two topics– rhetoric and literature—are especially intriguing and, in fact, his interest in both of these matters is also the central focus" of Schneeberger's own essay.

The next essay, by Nicolas Tredell, offers a particular "critical lens" on Jefferson. Specifically, Tredell seeks "to perform the task of the literary critic and analyze [Jefferson's] words—though this does not exclude ethical observations especially as, in Jefferson's case, words sometimes spoke louder than action, or were, more precisely, a form of action." Tredell focuses especially "on a selection of Jefferson's words that arguably acted to shape national identity, drawing on the Declaration of Independence (4 July 1776), the one complete book he published in his lifetime, *Notes on the State of Virginia* (1785), and his late unfinished *Autobiography* (begun 1821)."

Finally, the last of the critical context essays, by Robert Evans, examines the similarities between Jefferson's own writing (especially in the Declaration of Independence) and the ideas of Lord Kames, a thinker Jefferson deeply admired. Kames was not only a philosopher and political thinker but also a theorist about rhetoric, or good writing. Evans explores the relevance of Kames's very detailed ideas about writing to the kind of writing Jefferson himself did in the Declaration. Kames, Evans shows, particularly recommended writing that was clear, vivid, varied, logical, and well organized in every way and at every level, from the phrase to the sentence to the paragraph and then to the entire piece. But clarity, above all, was Kames's key interest.

Critical Readings: I

The first essay in the Critical Readings section is actually an interview with Dr. John B. Boles of Rice University, author of an important new biography of Jefferson. Boles's interview provides an exceptionally fine introduction to the essays that follows because he deals with many of the same issues those essays raise, including the vexed issue of Jefferson and slavery. Boles notes, for instance, that "Jefferson had plenty of evidence that achieving emancipation through legislation would be difficult, if not impossible. Every attempt he made failed." In fact, "just as he returned from his ambassadorship to France and became secretary of state, a huge controversy broke out in the Congress over two petitions to free slaves. Congressmen from South Carolina and Georgia," Boles reports, "went practically berserk in their opposition, threatening to destroy the union. This frightened every single Congressman, all of whom believed the union was a fragile experiment and likely to fail. At the same time," he continues, "most of them—Jefferson included—believed that slavery was an outmoded institution and was near extinction. They didn't know the exact process by which this was to happen, but it was commonly believed that slavery was a dying institution. Believing this," they wondered, "why risk destroying the union to attack an institution already on the way out? Of course," Boles concludes, "they were wrong; the union was strong (until finally disrupted by the slavery issue in 1861), and the invention of the cotton gin and the rise of cotton invigorated slavery after the early 1790s. But the Founders did not foresee these events."

In an essay on "Jefferson and the Long Eighteenth Century," Nicolas Tredell focuses "especially on [Jefferson's] relationship to eighteenth-century culture and literature and to the harbingers in that literature of the Romanticism that began to emerge near the end of the nineteenth century." Jefferson, he notes, "played a central role as the key drafter of the Declaration of Independence and as an active politician who would eventually hold the highest office in the United States." Thus, it is important to "consider how eighteenth-century ideas of reason, justice, equality, and interest permeated his cultural and political attitudes."

Robert Evans, in an essay on "Jefferson the Dramatist," argues that his famous "Dialogue between the Head and the Heart" really "deserves to be included in the standard anthologies of early American literature," from which it is now absent. Evans contends that "this text strongly displays Jefferson's sense of humor, his talent for re-creating credible speech, and his shrewd psychological insight. As a piece of writing," he asserts, "the 'Dialogue' is variously fascinating, especially in its complexities and ambiguities and in the complicated responses it can elicit from readers. It is," he concludes, "definitely one of Jefferson's most compelling texts and reveals his personality in many intriguing ways." However, Evans's main purpose is "to highlight the *literary* features of the 'Dialogue,' which can be considered one of the best examples of early American drama." His essay reprints the entire Dialogue with a numbered text.

In another essay on Jefferson as a writer, Kevin J. Hayes, a major scholar of American literature, explores "Jefferson's Proverbial Language." Examining some of Jefferson's letters to friends and family, Hayes suggests that to "entertain correspondents was one reason [he] used proverbs and proverbial phrases." He used them also to "endear himself to his readers, to experiment with the English language, to emphasize a point, to simplify complex ideas, to give new ideas a feeling of familiarity: all these reasons and more," Hayes contends, "account for Jefferson's use of proverbs. Oftentimes, he was not content to repeat proverbs in their orally circulated versions. Instead, he would alter traditional expressions to give them an aura of originality." Hayes suggests that this "dual impulse—to combine the traditional and the original—marks Jefferson's finest use of proverbs and proverbial phrases."

Steven D. Ealy, an expert on the writings of Robert Penn Warren, next examines Jefferson as seen through Warren's eyes, particularly in Warren's work *Brother to Dragons*, which exists in several different versions. Ealy suggests that in the period preceding the first publication of Warren's text, "the American image of Jefferson tended to be triumphant: Jefferson as the defender of enlightenment and prophet of the ultimate victory of man's unconquerable reason. No one before Warren," he continues "had characterized Jefferson as a slave of history rather than its master, a man of sorrow rather than of triumph, a critic of human nature rather than an advocate of man's perfectibility." But Ealy also argues that "Warren's initial poetic engagement with Jefferson in *Brother to Dragons: A Tale in Verse and Voices*, published in 1953, did not exhaust Warren's interest in and reflection on Jefferson. In 1976," Ealy notes, Warren "published a stage version of the poem and, in 1979, he issued a new version of the poem that was shorter and substantially rewritten." By comparing these different versions of Warren's text, Ealy shows that "Warren's understanding of Jefferson changed the longer he studied him."

Critical Readings: II

Also concerned with Jefferson's impact on later writers is an essay by Robert Evans, who suggests that "of all the 'founding fathers' of the United States, Thomas Jefferson was, for a long time, the most inspiring. Now he is without doubt the most controversial," partly because his lofty ideals have seemed to conflict with his disappointing practice as a slave-owner who failed to free his slaves. "Both aspects of Jefferson's reputation and legacy," Evans continues, "are reflected in a recent volume of poetry edited by Lisa Russ Spaar entitled *Monticello in Mind: Fifty Contemporary Poems on Jefferson.*" Evans surveys "some of the texts included in Spaar's collection and discusses them, for the most part, not so much as pieces of political rhetoric but as works of art. (In fact, the better they are as art, the more effective they are as rhetoric.)" The second half of his essay explores, in detail, a long poem titled "The Hand of Thomas Jefferson," by the distinguished poet Mary Jo Salter. Salter's work," he argues, "is one of the most important poetic texts Jefferson has ever inspired, at least in recent times."

Jefferson, however, has inspired not only recent writers but also recent filmmakers. One of these is Ken Burns. According to Kyla Free, "Burns had long wanted to make a film about Jefferson but has said he is glad other projects intervened. By the time he did get around to Jefferson," in 1997, "he had become the unrivalled American master of directing documentary films. He brought to the Jefferson undertaking close to twenty years of experience and expertise." Free reports that like "most of Burns's documentaries, his film on Jefferson received extremely positive reviews. Wholly negative reactions were almost non-existent," she observes, "and although the film did elicit a few mixed responses, most assessments were glowing." This documentary, she notes, "remains readily available on DVD and is probably the one film that most teachers of Jefferson use most often and that most non-professionals interested in Jefferson are most likely to view." Free's essay surveys early reviews of the film to discuss how and why the film was initially received.

Also concerned with Jefferson and film is an essay by Suzanne Strength on a 2000 television miniseries entitled *Sally Hemings: An American Scandal*. Hemings, of course, was the young slave with whom Jefferson was almost certainly sexually involved for many years. Strength shows that the CBS television program, "which starred Sam Neill as Jefferson and Carmen Ejogo as Hemings, provoked varied and widespread reactions. It was," she notes, "one of the top ten programs that week in the television ratings, and it received some positive, some mixed, and some very negative reviews from various critics." Interestingly, it "attracted mostly positive reactions from Jefferson's African American descendants, who were glad that the story they had known about for more than two centuries had now become very public knowledge." But some "other African Americans . . . were disgusted by the series." Strength reports that the "idea for the miniseries had come from Tina Andrews, a black actress and screenwriter who had written the script and worked for years to get the program made." The series won not only high ratings but also many awards and even resulted in a book written by Andrews that contained the script. Strength writes that her main purposes are "to survey Andrews's explanations of why she conceived the Jefferson-Hemings relationship as she did; to report reactions to the film (negative, mixed, and positive) by various critics; and, finally, to report how the film was received in the African American community, some of whom loved it, and some of whom despised it."

Finally, in an interview that nicely complements the earlier interview with John Boles, the prominent German Jefferson scholar Hannah Spahn offers "A View from Abroad." In comments that are both probing and often funny, Spahn discusses why and how she first became interested in Jefferson and how American writings about Jefferson look to someone who comes from a different national and scholarly tradition. Spahn writes that what first drew her to the field of American history and has fascinated her ever since "is the complex sense of continuity with the past that characterizes so many popular and scholarly approaches to American history and that I found to be particularly striking in the context of the founding period." Americans tend to treat the founders in general, and Jefferson in particular, as if they are still living beings whose imagined opinions on contemporary issues matter very much. Jefferson, especially, has become a much-debated figure who often inspires intense feelings, both pro and con, in many living Americans, including many academicians. To many people, he seems not so much a long-dead person from the past but a man who is, in many ways, still very much alive.

Resources

As has already been indicated, the Critical Readings section of the book is followed by a section devoted to additional "Resources," including a chronology of Jefferson's life, a listing of some of his most important written works, a bibliography of secondary scholarship (focused especially on Jefferson as writer), a biography of the volume's editor, and biographies of its various contributors.

Thomas Jefferson: Icon_____

John A. Ragosta[1]

A little more than twenty years ago, Conor Cruise O'Brien suggested that Thomas Jefferson should be struck from the Pantheon of American heroes because of his radicalism and racism. Today, student activists have renewed O'Brien's call.

Should O'Brien and Jefferson's critics be taken more seriously?

When I first attended the University of Virginia a number of years ago, I was warned that in Charlottesville people still talk about Thomas Jefferson, the town's most famous resident, as if he is in the next room—and there is some truth to that claim. In the University's hometown, Jefferson is invoked regularly as an authority on virtually any topic, and as if an observer of everyday life. And it is a bit odd.

This strange Charlottesville custom, though, simply amplifies a national tendency. Americans have a fetish for their Founding Fathers, with the Founders' images and advice (and even scores of spurious "quotations" attributed to them) finding their way into social media, commercial advertising, popular fiction, pop culture, and policy debates. And in our fixation on the Founders, Jefferson leads the pack. Jefferson reportedly appears more often in quotations and references on the Internet than any other of the Founders, and a quick search makes that easily believable. Almost 500,000 visitors a year find their way up the narrow, winding road in west central Virginia to Monticello, Jefferson's study in architecture, with Poplar Forest, his out-of-the-way second home in Virginia's southern Bedford County, logging tens of thousands of additional visits. More to the point, Jefferson is frequently quoted in modern political debates, by both Republicans and Democrats, and relied upon to advance positions, right and left.

Even when he was alive, and in the years shortly after his death, his legacy became almost synonymous with the American spirit.

After he retired from eight years as president, a period in which he had dominated the national scene, for 24 of the next 28 years avowed "Jeffersonians" occupied the Oval Office, a feat unparalleled in American history. A leading nineteenth century historian confidently declared that "If Jefferson was wrong, America is wrong. If America is right, Jefferson was right." (Parton iii.) Almost one hundred years later another biographer explained that "Without a close study of the man, . . . no proper understanding of America as it was and as it is today can be arrived at." (Schachner viii.) Release of a new biography of Jefferson has become an almost annual event. His image is on our coins and on our bills, and he is the penman of some of the most famous and important words in the English language. One modern historian noted simply that the Declaration of Independence, his most noted achievement, "invent[ed] America." (Wills.) Another, more wryly, concluded that "The virtual deification of Jefferson is ingrained in the public mind, sustained by popular biographers and scholars, supported by the mass media, and bolstered by recent presidents: William Jefferson Clinton, a Democrat, began the trek to his inauguration at Monticello; Ronald Reagan, a Republican, urged us to 'pluck a flower from Thomas Jefferson's life and wear it in our soul forever.'" (Finkelman 139.) Jefferson's admonition during his first inaugural address that "We are all republicans: we are all federalists," might well be modified to "we are all Jeffersonians."

Although pop culture has found a new Founder to embrace in the Broadway rap musical *Hamilton*—a paean to a devoted political opponent of Jefferson, there has been little noticeable impact on the continued popularity of the sage of Monticello or his centrality to the modern, popular understanding of America's Founders or America's Founding. No one is willing to stand against a Jeffersonian democracy, and few would openly challenge his vision. Jefferson's iconic status stands on a very broad and seemingly firm foundation.

With his presence so ubiquitous, we all, from across the political spectrum and across the nation, seem to feel somehow that we really know Jefferson. George Washington is impressive, but unapproachable. John Adams and Alexander Hamilton are brilliant and determined, but we do not sense a fraternal warmth in them.

James Madison, perhaps unfairly, seems too bookish. Patrick Henry, largely due to Jefferson's efforts to undermine the historic memory of a man whom he saw as a political traitor, is remembered as a two-dimensional character making inflammatory speeches. Not so Jefferson. Peter Onuf, America's preeminent Jefferson scholar, writes that Americans "think they know Jefferson because Jefferson—in visionary moments—seems to know them" (*The Mind* 1). Fifty years ago, *Life Magazine* spoke for our times in concluding that "Probably no great American of the past still seems so thoroughly alive" (qtd in Peterson 379). Having written so much on so many subjects—with over 19,000 of his letters being catalogued and edited and increasingly available free online—Jefferson's powerful mind and prolific pen seem to speak to each of us today, and he does so on virtually any topic. Jon Meacham was drawn into his orbit, saying that Jefferson "charms us" ("Leadership"). There is a historic intimacy with Jefferson. So that when we attempt to analyze and understand him, perhaps even to critique, we seem to be talking about an old friend. This, though, is a friendship worth exploring more carefully.

If we want to understand Jefferson and his hold on the American mind, there is no better place to start than his tombstone, which stands in a shady spot—chosen by Jefferson—in finely fenced grounds just down the hill from his beloved Monticello, his mountaintop home.

In papers found upon Jefferson's death were instructions for a marker or memorial if one was to be placed upon his grave. Unwilling to leave his own historic memory to chance, the sage of Monticello said that any memorial erected to his memory should read "Here was buried Thomas Jefferson, author of the Declaration of American Independence, of the statute of Virginia for religious freedom, and Father of the University of Virginia," and "not a word more." And, to his family, no less than his political supporters, his desire was as good as a command, and should you visit Charlottesville, take the road to his mountain aerie, and have the opportunity to venture down the hill from Monticello to see his grave site, you will see a monument so emblazoned. (See Jefferson, "Undated.") (You will actually be seeing the second monument at this location: The first was chipped away by rabid souvenir hunters in the nineteenth century, Americans who also thought that they somehow owned the iconic Jefferson and treasured a small broken piece of rock that seemed to connect them to the icon. That damaged grave marker is now on display at the University of Missouri [on land that was part of Jefferson's Louisiana Purchase].)

The stone memorial stands silent and dignified in a beautiful setting, but it is the message engraved on the black obelisk to which it owes its fame. Of course, there are two striking things about this epitaph: what it says, and what it does not say. The latter is often remarked upon. It does not mention that Jefferson was president, vice president, secretary of state, governor, member of Congress, ambassador, state representative—things that most of us would mention on a grave marker. It says nothing about the fact that he was a beloved husband, devoted father and son, doting grandfather for a bevy of children. It could say that he was a scientist, inventor, horticulturalist, meteorologist, architect, paleontologist, ethnographer . . . each important to Jefferson in its own way.

Instead, the list of accomplishments for which he wished to be remembered is pointedly clipped. Jefferson very intentionally focused the physical marker of his legacy upon political freedom, religious freedom, and educational opportunity. Why? Why was it more important for Jefferson to promote the memory of his involvement with those things rather than the scores of years devoted to government and community service or his deep devotion to his family or to science? What does this say about Jefferson and the legitimacy of our national fixation on the icon from Monticello?

At the most basic level, Jefferson wanted to be remembered for the battles that he fought and won for liberty in these inter-related areas: political freedom, religious freedom, and public education. Rather than a mere recording of former titles and offices, these accomplishments were forward-looking; they bespoke the hope of progress. It was these public "monuments" to liberty that framed both Jefferson's self-image and his popular image and legacy, and that led *Britannica* to describe Jefferson as "Long regarded as America's most distinguished 'apostle of liberty,'" a term used by commentators for two centuries, from Edgar Allen Poe to Jefferson's modern biographers, Dumas Malone and Joseph Ellis. Then and now, the nation seems to agree (see "Thomas Jefferson").

Jefferson and American Liberalism

This focus by Jefferson and the apostle's acolytes on the rights of the individual is liberalism, "tending towards individual freedom, democracy, or social equality . . . ," as the *Oxford English Dictionary* defines the term. The nation that Jefferson sought to build, the "liberal" nation that he wished to associate with his memory, was at heart built upon a vision of a free America, and free Americans, standing on a broad and firm foundation of political and religious liberty and educational opportunity. The very essence of Jefferson's vision for the new country was that Americans were to be unleashed from an old world that was based on hierarchy, aristocracy, repression, and tyranny.

Jefferson's seemingly unbounded belief in liberty speaks to what supporters (and sometimes detractors) see as American exceptionalism. This is a land of unlimited opportunity, each man his own king. In America, each person can make her/his own way. If things are not to your liking, "Go West!" and start anew. Apparently limitless open spaces fed this perspective in the early republic. Jefferson veritably crowed in his first inaugural address that America had land "for our descendants to the thousandth and thousandth generation." Americans—Jefferson's yeoman farmers—had the ability to have their own home, own land, . . . own small "empire of liberty" to do as they wanted, to pursue individual happiness seemingly without restraint. These characteristics and the progress of a young America were understood to stand in sharp contradistinction to the corruption and corrupting influences of European monarchies. Even freedom in Europe, where it survived, was more constrained, more hedged by government and the community.

The people who chose to emigrate here were adventurers, independent-minded, risk-takers, those willing to throw off their old life and try for a new life, free from the constraints of government, and church, and the old-world culture and society. The noted Harvard historian Bernard Bailyn explained this selective migration in the context of New England Puritans by noting that those who came "were not gentle souls. The timid, the unsure, . . . Those who left [Europe] were tougher, more defiant, more self-assured, more self-absorbed" (Bailyn 187). The same could be said of tens of thousands, millions of others who came to our shores. Focused on individual political and religious liberty and educational opportunity, freedom from restraint was the cry.

Jefferson spoke this philosophy of seemingly unbounded individual liberty as well as any. In the context of religious freedom, for example, he said "it does me no injury for my neighbour to say there are twenty gods, or no god. It neither picks my pocket nor breaks my leg" (*Notes* 265). As was often the case, Jefferson's turn of phrase was used to project a broader truth. We used to say colloquially that in the United States, a free country, I am free to do whatever I want with my freedom only stopping at my neighbor's nose. Jefferson said the same thing more poetically: "No man has a natural right to commit aggression on the equal rights of another; and this is *all* from which the laws ought to restrain him." (Jefferson, *Papers* [Retirement Series] 10:154 (emphasis added).) This was American liberty.

Jefferson's consuming focus on liberty had serious consequences for the relationship of government and the citizen. Among other things, it meant keeping government as small as reasonably possible, and as close to the people as possible (encouraging a strong states' rights doctrine). Similarly, his Statute for Establishing Religious Freedom, adopted by Virginia in 1786 and serving as an archetype for the First Amendment several years later, broke the time-honored chains between church and state—"kings, nobles, and priests" Jefferson would say—so that people could make religious decisions for themselves (Jefferson, *Papers . . . Digital* 10:245). He battled Alexander Hamilton's vision of a large government intertwined with business and financial interests because he feared the tyranny of a moneyed interest, a newly minted aristocracy, effectively controlling the people through cooperation with government. The statement that "That government is best which governs least," although a spurious

Jefferson quote (there is no record that he said it [see Jefferson, [Spurious Quotations]), certainly speaks for the apostle of liberty.

His passion for liberty was expansive, seemingly almost unlimited. As the Declaration made clear, if a government interfered with individual liberty ("life, liberty and the pursuit of happiness"), there was a right, nay, a "duty," of rebellion. Tellingly, Jefferson's original draft of the Declaration insisted that "all men are created equal & independent." But Jefferson went much further.

When farmers in western Massachusetts broke out in Shays' Rebellion in 1786, George Washington, James Madison, Alexander Hamilton, Henry Knox, and others openly worried about the future of the country. Americans had taken up arms against their own elective government, closing the courts and threatening mayhem. Washington was "mortified beyond expression" and demanded a firm response to the insurgents, or "anarchy & confusion must prevail" (Washington, *Papers* 4:297; 5:8). Even the revolutionary firebrand Samuel Adams was no less emphatic: "In monarchies the crime of treason or rebellion may admit of being pardoned, or lightly punished; but the man who dares to rebel against the laws of a republic ought to suffer death" (qtd in Lepore 22). A militia was called out, and a set battle was fought at the Springfield Armory—Americans v. Americans—with four insurgents killed and twenty wounded. Had the militia arrived a few hours later, the insurgents might have met them well-armed and determined. America's leading politicians feared the worst.

Not Jefferson.

When Jefferson, serving happily in Paris as ambassador, heard about the conflict and the deep concern of the other Founders, he dismissed their concerns as political hand-wringing. More than that, while he conceded that the insurgents had no cause for open rebellion, he seemed pleased that a free people had armed themselves and taken to the streets, proving that they were not fit subjects for a tyrannical government. "We have had 13. states independent 11. years. There has been one rebellion. That comes to one rebellion in a century and a half for each state. What country ever existed a century and a half without a rebellion?" Jefferson asks.

And what country can preserve it's [sic] liberties if their rulers are not warned from time to time that their people preserve the spirit of resistance? Let them take arms. . . . What signify a few lives lost in a century or two? The tree of liberty must be refreshed from time to time with the blood of patriots and tyrants. It is it's [sic] natural manure. (*Papers* 12:356).

To another correspondent he wrote "The spirit of resistance to government is so valuable on certain occasions, that I wish it to be always kept alive. It will often be exercised when wrong, but better so than not to be exercised at all. I like a little rebellion now and then" (*Papers* 11:174). Although the Shays' protestors certainly had grievances, Jefferson thought that they were fundamentally misguided on the central political issues, their acts "absolutely unjustifiable," he told Madison. Despite that, he hoped that their actions would "provoke no severities from their governments" (*Papers* 11:92). Jefferson's facile endorsement of blood for the tree of liberty was more focused on the value of rebellion-qua-rebellion in a country built on individual liberty.

Again in the 1790s, when "innocent blood" began to run in the streets of Paris, Jefferson reacted angrily to criticism of the French Revolution and of the growing mobs and lynchings. "It was necessary to use the arm of the people," our former ambassador mused, "a machine not quite so blind as balls and bombs, but blind to a certain degree." Casualties in the fight for liberty were inevitable, and necessary. "My own affections have been deeply wounded by some of the martyrs to the cause," he conceded, "but rather than it should have failed, I would have seen half the earth desolated. Were there but an Adam & Eve left in every country, & left free, it would be better than as it now is." Although this might seem to be mere poetic hyperbole, by the time that Jefferson wrote his Adam & Eve letter the mobs of Paris had already massacred more than a thousand (Jefferson, *Papers* 25:14).

When the Federalist Congress and President John Adams adopted the Alien & Sedition Acts—certainly deeply troubling legislation—Jefferson advocated firm opposition by the states in defense of liberty. He wrote the Kentucky Resolutions of 1798, his draft of which called for "nullification" of federal laws by states that unilaterally deemed federal action to be over-reaching. Other states were expressly urged to join in the opposition to federal power. Disunion seemed the inevitable result of Jefferson's actions; some leaders, including George Washington, Patrick Henry, and Alexander Hamilton, feared armed insurrection. A year or two later, when the election of 1800 hung in the balance in the Federalist-controlled House of Representatives because of the unexpected Electoral College tie between Jefferson and his running-mate, Aaron Burr, reports circulated, never quite disproven, that Virginia, led by its devout Jeffersonian governor, James Monroe, was beginning to amass arms and ammunition for possible action against the federal government. Jefferson warned Adams that there would likely be blood in the streets, "resistance by force & incalculable consequences," if Federalists interfered with Jefferson's elevation to the presidency (Jefferson, "Notes on Aaron Burr").

Individual liberty was the north star and the bellwether. Looking back, many conclude that nothing was more important for Jefferson.

Are you starting to feel a little uncomfortable?

You should be.

Liberty *Über Alles*, Jefferson, and Radicalism

Several decades later Jefferson's call for nullification became a battle cry for the Southern defense of slavery, a story that, while certainly relevant, need not be rehearsed here. In our own age, Jefferson's apparent fixation on individual freedom and the conflated states' rights, seemingly without restraint, has become a particularly popular motif and has been widely embraced by some of the most radical individuals and groups.

- Oklahoma City bomber Timothy McVeigh who killed 168 and injured 600 in an effort to foment rebellion against the federal government quoted Jefferson; his mugshot was taken in a t-shirt with the "blood for the tree of liberty" quote on the back.
- Clive Bundy and his armed supporters who blocked federal law enforcement from acting on a court order had a campsite that was marked by signs quoting Jefferson; one supporter—referring

blithely to killing federal law enforcement agents—posted this: "Thomas Jefferson wrote about this, stating that revolution is necessary to clean out the government. Should this situation escalate to violence, we might just see a housecleaning."

- White supremacists such as Hal Turner are fond of the "tree of liberty" quote. Jade Helm conspiracy zealots who insisted that the federal government, directed by President Obama, was invading Texas in 2015 to disarm the populace quoted Jefferson. Texas secessionists, including Debra Medina, warning of a coming "bloody war," rely on Jefferson. Historically, opponents of the civil rights movement threateningly referred to Jefferson's "tree of liberty."

- These views are not new. In 1948, an Alabama delegate to the Democratic Presidential Convention quoted "Jefferson's 'tree of liberty'. . ., menacingly, as he vowed that 'no southern jury would convict an employer for refusing to take a Negro into his white office force'" (Burstein, *Muse*, 129, quoting *Arkansas State P*, December 3, 1948).

- The so-called "Oath Keepers," private individuals who showed-up armed with semi-automatic rifles to "patrol" the streets of Ferguson, Missouri, after protests erupted over Michael Brown's shooting by the police, efforts that the St. Louis County Police Chief called "unnecessary and inflammatory," quote Jefferson's Kentucky Resolutions on their website. (They also use bogus quotes attributed to Jefferson about the right to keep and bear arms; see Larimer and Phillip.)

- The association of Jefferson with radical rebellion has spread internationally. Anders Breivik, who slaughtered 69 people at a youth camp in Norway in an effort to ignite an anti-Muslim race war and undermine feminism, embraced Jefferson's "tree of liberty" quote, featuring it in his lengthy rambling manifesto and repeating it in his opening statement at his trial.

- Jefferson has become the patron saint of private militias. As Conor Cruise O'Brien explained twenty years ago, his "tree of liberty" quote has become a "charter for the most militant segment of the modern American militias." Since then, the embrace of Jefferson by the radical right has only expanded (59).

In fairness, the embrace does not seem to be entirely misplaced. Jefferson's words strongly suggest a liberalism in which individual rights were to take precedent *über alles*. Jefferson seemed to be intoxicated by what Edmund Burke referred to as the "wild gas" of liberty, O'Brien suggests. Now Edmund Burke—one of the greatest British parliamentarians—was not opposed to liberty, but he had the temerity to suggest that individual liberty was not limited. When the French Revolution erupted, even before the French Terror set in, Burke expressed concern about the difference between liberty and licentiousness; he said that he would refrain from congratulating the French for their "spirit of liberty" until he knew how it maintained "morality and religion; with the solidity of property; with peace and order; with civil and social manner. All these (in their way) are good things too; and, without them, liberty is not a benefit whilst it lasts, and is not likely to continue long" (qtd by O'Brien 58). Burke might well have been speaking of Jefferson and modern Jeffersonians.

And I have not even begun to talk about Jefferson's fixation on personal liberty and states' rights and slavery, his racism, his long-running affair with one of his enslaved workers, and enslavement of his own flesh and blood.

One might ask whether radical groups have unfairly misinterpreted Jefferson, and there certainly is a lot of misquotation and simply fabrication of Jefferson quotes to go around. (The Thomas Jefferson Foundation, which owns Monticello, maintains a wonderful webpage on spurious Jefferson quotes; see Jefferson, [Spurious Quotations]). But in fairness to today's radicals, Jefferson was undoubtedly radical in his defense of individual freedom and states' rights. His "blood for the tree of liberty" and "Adam and Eve" letters, much less his Kentucky Resolution calling for states to nullify federal legislation, demonstrate that.

Certainly, I might conclude that many of these individuals and groups have wrongly identified the "patriots" and "tyrants" whose blood should water the tree of liberty, but that is the problem with radical liberty interpreted in a Jeffersonian voice: individuals seem empowered to make their own decisions and those decisions may differ fundamentally from those made by their neighbors.

Jefferson's language provides vigorous fuel for anarchy, for chaos, for hate. "[A]nyone . . . who is planning any act of mass destruction may invoke the sanction of [Jefferson] provided only that the act is deemed to be perpetrated in the holy cause of liberty," O'Brien warned (74). And liberty seems to be seen and defined in the eye of the beholder. The Apostle of Liberty, seconded by the unbridled spirit of free America, has been used to justify the radicalism of too many and continues to do so.

It is long past time to take Conor Cruise O'Brien's challenge, and the rising cries of modern critics, seriously. Does Jefferson go too far? Were his views too extreme? Should he be banished from the Pantheon of American heroes and leaders as a radical and racist? Is O'Brien correct in asserting that the "mystical side of Jefferson really belongs: among radical, violent, anti-federal libertarian fanatics" (71)? Are the students seeking to have Jefferson's statue removed from the University of Missouri and Hofstra University as a poor image for a liberal arts institution in a modern, multi-cultural society or the students engaged in a similar effort at Jefferson's alma mater, William & Mary, or his beloved University of Virginia right? Should we have listened more sympathetically when a group of students (and a few members of the faculty) asked the president of UVA to stop quoting Jefferson in public presentations? More importantly, we might ask, whatever his historic import, is Jefferson a fitting model for our time? Even setting aside his racism, is a single-minded mania for individual liberty or for states' rights formed in the eighteenth century relevant today? Is this what Vladimir Putin meant when he described western liberalism as "obsolete" (Blake)? "Liberal," after all, can also mean "unrestrained by prudence or decorum." Is the type of radicalism that has been wantonly and pervasively associated with Jefferson an unavoidable consequence of our fixation on the Founding Fathers and trying to apply their eighteenth-century wisdom, especially Jefferson's revolutionary vision of freedom, to complex twenty-first century problems? In venerating Jefferson, are we somehow complicit when his eighteenth-century radicalism encourages twenty-first century mayhem?

So, what to do with Jefferson?

Context Matters—A Lot

While the problems with Jefferson seem most immediate—perhaps in the same way that Jefferson seems the most immediate of the Founders—this is a problem, and a danger, that goes to the heart of our fixation on the Founders: Historians often remind us of the need to understand the context in which Jefferson and other Founders spoke, the context in which they developed and understood and applied principles of liberty upon a foundation of political, religious, and educational freedom. It is an admonition, however, that may be honored in the breach. But this is not merely an academic's lament. It holds the key to whether our fascination with the Founders will be essentially constructive or essentially destructive (or anarchic). In this case, Jefferson's statements, especially his endorsement of political violence, cannot be understood today without an appreciation of both the context of the eighteenth century and of the twenty-first.

First and foremost, Jefferson was a man of his time, a product of his age, and this had an enormous impact on his fixation on individual liberty. He spoke and acted at a time when the norm was people being controlled by others, economically, politically, religiously, and in their education. It was a time when the norm in government was control by the wealthy and well-born who believed that they could ride the rest of mankind, "booted and spurred" (To Roger Chew Weightman). Even in England, viewed as the very bastion of freedom in the mid-eighteenth century, most men could not vote. Birth continued to determine one's position in life. The press was not free (and there certainly was no free, rapid dissemination of ideas). Criminal defendants, for even very minor crimes, faced draconian penalties. Formal education was only available for the wealthy. Outside of England and America, the challenges posed by oppressive government power were yet far greater. Even in the United States, Jefferson saw that the institutions of the new republic were fragile, that the republican experiment in freedom could well fail. Most notably, when the Alien & Sedition Acts of 1798 essentially made it illegal to criticize the government and resulted in scores of newspaper editors being indicted and convicted, Jefferson feared that a "reign of witches" might undermine not just the new United States, but the hopes of free government generally (To John Taylor; *Papers* 30:389). Seriously worried, Jefferson warned James Madison that "if these papers fall, republicanism will be entirely brow-beaten" (To James Madison; *Papers* 30:300).

When the danger of tyranny was not just a slogan or paranoid nightmare, and the central challenge of the age was liberty, Jefferson could say with conviction "I prefer dangerous freedom over peaceful slavery" (the translation of Jefferson's Latin phrase *"Malo periculosam, libertatem quam quietam servitutem"; Papers* 11:92–93). He knew what slavery was, about the real absence of freedom, and the very real danger that freedom in the United States could slip away. The list he created for his personal memorial focused on individual liberty rather than his governmental service or family because liberty was the central issue of his time. The central issue of our day may be very different, certainly more complex.

Second, even in his own time, Jefferson's commitment to personal liberty was not simply about the individual pursuit of happiness (important as that was). Jefferson, a disciple of the Enlightenment and the Renaissance, developed a political view that freed and empowered the individual, not simply to pursue their own happiness, but in order to encourage the explosion of human potential, to propel the Enlightenment into all the corners of the world, to improve the local and worldwide community. Freedom, while an important goal, was also a means to an equally important end, Enlightenment. Educational opportunity would "form them [students] to habits of reflection, and correct action, rendering them examples of virtue *to others* & of happiness within themselves" (Rockfish Gap Report, *Papers* [Retirement Series] 13:213 (emphasis added)). In a similar fashion, Jefferson promoted free trade, which would benefit individual producers who had faced mercantilist restrictions under the old regime, but it would also benefit consumers and society at large. Jefferson developed an economic perspective that honored independent farmers on their private farms who could bid defiance to the world not simply for their own benefit, but in part so that, in their independence, a republican community would prosper both economically and politically. Religion, too, was to be free from government involvement and restraint. Making religion a private matter between a person and his god, Jefferson would say, was the morally correct thing to do for the individual. But beyond that, in an unholy alliance with government, religion was dangerous; the combination had created rivers of blood in Europe. "Millions of innocent men, women, and children, since the introduction of Christianity, have been burnt, tortured, fined, imprisoned" (*Notes* 267). Freed from government, religion was a force for good, not simply for the individual, but for society.

Others have argued that Jefferson valued individuals above government. "He was unperturbed by the thought of fracturing the nation itself for the benefit of the individuals in it," Edmund Morgan suggests (72). For example, when easterners complained that the Louisiana Purchase might result over the long term in westerners deciding to separate from the United States, Jefferson responded that "if they see their interest in separation, why should we take side with our Atlantic rather than our Missipi [sic] descendants?" He added, "God bless them both, and keep them in the union, if it be for their good, but separate them if it be better" (qtd in Morgan 73). This, though, can become a semantic game. While Jefferson certainly valued people over government, Morgan also recognizes that the "people" was also a collective concept for Jefferson as he clearly distinguished the nation (its people) from the government (70). In fact, one of the most revolutionary aspects of the Declaration of Independence—one often overlooked—is its firm assertion that Americans were "one people." The individual was freed not simply for their own benefit but for that of the "people."

After all, Jefferson's personal commitment to individual liberty was witnessed by a life dedicated to public service and must be understood in those terms. He was moved by the Scottish Enlightenment that, while certainly promoting personal liberty, insisted upon each individual's responsibility to participate in society and to do so with benevolence toward one's fellow man. Tellingly, as an adult, Jefferson became a great believer in the philosophy of Jesus (although he denied his divinity, resurrection, and Biblical miracles). He believed that Jesus was the greatest human philosopher and that Christianity was the best religion for a republic; central to his thinking in this regard was the fact that Christianity advocated love for one's neighbor, even one's enemy (see Ragosta 26).

For Jefferson, individual liberty was critically important not because it allowed a narcissistic pursuit of happiness to the exclusion of society (although people could certainly take it that way, and Jefferson was hardly a monk or ascetic) but because it gave human dignity to each individual, allowing each person to flourish and participate in, and contribute to, society. In a world controlled by tyranny, aristocracy, and hierarchy, dignity-granting freedom for the individual was essential for real community, for a republic, for enlightened progress. Individual liberty created the conditions for a vibrant community (that itself would guarantee freedom). But, in the age in which he lived, in which the challenge of his generation was creating a world in which people were free to think and live and govern, his interest and support for community seemed to be submerged in the demand to protect individual liberty. How different our world, in which the challenge for this and the next generation will be working within our interdependence to solve common problems.

Third, Jefferson's vision of independence was from an era when it seemed that land, and the freedom to act on one's own land, was limitless. A mere ten generations ago, even before the Louisiana Purchase, the sage opined that America would have open land for its people for thousands of years. In such a land, the independent-minded, free-spirited individuals who flocked to America could literally have their own place and think and do what they wanted, seemingly without affecting their neighbor. Beyond his positive embrace of the yeoman farmer, even in a world in which the largest American cities would today be viewed as small towns, Jefferson loathed urban centers, believing that urbanites lacked independence. "The mobs of great cities add just so much to support of pure government, as sores do to the strength of the human body," Jefferson wrote (*Papers* 8:426). Though Jefferson partied in Paris and had a hand in shaping Washington DC, he thought cities were dens of corruption and iniquity that would spoil the young American republic. It was important, indeed essential, in Jefferson's world that the country be populated primarily by individuals who had the independence that he believed only their own land could provide (*Notes* 275).

With this eighteenth-century mindset, Jefferson could not have imagined a world in which fracking or mining on your own land might affect your neighbors' groundwater or in which preservation of migratory species might require restrictions on private lands or in which grazing along streambeds could do irreparable damage to fragile, downstream ecosystems or in which use of private land could endanger the nation's airspace. His world of land-owning yeomen independent of their neighbors was worlds apart from an America in which problems of the common are often controlling and urban, even rural, populations that cannot exercise individual liberty without regard to others dominate U.S. demography. What a different world in which we live.

Jefferson, Slavery, and Racism

Perhaps the critical role of context—and the extent to which much of what is facilely seen as Jefferson's vision was dependent upon a world that is now fundamentally foreign—is nowhere more evident than in Jefferson's treatment of slavery and his racism. Let me note clearly, I am not making an excuse for Jefferson, as if slavery was not known to be morally repugnant in the eighteenth century: He and many other of the Founders certainly knew that it was. Yet, much of Jefferson's discussion of slavery and his unwillingness to intervene on the issue especially as he grew older is built upon his belief that formerly enslaved people, once freed (which he understood was inevitable), could not be permitted to remain in America; they must be colonized in Africa or the Caribbean or the west. Believing this, as Jefferson did, created an almost insurmountable problem for any plans for emancipation, causing Jefferson to avoid the issue.

Why did Jefferson think this? He explained that, in his time, the history of abuse of African Americans by whites was so raw, so immediate, so severe, so entirely consumed by a tyranny taught from childhood, "a perpetual exercise of the most boisterous passions, the most unremitting despotism on the one part, and degrading submissions on the other," that "the two races, equally free, cannot live in the same government" (*Notes* 270; *Works* 1:77). While Jefferson himself played a part in smudging the line between "the two races," he believed that slavery was so awful, that what had been done to African Americans was so horrid, that after emancipation the two peoples could not live together in peace. As the 1790s turned into the nineteenth century, "Jefferson feared that a conflagration similar to that in Haiti awaited Virginians, and 'only a single spark is wanting'" (qtd in Finkelman 134). Knowing intimately the terrors of slavery, he feared a race war because African Americans would take violent and understandable retribution. Pause on that point: Jefferson's ideas about race in America were founded upon his firm belief that the vicious abuse of African Americans inherent in the southern system of slavery would make a race war inevitable were enslaved people emancipated and the races tried to live together in America.

Our world certainly continues to face very serious racial challenges; yet would Jefferson, were he here today, see the possibility of whites and blacks and mixed-race peoples living in peace in a multicultural society as a complete impossibility? I hope not; I think not, but understanding this historic context is part of understanding Jefferson on slavery, just as understanding the context of his age is part of understanding the seeming radicalism of some of Jefferson's views on personal liberty, government, and violence.

A Modern World

Equally important, our modern context suggests the great care with which Jefferson's views on individual liberty and use of political violence must be considered. First, in the twenty-first century, our population (across race, gender, class, and creed) participates broadly in the political process and in education, with enormous implications. In 1798, when Jefferson urged "nullification" of federal laws, the country was facing laws under which a bevy of newspaper editors had been indicted and jailed, actively undermining the ability of people to participate effectively in the political process. (Previous studies have underestimated the breadth of the attack launched on the free press by the Sedition Act; see Bird.) Alternatively, when people had a broad and effective right to participate in the political process, both a right and a responsibility for Jefferson, he recognized that action in opposition to the government must occur within the political system. As Jefferson explained in 1817, once the law of majority rule is "disregarded, no other remains but that of force, which ends necessarily in military despotism" (*Papers* [Retirement Series] 11:434). Given Jefferson's commitment to majority rule, and the broad ability of almost all adults to participate in modern political discourse, perhaps recourse to non-political means can only be justified when someone (or a group) is effectively denied access to the political process and cannot gain access through legal means. (One might argue that the Civil Rights Movement of the 1950s and 1960s called for Jeffersonian resistance.)

Second, government power and liberty can no longer be seen as a binary in which any increase of governmental power inevitably and directly leads to a reduction in liberty as Jefferson thought at the turn of the nineteenth century (see Read). Even in his own time, Jefferson was arguably an outlier in this regard, but we certainly now know that private power, uncontrolled by government, can be and often is a real threat to individual liberty in a way that Jefferson could not imagine. Corporations, unions, associations . . . the accumulation of wealth and power in private hands without limits can all put private liberty at risk. For example, in the late nineteenth and early twentieth century antitrust laws were adopted that, by constraining the private liberty of some, protected the freedom of opportunity of many others. Government today through legislation and regulation engages in many such efforts to constrain private power in order to protect private freedom. Yet, Jefferson's soliloquies for violent opposition to government came in an era in which there seemed to him to be a simple dichotomy of government power versus private liberty.

Third, and this context is extremely important, the danger to others' legitimate rights, to society's interests, from the exercise of individual liberty is much greater today than it was or than it was perceived to be in the eighteenth century. Jefferson endorsed individual liberty as "unobstructed action according to our will"; yet he expressly recognized that "rightful liberty" must fall "within the limits drawn around us by the equal rights of others" (To Isaac Tiffany). He explained in his First Inaugural that "a wise and frugal Government . . . shall restrain men from injuring one another. . . ." Yet, while Jefferson recognized the principle, the risk posed by individual actions to the rights of others seemed more limited in the eighteenth century. Today, we recognize that our actions are far more likely to injure others than Jefferson could understand, especially were hundreds of millions, billions, of individuals simply to act with unbridled liberty.

Similarly, even before the cataclysm of the Civil War and the constitutional restructuring of federal relations, Jefferson recognized similar theoretical restrictions on the power of the states. While he reminded listeners to his First Inaugural that he would "support . . . the state governments in all their rights, as the most competent administrations for our domestic concerns, and the surest bulwarks against anti-republican tendencies," he vowed to also defend "the General government in its whole constitutional vigor, as the sheet anchor of our peace at home, and safety abroad" (*Writings* 494). Neither individual liberty nor states' rights could be viewed in isolation. O'Brien was simply wrong to conclude that Jefferson "was in the grip of a fanatical cult of liberty, which was seen as absolute to which it would be blasphemous to assign limits" (58), although the isolated quotations that are so popular with modern radical groups might suggest otherwise.

To talk of Jefferson and extreme individual liberty, states' rights, and small government, and apply his words today, without a proper appreciation of our extraordinary interdependence as a people that he could not have imagined—the impact of 7.5 billion people on the world (when in Jefferson's time the entire world population was probably less than one billion), global climate change, eco-system degradation, urban decay, public education for tens of millions of students, the increased reach and danger of criminal behavior, much less firepower, a racially-mixed society still sometimes struggling to find ways to live and work together. . .—is foolish. In the same vein, when the acting director of the Bureau of Land Management seeks to justify deregulation and sale of federal land by claiming that the Founders wished to sell public federal land, he engages in the most rank, reductive abuse of the historic record (see Knickmeyer and McCombs).

Facing social and environmental challenges that Jefferson could not have imagined, today a bureaucracy is needed to manage millions of acres of often fragile federal land impacting other ecosystems and possible extinctions, to maintain access to wild spaces that many millions of Americans can no longer obtain privately, to address immigration issues impacting millions, to provide health research on viruses that could impact us all, to manage weapons of mass destruction that could annihilate whole peoples and irreparably scar millions of square miles, to address trade disputes with over 100 trading partners from around the world. In this era of globalization and integration, the international community plays a much greater role in the life of Americans, and there is no going back, all of which requires a much more powerful national government and reasonable restraints on individual actions. A modern world requires some level of governmental regulation of broadcasting, and vehicles, and drugs, and the environment, and trade, and procurement . . . even for the most conservative, concepts that were literally beyond Jefferson. The world is no longer populated by white, independent farmers with a seemingly endless horizon and unlimited freedom to do as they please in their own small empire of liberty without harming others, and it cannot be. Small government today would be fundamentally different from small government in Jefferson's day. If we are concerned today about facile offers to water the tree of liberty with blood, or if we see the necessity of significant government regulation and some level of uniformity at the national level on a host of issues, this may not reflect the type of political hand-wringing that Jefferson breezily dismissed in the eighteenth century at the time of Shays' Rebellion and the French Revolution.

I do not mean to suggest that unlimited governmental power should be accepted nor that we casually surrender our freedoms, far from it. Perhaps we should embrace Jefferson's admonition that in a struggle between power and liberty, when in doubt, we should side with liberty. But one might well ask what are the limits to individual liberty in a modern society—a question and concern that is not evident in many of the popular Jefferson quotes about individual liberty and political violence both because he could not begin to see our interdependent society, and because he lived in a world that was truly challenged by fundamental economic, educational, political, and religious tyrannies.

Jefferson and Generational Sovereignty

Now, here is an important point: Jefferson would be the first to agree. Above all, he was a man of the Enlightenment who believed in reason and progress and application of new information and learning to problems. He referred dismissively to the "sanctimonious reverence" of those who look upon the Constitution or laws as somehow unchangeable mandates that cannot adapt to new times and new challenges. "Laws and institutions must go hand in hand with the progress of the human mind. As that becomes more developed, more enlightened, . . . institutions must advance also, and keep pace with the times." He scoffed at those who were hidebound by the past: "We might as well require a man to wear still the coat which fitted him when a boy, as civilised [sic] society to remain under the regimen of their barbarous ancestors" (*Papers* [Retirement Series] 10:226–27). No Founder was more concerned about overcoming the dead hand of the past than Jefferson. "[T]he earth belongs in usufruct to the living," he famously told Madison (*Papers* 15:392). Each generation must make its own laws, find its own path. Edmund Morgan concludes that "Jefferson's public career focused on securing for Americans a right of expatriation from the past" (77). The sage would agree with the modern political scientist who, in addressing his presidency, said "the degree to which a leader declines to modify his behavior in accordance with a changing external reality may be a measure of the degree of his failure as a leader" (Johnstone 29). And Jefferson did not fail as a leader. Jefferson believed in a government that was able to meet the challenges of its time, and he would certainly agree that the challenges of our time require different answers and actions than in 1800, actions that should not be constrained by the powerful poetic rhetoric of even the most intelligent eighteenth-century observer.

There is no need here for a specific argument about how big that government should be, about the specific powers of law enforcement, or industrial and environmental regulation, or the right to keep and bear arms, or federal land management. . . . But what I think is undeniable is that Jefferson's breathtaking devotion to individual liberty and states' rights, even to the point of rebellion and blood, a devotion that has become a veritable battle cry in some circles today, must be placed within the context of his time, and our time is very different. As Jill Lepore explains in a similar context, it is simply "ahistorical" to ignore such context, it "defies chronology, the logic of time."

What, Then, to Do with Jefferson?

What, then, can we learn from the Sage of Monticello? Is our study of the icon a waste of time? Was O'Brien right: Should he be chiseled off Mount Rushmore?

To answer those questions, one might return to the tomb.

In studying Jefferson over the past several years, two things are striking to me about the list from his memorial. First, each of the things that he hoped to have remembered relates to a topic involving freedom, certainly, but more fundamentally involving freedom of the mind as much, if not more, than unbounded liberty of action. Freedom of religion allowed one to think for oneself about enduring issues and principles. It did not, as Jefferson elsewhere noted, give one a right to violate otherwise valid, religiously-neutral laws adopted by a democratic majority (whether they involve criminal assault or discrimination based on race, gender, or gender orientation [*Papers* 1:547–48]). A sound education (a liberal arts education for Jefferson), if available, allowed one to question government, certainly, and to pursue individual opportunities, dreams, and goals, not to isolate oneself, but to engage in society intelligently and thoughtfully. At the top of his list, the freedom offered by the

Declaration of Independence, informed by a free and educated mind, allowed one to participate in a self-governing society, to join a community and for that nation to join a community of nations.

Perhaps even more importantly as we evaluate Jefferson's iconic role and ask whether he should be removed from the Pantheon of American heroes, it is significant that each of the achievements emblazoned on his tombstone was, and still is, aspirational.

We have not fully achieved political freedom, as we struggle with voting rights (and voter turnout) and how to manage wealth disparity and money in political campaigns, nor had people in Jefferson's time. He struggled with expanding voting rights for those who did not have the money to own land and with empowering frontiersmen who were underrepresented in the legislature; he urged a "geometrical progression" of taxes on wealth if wealth inequality threatened political harmony (*Papers* 8:682); he participated in the creation of political parties to try to give the voiceless a voice, although he struggled with the problems that parties and partisanship created. And he could not fathom women's participation in voting and politics, much less that of African Americans—and these failings cannot in justice and historical truth be ignored. Yet, he knew that times would change. Weeks before his death, poetically on July 4, 1826, 50 years to the day after the adoption of the Declaration, he wrote of his most famous monument

> May it be to the world, what I believe it will be, (to some parts sooner, to others later, but finally to all,) the signal of arousing men to burst the chains under which monkish ignorance and superstition had persuaded them to bind themselves, and to assume the blessings and security of self-government. . . . These are grounds of hope for others. (To Roger Chew Weightman)

He understood that much was yet to be done.

Similarly, we have not fully achieved perfect religious freedom, and separation of church and state, nor had people in Jefferson's time. He fought efforts to use the government's authority to propagate religion and declaimed against the New England clergy's death grip on their state and local governments. His late-in-life correspondence with John Adams is laced with examples of what he saw as continuing ecclesiastic tyranny. He grappled with complex questions of church and state that could not easily be answered, often goaded on by Madison. He tried to be guided by principle but knew that many conflicts lay ahead.

Affordable education for the people continues to be a goal that we have not met, nor had they in Jefferson's time. He was particularly unhappy that the education plan adopted by his state as it formed the University of Virginia was an inversion of what he had proposed, which included universal elementary school for all "free" children and public funding for secondary schools for gifted male students. When the University finally opened, he worried that the licentiousness of the students might undermine its educational mission and supported the strict disciplining of students, including a grandnephew, who disturbed the educational function of the University.

He knew of all these failures, all these shortcomings. The challenges, though, did not justify a retreat from the principles. Jefferson did not abandon his list.

In fact, I think that he was not providing a list for a tombstone simply of his achievements, impressive as they were; he was listing goals and dreams—knowing full well, I suspect, that the principles on which he based those dreams—equality, freedom of thought, educational opportunity—would continue to be goals for which we would be striving hundreds of years later. That is the real power of Jefferson's vision. Or, as Lincoln explained:

> All honor to Jefferson—to the man who, in the concrete pressure of a struggle for national independence by a single people, had the coolness, forecast, and capacity to introduce into a merely revolutionary document, an abstract truth, and so to embalm it there, that to-day and in all coming days, it shall be a rebuke and a stumbling-block to the very harbingers of reappearing tyranny and oppression. (*Complete Works* 533).

America has placed Jefferson on a pedestal for two hundred years. Although it is increasingly clear that many of the things that he said, even many of his most cherished ideas, taken out of the context of his time, are misleading, wrong-headed, in our time even dangerous, still he speaks to us today not of what was but of what we can be.

He speaks to us not of unbounded individual liberty to bid defiance to the world, but of the critical need for freedom of the mind for all people to allow participation in the world. He speaks to us not of the glories of a bygone era when liberty defined an unlimited American horizon, but of the hopes, dreams, and goals of the future—aspirations to political freedom, education, and religious freedom that will enrich the individual, and the community; aspirations that will continue to challenge our nation into the future.

Merrill Peterson, a great Jefferson scholar, once explained that Thomas Jefferson expressed what the "American people really felt and wanted." I think we might more accurately say that his vision expressed what we really want to feel about ourselves and our nation. Or, as Jefferson said in his old age, "I like the dreams of the future better than the history of the past" (*Papers* 10:285).

Political scientists and economists tell us that we live in a world of large government and finance that owes more of its origins to Alexander Hamilton than Thomas Jefferson. Still, as Andrew O'Shaughnessy says, Jefferson wrote our nation's "mission statement." Stephen Knott makes the point more broadly: "Jefferson's dream of an America constantly remaking itself and shedding the shackles of the past captures the American imagination, for dreams are frequently more appealing than reality, and it is easier to celebrate what might be than to defend what is" (26).

His vision speaks loudly to us of what we—and America—might be.

Why is Jefferson an icon? Not because he is a demigod, certainly, not because his world provides a direct model for ours, but because he is someone who strove for goals and on principles on which we want to strive. With a reasonable recognition of how different our times are than his, but perhaps how similar are our dreams, Jefferson's iconic role is safe.

Note

1. I would especially like to thank Peter Onuf, Johann Neem, and Billy Wayson for useful insights. The views expressed herein are the author's own and do not reflect the views of the Thomas Jefferson Foundation nor Virginia Humanities.

Works Cited

Bailyn, Bernand. *The Barbarous Years: The Peopling of British North America: The Conflict of Civilizations, 1600–1675*. Vintage Books, 2012.

Bird, Wendell. "New Light on the Sedition Act of 1798: The Missing Half of the Prosecutions." *Law and History Review*, Cambridge U P, vol. 34, no. 3, August 2016, pp. 541–614. doi.org/10.1017/S0738248016000201.

Blake, Aaron. "Trump's Apparent Ignorance of Basic Political Terms on Full Display Overseas." *The Washington Post*, 29 June 2019. www.washingtonpost.com/politics/2019/06/29/trumps-ignorance-basic-political-terms-is-full-display-overseas/.

Burstein, Andrew. *Democracy's Muse*. U of Virginia P, 2015.

Finkelman, Paul. *Slavery and the Founders: Race and Liberty in the Age of Jefferson*. Sharpe, 1996.

Jefferson, Thomas. "Notes on Aaron Burr," 15 Apr. 1806. *Founders Online*. National Archive. founders.archives.gov/documents/Jefferson/99-01-02-3574.

_____. *Notes on the State of Virginia*. Query XVII: Religion, 265. London: Stockdale, 1787.

_____. *The Papers of Thomas Jefferson Digital Edition*, edited by Barbara B. Oberg and J. Jefferson Looney. U of Virginia P, Rotunda, 2008–2015.

_____. *Papers of Thomas Jefferson (Retirement Series)*, general editor J. Jefferson Looney. Princeton U P, 2005.

_____. [Spurious Quotations.] www.monticello.org/site/research-and-collections/tje/spurious-quotations.

_____. From Thomas Jefferson to Isaac Tiffany, 4 Apr. 1819. *Founders Online*. National Archives. founders.archives.gov/documents/Jefferson/98-01-02-0303.

_____. From Thomas Jefferson to Roger Chew Weightman, 24 June 1826. *Founders Online*. National Archives. founders.archives.gov/documents/Jefferson/98-01-02-6179.

_____. Undated Memorandum on Epitaph. *Thomas Jefferson Papers*, Library of Congress. www.loc.gov/resource/mtj1.055_1135_1136/.

_____. *The Works of Thomas Jefferson*, edited by Paul Leicester Ford. 12 vols. G. P. Putnam's Sons, 1904.

Jefferson, Thomas. *Writings*, edited by Merrill D. Peterson. Library of America, 1984.

Johnstone, Robert M., Jr. *Jefferson and the Presidency: Leadership in the Young Republic*. Cornell U P, 1978.

Knickmeyer Ellen, and Brady McCombs. "Conservative Lawyer in Favor of Selling Public Lands Picked to Oversee BLM," *Denver Post*, 30 July 2019. www.denverpost.com/2019/07/30/bureau-land-management-william-perry-pendley/.

Knott, Stephen. "'Opposed in Death as in Life:' Hamilton and Jefferson in American Memory," in *The Many Faces of Alexander Hamilton: The Life & Legacy of America's Most Elusive Founding Father*, edited by Douglas Ambrose and Robert W. T. Martin. New York U P, 2006.

Larimer, Sarah, and Abby Phillip. "Who Are the Oath Keepers, and Why Has the Armed Group Returned to Ferguson?" *The Washington Post*, 11 Aug. 2015. www.washingtonpost.com/news/morning-mix/wp/2015/08/11/who-are-the-oath-keepers-and-why-has-the-armed-group-returned-to-ferguson/.

Lepore, Jill. *The Whites of Their Eyes: The Tea Party Revolution and Battle Over American History*. Princeton U P, 2010.

Lewis, Jan, and Peter S. Onuf. "American Synecdoche: Thomas Jefferson as Image, Icon, Character, and Self." *The American Historical Review*, vol. 103, no.1, Feb. 1998, pp. 125–36. *JSTOR*, www.jstor.org/stable/2650780.

Lincoln, Abraham. *Complete Works*, edited by John G. Nicolay and John Hay. Century Co., 1894.

Meacham, Jon. "Leadership Lessons from Thomas Jefferson," *Fortune*, 30 Nov. 2012. fortune.com/2012/11/30/leadership-lessons-from-thomas-jefferson/.

Morgan, Edmund S. *The Meaning of Independence: John Adams, George Washington, Thomas Jefferson*. U of Virginia P, 2004.

O'Brien, Conor Cruise. "Thomas Jefferson: Radical and Racist." *The Atlantic Monthly*, Oct. 1996. www.theatlantic.com/magazine/archive/1996/10/thomas-jefferson-radical-and-racist/376685/.

Onuf, Peter S. *The Mind of Thomas Jefferson*. U of Virginia P, 2007.

Parton, James. *Life of Thomas Jefferson*. James R. Osgood and Co., 1874.

Peterson, Merrill. *The Jefferson Image in the American Mind*. Oxford U P, 1960.

Ragosta, John. *Religious Freedom: Jefferson's Legacy, America's Creed*. U of Virginia P, 2013.

Read, James H. *Power versus Liberty: Madison, Hamilton, Wilson, and Jefferson*. U of Virginia P, 2000.

Schachner, Nathan. *Thomas Jefferson: A Biography*. Appleton-Century-Crofts, 1951.

"Thomas Jefferson." *Encyclopedia Britannica*. www.britannica.com/biography/Thomas-Jefferson.

Washington, George. *The Papers of George Washington Digital Edition* (Confederation Series), edited by Theodore J. Crackel. U of Virginia P, Rotunda, 2008.

Wills, Garry. *Inventing America: Jefferson's Declaration of Independence*. Mariner Books, 2002.

Thomas Jefferson: A Biography_____

Robert C. Evans

Thomas Jefferson was born on April 13, 1743, on a plantation named "Shadwell" near Charlottesville, Virginia.[1] His parents were Jane Randolph Jefferson (from a distinguished Virginia family) and her husband Peter, a prosperous farmer, surveyor, and cartographer. Thomas, their third child among ten altogether, showed an early interest in music and reading and, when nine years old, began studying Latin and Greek under William Douglas, a local preacher and schoolmaster. By his middle teens he was continuing such studies under James Maury, another local preacher with whom he also studied literature and mathematics. In 1760, he entered the College of William and Mary, where Jefferson (unlike many of his contemporaries) continued to be studious and where he came under the influence of a group of intelligent men that included William Small, Francis Fauquier, and George Wythe.

After years of further study, Jefferson eventually became a prominent lawyer and began to fulfill his boyhood dream of building a home on top of a hill near Charlottesville—a home he would call "Monticello" and which became a life-long project. Monticello, which became the center of Jefferson's existence, was not only a house but a plantation worked by approximately 135 slaves. On January 1, 1772, Jefferson married a young widow named Martha Wayles Skelton, whom he deeply loved and with whom he had six children, few of whom survived into full adulthood. Upon the death of Martha's father, John Wayles, Jefferson inherited even more property and more slaves, including a young girl named Sally, who was actually the result of Wayles's sexual involvement with one his slaves. Sally, then, was actually Martha's half-sister. Ironically, Jefferson himself would eventually become sexually involved with Sally in the years following Martha's eventual death. In the meantime, however, Martha and Thomas enjoyed what was, by all accounts, a truly loving marriage.

Jefferson's career might have remained confined to Virginia if the British government had not begun to arouse increasing anger among all the American colonies by treating the colonies in ways their citizens considered high-handed and even tyrannical. Opposition to such treatment rapidly grew, leading to actual armed conflict in early 1775. By this time Jefferson had long been serving as a legislator in Virginia and had become an especially vocal opponent of British rule. Later in 1775, he and other representatives of the thirteen colonies created a Continental Army, headed by George Washington, and then began plans to officially break from Britain. The learned, talented Jefferson was selected to put the delegates' ideas down on paper, thus producing one of the most famous and important documents ever written: The Declaration of Independence.

As the colonists fought British armies to fulfill the Declaration's goals, Jefferson was back in Virginia, serving in the legislature between 1776 and 1779 and fighting especially for religious freedom in his home state. By the summer of 1779, he had been elected governor of his state, where he helped direct the sometimes unsuccessful American war efforts. By 1781 he had left the governorship and retired to Monticello and had begun writing a book titled *Notes on the State of Virginia*, which described the area's numerous traits and features in voluminous detail while also outlining many of Jefferson's own most important ideals. Although he considered black people inferior to whites, he hoped that slavery would someday be abolished, and he even made repeated but always unsuccessful proposals to abolish it. Eventually he came to feel that abolition would never take place in his own lifetime, and he has also been criticized for failing to free his own slaves—a failure than can be attributed to many complicated reasons.

One especially important event in Jefferson's own life was the premature death of his wife. She passed away on September 6, 1782, at the young age of 34. She had asked Jefferson to swear to her that he would never marry again. After Martha's death, the broken-hearted Jefferson returned to political activities. He served in the so-called Confederation Congress and, most famously, in 1785 was appointed to represent the United States in France. By

1789 he had returned to America, where George Washington soon appointed him to the position of secretary of state. While serving under Washington, Jefferson came into increasing conflict with "the Federalists," headed by Alexander Hamilton, who wanted a strong central government, as opposed to Jefferson's ideal of states' rights. Eventually, early in 1794, Jefferson resigned his position and returned to Monticello. But by 1797 he was nominated by the Republicans to become Washington's successor as President—a contest he lost narrowly to John Adams, a former friend who had become his rival but who would eventually become his friend again, near the end of both men's lives. Jefferson's loss of the presidential election meant that he would serve as Vice President—a job which, then as now, involved little real power. Jefferson had his second chance to become President in 1800, when he and Aaron Burr received exactly the same number of electoral votes. Ultimately, Jefferson became President and Burr became Vice President.

Jefferson served two terms as President, sometimes using his own power and that of the Federal government in unexpected ways. Perhaps the most famous example of such behavior was his negotiation with France of the so-called "Louisiana Purchase." This involved buying not simply the area we now call Louisiana but, in fact, a huge swath of land beyond the Mississippi River. Suddenly the United States stretched all the way from the Atlantic to the Pacific Oceans; overnight, it had become one of the largest countries on Earth. Other famous events during Jefferson's two terms as President included the Lewis and Clark expedition to explore the new territories; war with North African pirates who had been harassing American ships at sea; unsuccessful efforts to impeach Federalist judges; and a disastrous embargo against the purchase of European goods—a policy Jefferson pursued to keep the United States out of foreign wars but one that badly damaged the American economy. By early 1809, however, Jefferson's second term as President had ended, and he had retired once more to Monticello. He constantly altered and enlarged the house there, using his work on it as a process of experimentation in architecture and the development of all kinds of practical gadgets.

But Jefferson, by this time, was also keenly interested in founding an institution of higher learning. His last grand project, the University of Virginia, finally opened in 1825, a little more than a year before Jefferson's death. By this time, he had long since reconciled with John Adams of Massachusetts, and the two old men had begun exchanging a now-famous series of letters. In a coincidence that still seems astonishing, Jefferson and Adams both died on the same date: July 4, 1826—fifty years to the day that they had both signed the Declaration of Independence. Jefferson was buried at his beloved Monticello, under a modest tombstone that, as he himself had dictated, said nothing about his political offices but instead emphasized his intellectual accomplishments: "Here was buried Thomas Jefferson, author of the Declaration of American Independence, of the Virginia Statute for Religious Freedom, and father of the University of Virginia."

Note

1. The basic facts of Jefferson's life are laid out clearly in the article on him at Biography.com, from which I have drawn heavily here. For more detailed biographies, see, for instance, John B. Boles, Fawn M. Brodie, Joseph J. Ellis, Kevin J. Hayes, Jon Meacham, and Merrill D. Peterson, to mention just a few.

Works Cited

Boles, John B. *Thomas Jefferson: Architect of American Liberty*. Basic Books, 2017.

Brodie, Fawn M. *Thomas Jefferson: An Intimate History*. Norton, 1974.

Ellis, Joseph J. *American Sphinx: The Character of Thomas Jefferson*. Knopf, 1997.

Hayes, Kevin J. *The Road to Monticello: The Life and Mind of Thomas Jefferson*. Oxford U P, 2008.

Meacham, Jon. *Thomas Jefferson: The Art of Power*. Random House, 2012.

Peterson, Merrill D. *Thomas Jefferson and the New Nation: A Biography*. Oxford U P, 1970.

_____, editor. *Thomas Jefferson: A Reference Biography*. Scribner, 1986.

"Thomas Jefferson Biography." Biography.com. 5 Sept. 2019. www.biography.com/us-president/thomas-jefferson.

CRITICAL
CONTEXTS

Thomas Jefferson's Church: Religious Services in the U.S. Capitol Building_____

Daniel R. Roeber

One of the most notable and controversial of Thomas Jefferson's writings on the subject of politics and religion is his January 1, 1802 letter to the Danbury Baptist Association. The Danbury Baptists, concerned about their religious liberty as a minority group in Connecticut, asked the new president to clarify his view. In response Jefferson wrote:

> Religion is a matter which lies solely between man and his God, that he owes account to none other for his faith or his worship. I contemplate with sovereign reverence that act of the whole American people which declared that their legislature should "make no law respecting an establishment of religion, or prohibiting the free exercise thereof"; thus building a wall of separation between church and state. (qtd in Harris and Kidd 152)[1]

This paradigm-creating phrase, "wall of separation between church and state," has been the touchstone for discussions of religious freedom, especially over the past century.

What is striking about this letter is not only the content, but also the timing: New Year's Day 1802 was a Friday. Two days later, Jefferson attended a religious service in the then-current Hall of Representatives in the Capitol Building. To understand Jefferson's motivation, one must consider the role of cheese: a group of Baptists in Cheshire, Massachusetts, were particularly fond of Jefferson and wanted to show their appreciation to him in a big way. They milked 900 cows and used their product to create a 1,234-pound block of "mammoth cheese"—four feet in diameter and eighteen inches tall. Inscribed on the red crust may have been a Jeffersonian motto, "Rebellion to tyrants is obedience to God" (see Dreisbach [10], who notes that the quote cannot be verified). The cheese was delivered to

Jefferson on New Year's Day by two members of the town, one of whom was John Leland, the town's Baptist divine. Jefferson invited him to be the speaker at the Capitol religious service on Sunday.[2]

This event provides a humorous entrance into the connection between politics and religion at the nation's founding. Apprehending Jefferson's views on religion and politics is both confusing and important, for Jefferson more than any other founder shaped the language of church-state separation.[3] He was the author of Virginia's 1777 Act of Establishing Religious Freedom, which influenced the language used in the religious clauses to the Bill of Rights. Jefferson's letter to the Danbury Baptists is widely cited by groups and individuals dedicated to the separation of church and state. In fact, the Supreme Court has used the phrase as evidence several times in both majority and minority opinions on religiopolitical issues.[4]

The juxtaposition of Jefferson's carefully worded influential letter to the Danbury Baptists and his presence at a religious service in the Capitol Building is striking. An outside observer could hastily conclude that Jefferson's words and actions were not consistent during this first weekend of 1802. But the events of this weekend, and the hundreds of other religious services in the Capitol Building as well as other government buildings in the city of Washington, point to something else: Jefferson and others recognized the benefits of developing a national identity that transcended interdenominational division.[5]

This essay will narrate particular occurrences in which the Capitol Building in Washington, DC was used for religious services and consider the rationale behind such events. I argue that these events show that policies of religious liberty in the Constitution represented a response to a history of religious oppression and dissension in Europe, as well as an attempt to find unity amidst the colonies' diverse religious perspectives. While a sense of the religiosity (and the cultural and political power of an assumed pan-Protestant identity) of the nation can be ascertained from these events, the services speak more to a civil religion that was a foundational part of the country's emerging national identity. The civil religion manifest in the frequency and variety of religious services at the Capitol reinforced the republican ideal of government by broadcasting respect for different opinions and by educating attendees in the variety of theological views espoused by American citizens. These services provided a forum celebrating American religious freedom as a contribution to good government.

Religious Activities in Government Buildings

Little has been written about religious activity in the Capitol or other government buildings. One work that does include a brief discussion of the topic is James H. Hutson's *Religion and the Founding of the American Republic*, a companion book to the 1996 exhibition of the same name at the Library of Congress. Besides Hutson's useful work, further primary sources such as diaries, personal correspondence, and newspaper advertisements provide records of religious services that occurred in the Capitol Building. Compiling these sources provides a picture of varied comprehensiveness with regard to the nature and substance of the services.

The Revolutionary era is a period of transition vis-à-vis religious liberty in the United States. The untried confederacy was seeking an identity that would include all thirteen colonies and the varied denominations of Christianity they espoused. Just a few decades before, many colonies had their preferred denomination at the expense of others, though the situation was evolving, as historian Wilhelmus Bryan notes:

> "The rigors of religious intoleration and persecution as expressed in the laws [of the colonies] were severe and complete. But it is a pleasant reflection . . . that for some years prior to the revolution, while the laws remained unchanged, their enforcement gradually became less vigorous, owing in part to the common danger felt in communities close to the frontier . . . and the need of united action with the mother country." (*History* 1:80)

The final decades of the eighteenth century saw the repeal of laws restricting the practice of Catholicism, and the use of taxes to support clergy of a preferred denomination waned. Still, an underlying tension concerning the direction of the country remained and demonstrated two realities of the time, as Harry Stout describes: "one [reality was] political and constitutional, which explicitly separated church and state and left God out of the formulation; and the other [was] rhetorical and religious, in which 'America' inherited New England's colonial covenant and where God orchestrated a sacred union of church and state for his redemptive purposes" (63). Tension like this could cause violent division and could jeopardize any notions of a national unity.

Conceptions of nationalism were also inconsistent in the nascent republic. Certainly desires for a stronger national government were opposed by groups more interested in maintaining power at the state level. Beyond this, Benjamin Park's recent work illustrates that allegiance to a federal body was a divisive issue that developed at different rates throughout the nation. He writes, "nationalism was never a set of static, self-dependent principles that were agreed upon by a majority of citizens. Rather, conceptions of national identity—and even the 'nation' itself—varied dramatically during the early republic period, and a homogenized understanding distorts a dynamic and diverse reality" (6). The new federal government was faced with a problem: in light of religious and political differences, how could the United States develop a coherent and compelling national identity?

Contained within the Constitution was the plan to establish a seat of the federal government that would be separate from the states. The debate over where the land would be located is a story in itself (see, for example, Yazawa and also Bowling, "A Capital"), but under George Washington's leadership, and in response to the 1790 Residence Act, a plot of land ten miles square on the Potomac River was designated as the capital district. The land came from both Maryland and Virginia and encompassed the settlements of Georgetown and Alexandria, but was primarily an open wilderness ready to become a new city for the federal government.

The construction began during the final decade of the eighteenth century with the building of roads, houses, the first stages of the

Capitol Building (see Bowling, "The Year" and also Allen), and the seemingly proactive construction of a Presbyterian church:

> . . . the summer of 1794 places the Presbyterian Church in the front rank in the pioneer religious work started in the new city. At that time a population had just begun to gather, for only the year before the cornerstones of the Capitol and the White House had been laid and the lines of only a few of the streets had been cut through the forests, while the erection of houses had scarcely been started. A year later the population of the city was estimated to be only 500, so that it will be perceived that the promoters of church work, as well as those identified with the material development drew largely upon the hopes of the future of what was to be the capital city of the American Republic. (Bryan, *Beginnings* 52)

Though a Presbyterian church was out of place in its Episcopal environs, the erection of that church was not wholly surprising considering the influence of the denomination in New England. Such influence was expanding: John Witherspoon, then president of Princeton University, assisted in the writing of the Constitutions for both the United States and the Presbyterian church. References to the Presbyterian church in Washington are absent until 1800. However, another early church building was referenced in a November 16, 1800 letter from early Washington settler Margaret Bayard Smith, the wife of a newspaper publisher: "At this time the only place for public worship in our new-city was a small, a very small frame building at the bottom of Capitol Hill. It had been a tobacco house belonging to Daniel Carrol and was purchased by a few Episcopalians for a mere trifle and fitted up as a church in the plainest and rudest manner." She also notes that no more than fifty or sixty people could fit in the building and that the service usually had about twenty (see Smith and Hunt 13; see also Robertson). Evidently the plans for the new city were attracting religious houses of worship. This development seems more pragmatic than planned, as leaders who desired the new capital to be a cultural as well as political capital discussed "a library, a botanic garden, museums to enhance knowledge and fan the flames of American patriotism, an archives to preserve the nation's documentary history, scientific societies, and an experimental agricultural station," but not a church (see Bowling, "A Capital" 49–50).

Specific Services

Amidst the establishment of churches and the construction of the city came a newspaper mention of a religious service occurring in the partially completed Capitol Building:

> CITY of WASHINGTON, June 19 [1795]. It is with much pleasure that we discover the rising consequence of our infant city. Public worship is now regularly administered at the capitol, every Sunday morning, at 12 o'clock by the reverend Mr. Ralph, and an additional school has been opened by that gentleman, upon an extensive and liberal plan. ("Domestic Intelligence")

While the unfinished Capitol Building may have filled an immediate need for a physical space, the presence of Presbyterian and Episcopal churches in the area would have met at least some of the need for religious services. So, were services in the Capitol Building meeting necessary? Ida A. Brudnick argues yes: in a report for the Congressional Research Service, she writes, "When Congress moved to Washington in 1800, houses of worship were so few that the chaplains took turns conducting Sunday services in the House chamber—now Statuary Hall" (1). John Quincy Adams, at this point a senator, agreed with this sentiment three years later: "There is no church of any denomination in the city" (see Adams and Adams 1:268). Adams's incorrect statement can be attributed to his arrival in Washington only two days before. Churches did exist, but as a whole Washington was little more than a construction site. Fredrika J. Teute notes, "Early on, the functions of the city were so purely political that a private side to life hardly seemed to have existed. Boarding houses accommodated members of the government's three branches and served as informal caucuses for politicking. Domesticity resided back in the home districts where wives and children had been left behind" (90; see also Young).

What were apparently unofficial services became, during the turn of the century, sanctioned gatherings. The Annals of Congress on December 4, 1800 contain a short note on the subject: "The Speaker informed the House that the Chaplains had proposed, if agreeable to the House, to hold Divine service every Sunday in their chamber" (10 *AOC* 797). No further debate is recorded, and the issue is not raised in the proceedings of the Senate. The House spent more time that day debating the need for and location of stenographers to record the debates in the House. In addition to being used for regular services on Sundays, the Capitol also hosted services on holidays like the 4th of July. An June 18, 1801 letter from David Austin to Thomas Jefferson states, "a discourse should be delivered in the Capitol, to any disposed to attend." That Austin would make the request to the President deserves consideration. One might assume that the chaplains would oversee such services (in addition to the Sunday services) as well. The records of the National Archives list thirteen letters sent to Jefferson by Austin before this request; his first letter indicates no earlier acquaintance between the two, so there is no special relationship here. Why would Austin make this request directly to the President? Whatever the reason, Austin received an affirmative reply and delivered a sermon based on Psalms 22:28: "For the kingdom is the Lord's: and he is the Governor among the nations."

The rush to move Congress to Washington in 1800 did not ultimately help John Adams's bid for reelection, and Thomas Jefferson came to power as the new President. In the early years of his presidency, Jefferson wrote the letter of response to the Danbury Baptist Association, and two days later he attended a U.S. Capitol church service. As a matter of fact, Jefferson made a habit of attending Sunday church services while in Washington both as Vice President and President (see Hutson, *Religion* 84.) He did so first at the tobacco house turned Episcopal Church, although, as already noted, he had few options. As a contemporary of Jefferson wrote, "He could have had no motive for this regular attendance, but that of respect for public worship, choice of place or preacher he had not, as this, with the exception of a little Catholic chapel was the only church in the new city" (see Smith and Hunt 13). During his presidency Jefferson regularly attended services in the U.S. Capitol Building, even sitting in the same seat each week. Smith records as much in her letters: "The custom of preaching in the Hall of Representatives had not then been attempted, though after it was established Mr. Jefferson during his whole administration, was a most regular attendant. The seat he chose the first Sabbath, and the adjoining one, which his private secretary occupied, were ever afterwards by the courtesy of the congregation, left for him and his secretary" (Smith and Hunt 13).

One might argue that, for Jefferson, this was the "most conspicuous form of public witness possible, regularly attending worship services where the delegates of the entire nation could see him—in the 'hall' of the House of Representatives" (Hutson, *Religion* 83). This public view assisted him politically, for it silenced critics who were less than kind about Jefferson's perceived lack of faith. Although the Congregational minister and Jefferson opponent William Cutler thought Congress was "insulted by the introduction of Leland, the cheesemonger, as a preacher" in the January 1802 service, he also recognized the political value of such a move. He wrote later regarding Jefferson's attendance at the services, "Although this is no kind of evidence of any regard to religion, it goes far to prove that the idea of bearing down and overturning our religious institutions, which, I believe, has been a favorite object, is now given up. The political necessity of paying some respect to the religion of the country is felt" (Cutler, Cutler, and Egle, *Life*, 58–59, 119).

The ecumenical nature of the services shed some light on why Jefferson felt comfortable participating. As Hutson argues, "The nondiscriminatory manner in which the nation's various Christian denominations were permitted to conduct congressional church services seems to have shielded them from controversy and made them politically safe for Jefferson to attend" (*Religion* 86). Jefferson celebrated the diversity of people who were, as he said in his first inaugural speech, "enlightened by a benign religion, professed, indeed, and practiced in various forms, yet all of them inculcating honesty, truth, temperance, gratitude, and the love of man" (*U. S. Presidential* 30). Certainly people noticed Jefferson and treated him with great respect. Catharine Mitchill, the wife of a Senator from New York, once noted in a letter her social faux pas of stepping on Jefferson's foot after a service. In her words, she was "so prodigiously frighten'd that I could not stop to make an apology, but got out of the way as quick as I could." In a celebration of Republican freedom, Mitchill goes on to note, "Now I suppose if this had been King George or the Emperor of France I should have had my Head cut off for the insult. But thank heaven we Fredonians [an informal term for colonists after the Revolution] have no such tyrants to reign over us" (qtd in Sung 175).

But the argument can be taken further, as it is elsewhere (again by Hutson): "While it is certainly true that Jefferson did not, like James I, publicly exult in his role as a nursing father of the church, an argument can be made that, within the space left by his principled aversion to the use of state power to promote religion, he played the part" (*Forgotten* 63). In addition to attending the services in the Capitol Building, Jefferson assisted young churches in the city of Washington by allowing services in multiple government buildings and provided money for the building of churches in the area.

Jefferson's successor, James Madison, attended religious services in the Capitol as frequently as Jefferson. Madison "evidently thought that the Constitution conferred some modest degree of authority that would permit the national government to support Christianity in a non-discriminatory, non-coercive way" (Hutson, *Religion* 78). A Christian service that was broadly Protestant would surely belong in this category of authority. It is unclear if James Monroe followed his predecessor's example. A British traveler recorded in an 1823 periodical his attendance at a service in the House of Representatives, and after he had a meal, he "sat in the seat next to the President's in the Episcopal Church, where we had an excellent sequel to our morning's sermon" ("Remarks"). Monroe could have been in both services, but he could also have been absent from both, his designated place left empty.

John Quincy Adams is a useful source for this subject because of his detailed memoirs as well as his long tenure in Washington, starting as a Senator in 1803, then Secretary of State and President, and finally a Representative until his death in 1848. His first Sunday was spent at the Capitol, as noted earlier, and he attended services there off and on throughout his tenure in the capital city. This is not to say that doing so was always enjoyable. For example, his memoirs record Adams's attendance at the Capitol for two weeks in May 1842 when a Mr. Maffitt was preaching. The first week's sermon, when Mr. Maffitt took Luke 15 as his text, was viewed by Adams as a "stab, Joab-like, under the fifth rib" directed at him by a preacher whose sermon was "certainly given in no Christian spirit." Adams judged the public speaking ability of the preacher as well, believing his oratory to be "superficial, flashy, and shallow, but very attractive" (Adams and Adams 11:160). The following week, when the subject was the resurrection, Adams viewed the topic as "too capacious for the grasp and too weighty for the poise of Mr. Maffitt" (Adams and Adams 11:164). Another sermon by an unnamed preacher was called "galimatias" (i.e., confused talk or gibberish; Adams and Adams 11:196). Responses like these are scattered throughout Adams's memoirs.

The Nature of the Religious Services

Describing the general nature of a religious service over the course of almost seventy years, with limited and piecemeal information, is an imposing task. The general structure for the religious services is clear: the chaplains of each house organized the services and would preach on alternate weeks. Occasionally visiting clergy were invited to preach as well; as Smith notes, "those of distinguished reputation attracted crowed audiences and were evidently gratified by having such an opportunity for the exercise of their talents and their zeal" (Smith and Hunt 15).

If there is a common trait for these services, it would be a lack of general organization. The role of chaplain began as a part-time task taken on by members of the clergy with responsibilities elsewhere. The work of the chaplain included preaching in these services, though Jefferson invited Leland to speak and other guest preachers, approved by the Speaker of the House, participated as well. The meeting place changed depending on the week—early locations in the Capitol included such locations as the north wing; "the Oven," a temporary meeting place for the House of Representatives that was removed in 1804; the Supreme Court chamber in the basement; and what is now known as Statuary Hall. An entry in Adams's memoirs records him one Sunday going from room to room until he found the actual gathering—apparently the meeting place was not always known.

The services made full use of the room the congregants were meeting in, regardless of the actual room. When meeting in the House Chambers, the rostrum of the Speaker of the House was utilized as the pulpit. The nature of the religious services in the Capitol is telling: their function was much more than simply religious observance. According to one of the attendees of the early services, Washington resident Margaret Smith, at times the events did not look like religious services, but more like social gatherings. She writes,

> I have called these Sunday assemblies in the capitol, a congregation, but the almost exclusive appropriation of that word to religious assemblies, prevents its being a descriptive term as applied in the present case, since the gay company who thronged the H.R. looked very little like a religious assembly. The occasion presented for display was not only a novel, but a favourable one for the youth, beauty and fashion of the city, Georgetown and environs (Smith and Hunt 13–14).

Not only were these services fashionable—they were popular as well, as the chairs would be packed into the room and completely occupied, even on the platform behind the Speaker's chair. According to Smith, "This sabbath-day-resort became so fashionable, that the floor of the house offered insufficient space, the platform behind the Speaker's chair, and every spot where a chair could be wedged in was crowded with ladies in their gayest costume and their attendant beaux and who led them to their seats with the game gallantry as is exhibited in a ball room" (Smith and Hunt 14).

The music added to the festive atmosphere, the opposite of a typical worship service for the time,[6] as the United States Marine Corps Band accompanied the singing, at least for a while. Smith describes the music as "little in union with devotional feelings, as the place. The marine band, were the performers. Their scarlet uniform, their various instruments, made quite a dazzling appearance in the gallery." In her mind, "The marches they played were good and inspiring, but in their attempts to accompany the psalm-singing of the congregation, they completely failed and after a while, the practice was discontinued,—it was too ridiculous" (Smith and Hunt 14). A service in February 1841 was staider, as John Quincy Adams notes in his memoir—"There was a small choir of singers in the front galleries, who sung the hymns" (Adams and Adams 10:435).

The religious services were progressive for both their ecumenism and their allowance of female preachers. Smith notes, "Even women were allowed to display their pulpit eloquence, in this national Hall. . . . The admission of female preachers has been justly reprobated: curiosity rather than piety attracted throngs on such occasions" (Smith and Hunt 15). The first woman known to preach at the Capitol was Dorothy Ripley, a British Methodist missionary, on January 12, 1806. The first time a woman preached in the Capitol was likely the first time a woman was allowed to speak at a formal gathering in the Capitol at all. When granted permission to preach by the Speaker of the House, Nathaniel Macon of North Carolina, Ripley asked "the Lord [to] direct my tongue, and open my mouth powerfully, that His Name (by a woman) may be extolled to the great astonishment of the hearers, who no doubt will be watching every word to criticize thereon" (240). Twenty-one years later Ripley was followed by another female preacher, Harriet Livermore, who also spoke in 1832, 1838, and 1843. While Ripley was an outsider, Livermore was the daughter and granddaughter of former Congressmen. It is said that her first engagement drew a packed crowd, so much so that John Quincy Adams "sat on the steps leading up to her feet because he could not find a free chair"

(Hutson, *Religion* 87). Another witness of the event noted that the Avenue leading into the building "was full of persons excluded." Livermore's text was 2 Samuel 23:3–4—"He that ruleth over men must be just, ruling in the fear of God. And he shall be as the light of the morning, when the sun riseth, even a morning without clouds, as the tender grass springing out of the earth by clear shining after rain." The observer's account notes that the message "was intended principally for the rulers of the nation," though she considered as well "the whole multitude—the rulers of schools—the rulers of families: and as individuals, the rulers of our passions." Her sermon was eloquent and well received, drawing "the profound attention and sympathy of the audience" ("Miss Livermore").

Conclusion: Thomas Jefferson and his Wall of Separation
What does the fact that Thomas Jefferson attended religious services at the U.S. Capitol Building reveal about his personal beliefs? Very little. Correlating attendance at religious events with theological views is fraught with methodological difficulties. For one, many factors played into Jefferson's decision to attend. Jefferson's motivation to be present at these services could have been an adherence to what would have been culturally normative for the time. Political motivations must be considered as well. In view of political adversaries who called him an atheist, Jefferson's attendance at (very public) religious services provided a clear retort to their accusations. Even without considering these factors, attending a religious service does not mean agreement with the beliefs of the speaker, especially with a varied lineup of guest preachers. What Jefferson personally believed is unclear.

A more instructive direction considers how Jefferson's attendance at these services sheds light on his views vis-à-vis the relationship between church and state. Jefferson remains one of the most prominent voices regarding the development of religious freedom in Virginia as well as in the newly formed government. His writings on the matter, be it in the legal record or private correspondence, have been quoted in multiple Supreme Court decisions. In light of this fact, the juxtaposition of Jefferson's letter to the Danbury Baptist Association and his presence at a religious service with a preacher *he chose* should not be ignored. The wall of separation between church and state that was created by the First Amendment is alive and well, but for Jefferson, that wall was permeable.

Notes

1. The original document has the word "eternal" before "separation," but it was crossed out. Letters to two of Jefferson's cabinet members who lived in New England, Attorney General Levi Lincoln and Postmaster General Gideon Granger, to vet the political import of the letter, illustrate the thought and effort that went into Jefferson's reply. Granger believed the letter would "give great Offence to the established Clergy of New England while it will delight the Dissenters as they are called." In summary: "He cannot therefore wish a Sentence changed, or a Sentiment expressed equivocally." (December 1801 letter from Gideon Granger to Thomas Jefferson, in Dreisbach and Hall [528]). One must note the controversy rather than the clarification this letter created, both then and at present. For example, a "wall of separation" is restrictive in two directions, whereas the Constitution restricts acts of Congress against respecting a particular religion. Federalists, already no friends of Jefferson, saw this letter as furthering political atheism. See Daniel L. Dreisbach and James H. Hutson.

2. See Pasley (31–36). Criticism of Leland's message illustrates the overt political divisions of the time. A Congregationalist clergyman and Federalist congressman named Manasseh Cutler referred to Leland as "the cheesemonger, a poor, ignorant, illiterate, clownish preacher" who, in alluding to Jefferson, "bawled with stunning voice, horrid tone, frightful grimaces, and extravagant gestures. . . . Such an outrage upon religion, the Sabbath, and common decency, was extremely painful to every sober, thinking person present." See 4 January 1802 Letter from Manasseh Cutler to Joseph Torrey, qtd in Cutler and Egle, 2:66–67.

3. The other major founder whose thought held sway was James Madison, though Muñoz argues that George Washington deserves consideration as well.

4. The first mention of the document by the Supreme Court was for *Reynolds v. U.S.*, 98 U.S. 145 (1878), a case about religious liberty and the concept of religion (which is not defined by the Constitution). Other notable cases that referenced the document include *Everson v. Board of Education*, 330 U.S. 1 (1947), which debated the use of government funds to bus students to a Catholic school; *Engle v. Vitale*, 370 U.S. 421 (1962) which ruled unconstitutional mandatory school prayer; *Epperson v. Arkansas*, 393 U.S. 97 (1968), over an Arkansas law that prohibited the teaching of evolution; and *Lemon v. Kurtzman*, 403 U.S. 602 (1971), over funding secular subjects and materials in religious schools. This final case created the "Lemon test" to see if the Establishment Clause was being transgressed or not.

5. Religious services occurred in the Treasury and War Office buildings as well; see Hutson, *Forgotten Features* 63.

6. Although church services at the time were generally more solemn affairs with long expositions of scripture, the camp meetings occurring at the same time during the so-called Second Great Awakening were far from tame, with "elemental religious feelings" and "unusual bodily effects—the jerks, dancing, laughing, running, and 'the barking exercise'" (see Noll 267). The atmosphere of the services at the Capitol would vary greatly depending on the week, but the emotion would fall between these two extremes.

Works Cited

Adams, John Quincy, and Charles Francis Adams. *Memoirs of John Quincy Adams, Comprising Portions of His Diary from 1795 to 1848*. Lippincott, 1874.

Allen, William C. *"In the Greatest Solemn Dignity." The Capitol's Four Cornerstones. Senate Document / 103rd Congress, 2nd Session. Senate; No. 28* (Washington, DC: 1994).

Annals of Congress. memory.loc.gov/ammem/amlaw/lwac.html.

Austin, David. 18 June 1801 Letter to Thomas Jefferson. *Founders Online*. National Archives. founders.archives.gov/documents/Jefferson/01-34-02-0297.

Bowling, Kenneth R. "A Capital before a Capitol: Republican Visions," in Donald R. Kennon ed. *A Republic for the Ages: The United States Capitol and the Political Culture of the Early Republic* (1999), U. of Virginia P. pp. 36–54.

_____. "'The Year 1800 Will Soon Be upon Us': George Washington and the Capitol," in Donald R. Kennon, ed., *A Republic for the Ages: The United States Capitol and the Political Culture of the Early Republic* (Charlottesville, VA: U of Virginia P, 1999) pp. 55–63.

Brudnick, Ida A. *House and Senate Chaplains: An Overview.* Congressional Research Service. CRS Report. R41807 (2011). www.senate.gov/CRSpubs/bf55b1cc-a690-48a0-a95d-94d7a07afb08.pdf.

Bryan, Wilhelmus Bogart. *The Beginnings of the Presbyterian Church in the District of Columbia.* Columbia Historical Society, 1905, p. 43–66. babel.hathitrust.org/cgi/pt?id=hvd.32044100164169&view=1up&seq=74.

_____. *A History of the National Capital from Its Foundation through the Period of the Adoption of the Organic Act*, 2 vols. Macmillan, 1914.

Cutler, William Parker, Julia Perkins Cutler, and William Henry Egle, editors. *Life, Journals and Correspondence of Rev. Manasseh Cutler, Ll.D*, 2 vols. Robert Clarke & Co., 1888.

"Domestic Intelligence." *Federal Orrery*, 2 July 1795, p. 1. Church in the U.S. Capitol, Wallbuilders, wallbuilders.com/church-u-s-capitol/.

Dreisbach, Daniel L. *Thomas Jefferson and the Wall of Separation between Church and State, Critical America.* New York U P, 2002.

Dreisbach, Daniel L., and Mark David Hall. *The Sacred Rights of Conscience: Selected Readings on Religious Liberty and Church-State Relations in the American Founding.* Liberty Fund, 2009.

Harris, Matthew L., and Thomas S. Kidd. *The Founding Fathers and the Debate over Religion Revolutionary America: A History in Documents.* Oxford U P, 2012.

Hutson, James H. *Forgotten Features of the Founding: The Recovery of Religious Themes in the Early American Republic.* Lexington Books, 2003.

_____. *Religion and the Founding of the American Republic.* Library of Congress, 1998.

_____, and Thomas Jefferson. "Thomas Jefferson's Letter to the Danbury Baptists: A Controversy Rejoined." *The William and Mary Quarterly* vol. 56, no. 4, 1999, pp. 775–90. *JSTOR*, www.jstor.org/stable/2674235.

Kennon, Donald R, editor. *A Republic for the Ages: The United States Capitol and the Political Culture of the Early Republic.* U P of Virginia, 1999.

"Miss Livermore." *National Intelligencer,* 13 Jan. 1827, p. 1.

Muñoz, Vincent Phillip. "Religion and the Common Good: George Washington on Church and State." *The Founders on God and Government,* edited by Daniel L. Dreisbach, Mark D. Hall, and Jeffry H. Morrison. Rowman & Littlefield, 2004, pp. 1–22.

Noll, Mark A. *A History of Christianity in the United States and Canada.* Eerdmans, 1992.

Park, Benjamin E. *American Nationalisms: Imagining Union in the Age of Revolutions, 1783–1833.* Cambridge U P, 2018.

Pasley, Jeffrey L. "The Cheese and the Words: Popular Political Culture and Participatory Democracy in the Early American Republic." Pasley, Robertson, and Waldstreicher, pp. 31–56.

Pasley, Jeffrey L., Andrew W. Robertson, and David Waldstreicher, editors. *Beyond the Frontiers: New Approaches to the Political History of the Early American Republic.* U of North Carolina P, 2004.

"Remarks of an English Traveller in the United States." *The Columbian Star,* 11 January 1823, p. 1.

Ripley, Dorothy. *The Bank of Faith and Works United.* G. Clark, 1822.

Robertson, Nan. *Christ Church, Washington Parish: A Brief History* (2016), 2–4, washingtonparish.org/wp-content/uploads/2013/09/Christ-Church-History-2015-Final2.pdf.

Smith Margaret Bayard, and Gaillard Hunt. *The First Forty Years of Washington Society, Portrayed by the Family Letters of Mrs. Samuel Harrison Smith (Margaret Bayard) from the Collection of Her Grandson, J. Henley Smith.* Scribner's, 1906.

Stout, Harry S. "Rhetoric and Reality in the Early Republic: The Case of the Federalist Clergy," in *Religion and American Politics: From the Colonial Period to the 1980s,* edited by Mark A. Noll. Oxford U P, 1990, pp. 62–76.

Sung, Carolyn Hoover. "Catharine Mitchill's Letters from Washington 1806–1812." *The Quarterly Journal of the Library of Congress, Library of Congress Manuscript Div.,* 34, no. 3, 1977, pp. 171–89.

Teute, Frederika J. "Roman Matron on the Banks of the Tiber Creek: Margaret Bayard Smith and the Politicization of Spheres in the Nation's Capital." In Donald R. Kennon, ed., A Republic for the Ages: The United States Capitol and the Political Culture of the Early Republic (Charlottesville, VA., 1999) pp. 89–121.

U.S. Presidential Inaugural Addresses from Washington to Obama. Floating P, 2009.

Yazawa, Melvin. "Republican Expectations: Revolutionary Ideology and the Compromise of 1790." In a Republic for the Ages: The United States Capitol and the Political Culture of the Early Republic, edited by Donald R. Kennon, pp. 3–35. Charlottesville: Published for the United States Capitol Historical Society, by the U P of Virginia, 1999.

Young, James Sterling. *The Washington Community, 1800–1828.* Columbia U P, 1966.

Jefferson as Reader and Writer_____

Brandon Schneeberger

Thomas Jefferson is best remembered today as one of the most significant of all the so-called "Founding Fathers" of the United States. Jefferson not only wrote the Declaration of Independence, the key document in creating the new republic, but also served the young nation as secretary of state, ambassador to France, and then, for two terms, as its third president. It was Jefferson who, through the Louisiana Purchase, instantly doubled the country's size, and it was Jefferson who oversaw some of the nation's earliest military engagements, especially the war with the Barbary pirates. But Jefferson—legislator in Virginia, governor of that state, and founder of the University of Virginia—was not only a practical politician. He was also a very well-read man who once said that he could not live without books. Over the course of his long life he amassed the largest library in his state—a collection that eventually became the nucleus of the newly founded Library of Congress. What, exactly, did he read? And, in particular, how did his reading affect his ideas about the nature and purposes of good writing? Answering these sorts of questions is the main purpose of the present essay.

Eleanor Berman: *Thomas Jefferson among the Arts*

One especially valuable book about Jefferson as a reader and writer remains Eleanor D. Berman's 1947 monograph titled *Thomas Jefferson among the Arts: An Essay in Early American Esthetics.* This volume was published by a relatively small press and is now difficult to find in most libraries. (Worldcat.org lists less than 400 copies worldwide.) All the more reason, then, to summarize her findings here. As her title and subtitle suggest, Berman was less interested in Jefferson's reading of works in political philosophy or practical statesmanship than his reading of works about matters he himself classified as the "Fine Arts," including painting, sculpture, architecture, gardening, music, rhetoric, and literature. Berman's interest in his responses to these last two topics—rhetoric and literature—are especially intriguing and, in fact, his interest in both these matters is also the central focus of the present essay.

In her tenth chapter—"Jefferson and the Art of Rhetoric"—Berman begins by noting that Jefferson learned much about rhetoric from several of his earliest teachers, but she also mentions numerous books on the topic included in a catalog he prepared, in 1815, of books from the library he had amassed by that time. One of his subcategories, which included books on "Logic, Rhetoric, [and] Orations," included (according to Berman)

> Aristotle's *Logic,* Condillac's *Logic* (2 vols.), as well as works on logic by Aldrich, Crackenthorpe, Wallis and Watts. The second subdivision lists Aristotle's *Logic,* Cicero's *Orator,* as translated by Guthrie, two volumes of Cicero *On Oratory,* Quintilian's *Institutiones Oratoriae,* Demetrius Phalereus' *de Elocutione,* Vosii's *Rhetorica,* Adams' *Lectures on Rhetoric and Oratory,* Blair's *Lectures on Rhetoric,* Cambray *On Eloquence,* Dugard's *Rhetorices Elementa,* Mason *On Poetical and Prosaic Numbers and Elocution,* Sheridan on *Elocution,* and Ward's *Oratory.* The third subdivision, "Orations," lists speeches by Aeschines, Deinarchus, Andocides, Lysias, Isaeus, Antiphon, Herodes, Antisthenes, Alcidamas, Lycurgus, Demades, Gorgias, Demosthenes, Isocrates, Quintilian, Cicero, and Seneca among the ancients, while the eloquence of Jefferson's own time is represented by Birch's *Virginian Orator,* the *Boylston Prize Dissertations, Orations of the 4th of July* and on the *Boston Massacre of March 5, 1770;* by Curran's *Forensic Eloquence,* and by *Eulogiums on Washington.* Guthrie's version of Cicero's *Orations* appears again in this list, probably by mistake. Of the orations of antiquity, Jefferson's collection lacked only Hyperides of the ten Attic orators recognized by the Alexandrine canon. Since the fragments of six of Hyperides' speeches were only recovered from papyri after 1847 [Hyperides is known to modern times as "the Sheridan of Athens"] this is not surprising. It is safe, however, to assume that Jefferson had some knowledge of Hyperides, as he and John Adams from time to time discussed Dionysius of Halicarnassus in their correspondence, and the second part of the treatise "On Imitation" in the latter's *Scripta Rhetorica* considers fragments of Hyperides. (190–91).

This is, needless to say, an impressive list, but it is worth remembering that by the time Jefferson compiled this catalog he was near the end of his life. The library he had used as a young man was probably far less comprehensive than the 1815 catalog would suggest.

Berman argues that in "Jefferson's mind rhetorical or classical education would be useful not only to lawyers but to nearly every variety of citizen" (191). This, she says, explains why he gave rhetoric and oratory such a prominent place in his plans to promote public education (194). Rhetoric, she says, was a subject he wanted to see "universally taught" (195). She reports that "what Jefferson preferred in the ancients was what perhaps was closest to his own theory and practice of expression: it was logical form, clear and distinct conception and compact statement" (195). According to Berman,

> To Jefferson the lasting cause which all speaking and writing should serve are the liberties of the citizens of a state. For the upkeep of such liberties he felt that there is needed an art of writing and speaking which should keep communication simple, flexible, lively, clear and distinct. He deprecated to John Waldo the Edinburgh reviewers who "set their faces against the introduction of new words in the English language" and who "feared that the writers of the United States would adulterate it." He looked forward to an American style in English, and as a base for it he counted not only on Shakespeare and other English classics, but on a knowledge of Anglo-Saxon origins and Greek and Latin roots. (196–97)

He wrote to a friend, "I set equal value on the beautiful engraftments we have borrowed from Greece and Rome. . . . I am equally a friend to the encouragement of a judicious neology [i.e., the creation of new words]; a language cannot be too rich. The more copious the more susceptible of embellishment it will become" (197). This interest in creating new words suggests, in Berman's opinion, that although he valued the ancient Greek and Roman classics, he "was neither fanatical nor lacking insight into their deficiencies" (200). Nor was he unwilling to reject aspects of the English literary tradition: "In poetry he deprecated rhyme and preferred the measured beat of blank verse. He thought rhyme was a childish thing" (201).

Jefferson's Rhetorical Criteria

The standard criteria for Jefferson regarding rhetoric was its social use for expression and communication, and he likely would have lauded Sallust's statement that "it is glorious to serve one's country by deeds; even to serve her by words is a thing not to be despised" (201). In Sallust's account of *The War with Catiline*, in fact, "Cato's ringing words affirmed an ideal that to Jefferson was the lasting cause which all speaking and writing should serve—the liberties of the citizens of a state" (202). Jefferson's admiration of the classics, however, did not extend wholly to Cicero. Interestingly, while he recommended Cicero to students, and transcribed twenty-one passages of Cicero in his *Literary Bible*, the classical rhetorician was not among his favorites. He described him as "diffuse, vapid, rhetorical, but enchanting" and added that "his prototype, Plato, eloquent as himself, dealing out mysticisms incomprehensible to the human mind, has been deified by certain sects" (206). Instead of Cicero, the classical writers he finds the greatest models for oratory are Livy, Tacitus, and Sallust, but "most assuredly not in Cicero" (206). Indeed, Jefferson doubted whether "there is a man in the world who can now read one of his [Cicero's] orations through but as a piece of task work" (206).

Cicero, however, is a writer who may be useful when it comes to the law. As the social uses of expression and communication are naturally applied to the profession of the law, it is in Jefferson's thoughts about this profession that he indicates his criteria for writing that is clear, distinct, accurate, brief, and simple, as opposed to the "tautologies, redundancies, and circumlocutions that characterize the 'barbarous' style of the law" (203). Berman also asserts that Jefferson, despite his hatred for legal language, still believed the law had great social value (203). He wrote to his son-in-law, Thomas Mann Randolph, that to study the profession of law alongside farming was a "wise combination since one would relieve the other." He considered law useful not only to himself but also to his neighbors and the public. Law was, Jefferson wrote, the "most certain stepping stone to preferment in the political line" (208).

In a letter written in the 1820s to the president of the Jefferson Debating Society, Jefferson noted that he believed Livy, Sallust, and Tacitus were, in his own words, "preeminent specimens of logic, taste, and that sententious brevity which, using not a word to spare, leaves not a moment for inattention to the hearer" (210). He thought that a few key characteristics of compositions include brevity, clarity, distinctiveness, diversity, forcefulness, and sympathy. These, along with an "honest heart" and "knowing head" (212), are especially important for Jefferson, argues Berman, because they reduce the chances for audiences to grow inattentive. Jefferson lauded these writers because he saw them as models of brevity and simplicity, especially for audiences on whom "froth and fancy would be lost in air" (211). The central faults in contemporary rhetoric, he thought, were extended and rhetorically complex speeches, whether they included "eulogy, inflation, vagueness, hyperbole, or amplification" (212). These speeches, Jefferson wrote, are "disgusting and revolting," and they do not persuade, for "Speeches measured by the hour, die with the hour" (210). Additional oratorical vices included "elaborate philippic and diatribe done with 'passions vehement and viperous . . . catching at every gossiping story . . . supplying by suspicions what could (be found) nowhere else [and] . . . arguing on . . . motley farrago as if established on gospel evidence'" (212).

At the end of her chapter on Jefferson and rhetoric, Berman offers the following summary of Jefferson's rhetorical views:

> It is clear that he wanted every form of composition—the oration, the essay, the letter, to be brief, clear and distinct, diversified, yet forceful and sympathetic. He favored the use of new words where it seemed desirable, and he deprecated rigid adherence to rules. He felt that the speaker must think of his audience and suit his arguments to them. In order to achieve this, he advised frequent presentation of speeches and the like before capable judges. He deprecated the use of notes. He deprecated pedantic adherence to grammar, purisms, wire-drawn expressions and barbarisms. He deprecated technicalities, especially such as are so conspicuous in the law. He deprecated straining for

effect or originality. He urged in the dealing with any subject the boldness of an honest heart and a knowing head. He urged the development of an argument on the basis of exhaustive research and, as nearly as possible, perfect knowledge employed with a strict logic. He was averse to overstatement and philippics, even on issues where his passions were strong. He forbade gossip, innuendo, intrigue, chicanery and dissimulation. Vehemence of any kind was anathema to him. To achieve the positive qualities of writing and speaking that he desired, and to escape the negative, he urged the study and imitation of the finest models in the art of reasoning. (212–13)

Jefferson as a Literary Critic

In addition to emphasizing Jefferson's admiration for classical rhetoricians, Berman notes in her eleventh chapter— "Jefferson as Litterateur and Critic"— his literary interest in several Greek authors, including Homer, Herodotus, Euripides, Anacreon, and Quintus Smyrnaeus (218). She especially notes his deep love for Homer, whom he called "that first of poets as he must ever remain, until a language equally ductile and copious shall again be spoken" (218). His love of Homer was so great that he inscribed upon his wife's tomb lines from the *Iliad*: "If in the house of Hades men forget their dead / Yet will I even there remember my dear companion" (218).

Berman records that Jefferson admired several works of Euripides, including *Hecuba, Orestes, Phoenissae, Medea,* and *Hippolytus* (218). In what has been titled *The Literary Bible of Thomas Jefferson*, Jefferson's literary commonplace book published by Gilbert Chinard in 1928, Jefferson leaves out any reference to Plato; and, in fact, Berman explains that Jefferson felt a deep antipathy toward that Greek philosopher (218). She argues that "the aristocratic, mystical elements in the philosopher's thinking were most uncongenial both to his [Jefferson's] rationalism and his egalitarianism" (218–19). Indeed, writing to John Adams about Plato's *Republic*, Jefferson describes it as containing "whimsies," "puerilities," and "unintelligible jargon" and claims he "laid it down often to ask myself how it could have been that the world should have so long consented to give reputation to such nonsense as this" (219). However, if Jefferson did not care for the famous Greek philosopher, he did have great respect for the thought of the Roman thinker Cicero. While he dismissed Cicero as a rhetorician, he was nevertheless fond of him as a philosopher. He also valued Epicurus. As he tells William Short in a letter, "I too am an Epicurean. I consider the genuine (not the imputed) doctrines of Epicurus as containing everything rational in moral philosophy which Greece and Rome have left us" (219).

Berman cites a number of influential English writers included in Jefferson's *Literary Bible*, including Lord Bolingbroke, who exceeds any other English writer in the number of extracts Jefferson quoted (230). Compared to fifty quotations from Bolingbroke, Alexander Pope has only ten, not including the quotations from his translations of Homer (230). Berman suggests that Jefferson's extracts from Pope's Homer translations more accurately indicate his appreciation of the Greek poet than the English author (230) and adds that neither "Pope's aristocratic point of view, his fairly parochial estheticism, nor his concurrence in the *status quo* could endear him to the Virginian" (230). According to Berman, a much more congenial poet for Jefferson's temperament was John Milton, especially in *Paradise Lost*. Indeed, she thinks that "the nobility of [Milton's] verse and the moral elevation of his subject matter" made an enduring influence on Jefferson (230).

English literary influences upon Jefferson also included various poets and dramatists, especially Shakespeare. Jefferson once wrote that "Shakespeare must be singled out by one who wishes to learn the full powers of the English language" (230). Other dramatists he valued included Thomas Otway, John Dryden, William Congreve, Edward Young, and Nicholas Rowe, and the poets he appreciated included James Thompson, Mark Akenside, John Langhorne, and "the two leading members of the 'graveyard' school—[Edward] Young and [Robert] Blair" (231). But, Berman notes, Jefferson's reverence for the great English poets, even Shakespeare, is paralleled by what she calls a "preoccupation . . . difficult for us to understand": his "exaggerated admiration" for the perhaps imaginary or invented poet Ossian, whom Jefferson defended even well after his supposed antiquity was revealed to be false (230). Jefferson wrote that if

Ossian's poetry is "not ancient" it is "equal to the best morsels of antiquity" (230). All in all, Berman asserts that Jefferson's tastes were largely shaped by his era, whether those tastes involved literature, music, architecture, gardening, painting, or sculpture (231).

One English literary figure Jefferson did not like is Samuel Johnson, whom Berman describes as "violently anti-American" (227). Jefferson regretted the influence of Johnson's famous dictionary, asserting that Johnson too often attributed Latin and Greek origins to English words instead of stressing Anglo-Saxon roots (228). Berman explains that Jefferson particularly disagreed with Johnson in matters concerning the philosophy of language, following instead the rational empiricism of Logan, George (227). Unlike Johnson, Jefferson "adhered to the progressive, dynamic conception of language as against the static" (227). Jefferson wrote that "Dictionaries are but the depositories of words already legitimated by usage. Society is the workshop in which new ones are elaborated. . . . And if, in this process" of developing the English language "our trans-Atlantic brethren shall not choose to accompany us, we may furnish, after the Ionians, a second example of a colonial dialect improving on its primitive" (227). In general, Jefferson lamented the influence of Johnson's dictionary, believing that a strict adherence to it as authority would stifle the language from developing as it should (228). Instead of looking backward, Jefferson believed that authentic progress would only occur when there were a larger number of writers in America. He admitted, however, that America currently had "no distinct class of literati. . . . Every man is engaged in some industrious pursuit, and science is but a secondary occupation, always subordinate to the main business of his life" (228). He looked forward to a day in which the American use of language would someday have a "new character" that might " separate it in name as well as in power, from the mother-tongue" (228).

Jefferson the Writer

Berman discusses Jefferson not only as a reader but also as a writer. She argues that his practice of and attitude toward writing must be viewed within the "framework of his activity as a revolutionary and as the architect of a rising democracy" (229). She thinks Jefferson's writing was explicitly purposeful, intended to rouse others to action. Jefferson was, according to Berman, not a great orator, but she claims he excelled especially in "the chiselled phrase [that] lived on paper rather than in the momentary quivering of the air" (229). While he composed best in solitude, "every bent of his mind and heart was suited for becoming the scribe of the Revolution" (229).

Berman argues that although Jefferson had a deep interest in literature, he did not believe he had the creative imagination for writing. In a letter to [William] Short he writes that he "never had that sort of poetical fancy which qualifies for allegorical devices, mottoes, etc. Painters, poets, men of happy imagination can alone do these things with taste" (232). Jefferson read not for pleasure but for profit, but, as Berman notes, to read for profit in Jefferson's time was to read for pleasure (232). Berman continues:

> Certainly Jefferson, who declared to John Adams that "I cannot live without books"; who was so sensitive to literary style that he never read a work in translation if he could do so in the original; and who was so responsive to the nuances of language that he advocated the publication of the county dialects of England because we would find in Shakespeare "new sublimities which we had not tasted before"— certainly such a man cannot with justice be described as having read for profit rather than pleasure. He read because books symbolized knowledge, power, the joy of contact with great spirits, the joy of meeting new ideas. Certainly his intention to learn Gaelic so that he could taste the "sublime" beauties of Ossian in the original bespeaks the passionate reader, not the purely acquisitive one. (232)

According to Berman, when "considering his literary esthetic it must be remembered that he stemmed out of a period in which meaning was still a basic component of creative writing. . . . Form and content, style and message were no less indissolubly joined than profit and pleasure" (233). Jefferson, however, was less interested in form than in content, and this helps explain his long-lasting interest in Greek and Latin, an interest that led to his "astonishing aptitude for practical linguistics" (220).

Berman characterizes Jefferson the writer as a "bold experimenter" who appealed not to the authority of tradition but to usage (221). He wrote of his own habit of producing "much hasty writing," which was "more indebted for style to reading and memory, than to rules of grammar" (221). "I have been pleased to see," he wrote to one friend, "that in all cases you appeal to usage, as the arbiter of language; and justly consider that as giving law to grammar, and not grammar to usage" (221).

Although Jefferson may not have been an author of "literature" per se, he still understood that an overly pedantic dependence on and admiration for the classics could impede a writer's creative imagination, and he believed that the classics should ultimately be approached, as Berman explains, with the "boldness of the creative artist" instead of the "rigidity of the academician" (221). Jefferson wrote to another friend, "I concur entirely with you in opposition to Purists, who would destroy all strength and beauty of style, by subjecting it to a rigorous compliance with their rules" (221–22). He, therefore, longed for an American style of writing that would be someday free from the older English style (222).

Near the end of her chapter on Jefferson as critic, Berman discusses some of his written works, notably his *Thoughts on English Prosody* and his *Essay on Anglo-Saxon*. She explains that Jefferson lost interest in poetry and fiction as he grew older, because aging, in his words, "withers the fancy as the other faculties of the mind and body" (235). But Berman argues that his interest in poetry remains evident through his *Thoughts on English Prosody*—that is, metrical rhythm. Jefferson complemented his interest in prosody with "a sustained absorption in the origin and development of the English language" (238). When he was eighty-two years old, he claimed that studying Anglo-Saxon was a hobby that "too often runs away with me" (239). In fact, he became the first person to suggest that American colleges include Anglo-Saxon in the curriculum, and in 1798 he would write his *Essay on Anglo-Saxon*, in which he argued that it is the basis of our language (240). Bernard explains that in this

Essay Jefferson rejected "the mysterious jargon in which the scholars wrapped their lore to mystify and overawe the unlettered masses" (240). As with his rules for rhetoric, he advocated a simplification in education that did away with "needless complexities" (240). This was, as Berman puts it, a "'common-sense' approach," since he "believed in the ability of the common man to understand what was properly explained to him" (240).

The *Essay* reveals, as well, Jefferson's understanding that studying Anglo-Saxon would result in a greater appreciation of other English authors, notably Shakespeare and Milton. Indeed, studying Anglo-Saxon would

> richly repay us by the intimate insight it will give us into the genuine structure, powers and meanings of the language we now read and speak. We shall then read Shakespeare and Milton with a superior degree of intelligence and delight, heightened by the new and delicate shades of meaning developed to us by a knowledge of the original sense of the same words. (241)

More importantly, however, Jefferson believed that studying Anglo-Saxon could have political benefits as well, for he believed that it could play a role in bringing together America and England. Jefferson believed that by mutually understanding the roots of their common language, both countries would "yoke [themselves] jointly to the same care of human happiness, and vie in common efforts to do each other all the good we can—to reflect on each other the lights of mutual science particularly, and the kind affections of kindred blood" (242).

As in her tenth chapter, Berman wraps up her eleventh with a helpful summary:

> We have then, in Jefferson, a literary craftsman of high order, whose pen had the honor of producing the chief document of the American Revolution; a keen student of the laws of language, particularly in regard to the development of an American speech; a lover of literary style, a translator, and the author of essays on prosody and Anglo-Saxon which reveal both literary scholarship and linguistic

attainments; a lover of books, who saw in their dissemination one of the bulwarks of democratic thought; a vigilant protector of the rights of authors and of the freedom of the press. He was above all an enlightened litterateur-statesman who, despite his intense Americanism, saw "the great republic of letters" as a "great fraternity spreading over the whole earth." It need hardly be added to this, as in his attitudes towards each of the other arts, [that] he was consistently the man of the Enlightenment, the revolutionary statesman, the humanist, utilitarian and progressive. (251)

Conclusion

Berman's book remains an especially valuable overview of Jefferson not only as a writer himself but as a student of good writing. Her survey of what he read and what he thought about his reading is as important today as it was when it was first published more than seventy years ago. Berman herself was an excellent reader, writer, historian, and critic—a fine scholar whose scholarship is still worth reading today.

Work Cited

Berman, Eleanor Davidson. *Thomas Jefferson among the Arts: An Essay in Early American Esthetics.* Philosophical Library, 1947.

Thomas Jefferson: Words for a Nation

Nicolas Tredell

In his writings and speeches, Thomas Jefferson, the prime author of the Declaration of Independence and the third President of the United States, developed a potent, elegant, and eloquent set of discourses on national identity, drawing on a wide variety of sources and resources within and outside himself. On April 29, 1962, 136 years after Jefferson's death, one of his successors, the thirty-fifth President of the United States, John F. Kennedy, observed that the dinner he was then hosting for all living Nobel Prize winners in the Western hemisphere was "the most extraordinary collection of talent, of human knowledge, that has ever been gathered together at the White House, with the possible exception of when Thomas Jefferson dined alone." In his observation Kennedy perceives that Jefferson's capacious mind, his wide spectrum of philosophical, cultural, literary and scientific interests, his ability to respond to, animate and shape the spirit of the age and his remarkable political achievements in attaining the highest office in the land, retaining it for the full two terms and, above all, elevating its dignity, made him, in effect, into a multiplicity of people, a true forerunner of the poet Walt Whitman who famously announced in *Song of Myself* (1855), halfway through the decade in which, arguably, American literature made its own declaration of independence: "I am large. . . . I contain multitudes" (737).

This is not to deny that Jefferson's multitudinousness included both political and personal attitudes and actions that were and are open to challenge and censure. Even in his own lifetime, he was subject both to sustained and reasoned public criticism, and (centuries before social media) to what we would now call trolling in the form of virulent abuse and death threats sent through the mails. From a twenty-first-century perspective, his public utterances about African Americans and Native Americans endorse ideas of racial inferiority and exclusion that contradict his stress elsewhere on enlightenment and equality. Looking at his private life, anecdotal, circumstantial, and DNA evidence allows us reasonably to infer that he had a relationship, which produced children, with his wife's half-sister, Sally Hemings, who was a member of his household staff; today this seems to exemplify the sexual and racial exploitation of a mixed race woman by a powerful white male predator. Jefferson was like Whitman not only in containing multitudes but also in his capacity to contradict himself.

This essay does not seek to assess the whole gamut of Jefferson's actions, which is the task of the historian and biographer, but to perform the task of the literary critic and analyze his words—though this does not exclude ethical observations especially as, in Jefferson's case, words sometimes spoke louder than action, or were, more precisely, a form of action. We will focus on a selection of Jefferson's words that arguably acted to shape national identity, drawing on the Declaration of Independence (July 4, 1776); the one complete book he published in his lifetime, *Notes on the State of Virginia* (1785); and his late unfinished *Autobiography* (begun 1821).

The Declaration of Independence

At the age of 33, Thomas Jefferson assumed a grave and momentous responsibility: that of drafting the creed of a new nation, a nation coming into being as he wrote and, in part, because of what he wrote. In analyzing any historical situation, particularly when approaching it from a literary perspective, it is important neither to overestimate the power of language nor to underestimate political, social, military, economic, and other forces; but it remains a reasonable inference that in the case of the Declaration of Independence, at that decisive historical conjuncture, Jefferson's words, amended by cosignatories such as John Adams and Benjamin Franklin but still largely originating with him, would significantly arise from and help to shape the identity of the emergent new country and would continue to reverberate, like any text widely perceived as foundational, through later centuries.

The Declaration can be characterized in several ways. It was a performative utterance, like a promise. Just as making a promise performs the act of promising, so making a declaration of independence performs the act of declaring independence; but it does not thereby achieve independence, any more than making a promise fulfils a promise: both require an usually complex concatenation of further acts. The Declaration was also a piece of polemic, of propaganda, written in the heat of a fiercely incandescent moment; but its anger was tempered by reason. It could and did offer vehement condemnation; but it also employed concepts and rational assertions. In that latter respect, it was an apologia, a formal defense of a particular set of opinions and lines of conduct. If, in the seventeenth century John Milton, in his epic poem *Paradise Lost* (1667), had offered to justify the ways of God to man; the Declaration offers to justify the ways of man to man (and the gendered noun is appropriate—although the Declaration uses the term "people" 14 times, it never explicitly mentions "woman" or "women"). Its long one-sentence opening paragraph concludes with an acknowledgement of the duty to justify the action it is performing in the forum of global debate (even if this was, in the late eighteenth century, a fairly exclusive forum): "a decent respect to the opinions of mankind requires that they should declare the causes which impel them to the separation."

The Declaration smacks of the courtroom as well as the forum. Jefferson had trained and practiced as a lawyer, and the document combines the functions of statements for the defense and prosecution, though with different figures in the dock in each case—one of whom, as it happens, is also the defense counsel, who is providing a preemptive exculpation of himself and his fellow signatories, who could have found themselves literally in the dock charged with treason, a capital crime, if the British had defeated the revolutionary forces—a point summed up in the famous statement attributed to Benjamin Franklin urging solidarity among his cosignatories: "Gentlemen, we must all hang together or assuredly we shall all hang separately." The Declaration mounts its defense on the ground of natural rights sourced from God: "all men are created equal" and "are endowed by their Creator with certain unalienable Rights"—and on the violation of these by the figure who is the chief target of the prosecution: "the present King of Great Britain," George III.

By focusing on the king, the Declaration personalizes its more general and abstract case against the colonial power, making the British monarch into an embodiment of the desire for "absolute Despotism," "absolute Tyranny," "absolute rule," "whose character" is "marked by every act which may define a Tyrant." The Declaration supplies a series of what might, in legal terms, have the status of allegations against George III but are presented as "Facts"; this appeal to supposedly empirical evidence is characteristic of Jefferson's eighteenth-century formation. Rhetorical techniques reinforce the empirical appeal: eighteen of the allegations start with "He has," employing the device of anaphora, that kind of repetition, at the beginning and end of phrases, which serves to drive home a message, rather like Perry Mason's "Isn't it true . . . ?" in the TV version of Erle Stanley Gardner's novels when he is closing in on the true perpetrator of the crime of which his client has been falsely accused. The thirteenth clause has nine sub-clauses detailing the "Acts of pretended Legislation" to which George III has given his assent—but these also use anaphora in the shape of the "For" that begins each subclause, as in "For imposing Taxes on us without our Consent."

At the start of the main subclauses, there is one significant variation: the sixteenth clause starts with "He" but replaces the past participle "has" with the present tense: "He is"; and the immediacy of the charge is emphasized by the phrase that follows: "at this time," reinforcing a sense of immediate threat: this is happening now. It is the kind of urgency associated with Paul Revere's ride on April 18, 1775 (later much mythologized, not least in Longfellow's 1860 poem) to warn of British troops approaching Lexington and Concord, or with the Minutemen of the Revolutionary War who held themselves armed and ready to respond at a moment's notice to threats of military attack. The language at this point is especially strong: "He is at this time transporting large Armies of foreign Mercenaries to compleat the works of death, desolation, and tyranny, already begun with circumstances of Cruelty & perfidy scarcely paralleled in the most barbarous ages, and totally unworthy the Head of a civilized nation." "Death," "desolation," "tyranny," "Cruelty," "perfidy"; the five nouns are an inventory of apocalyptic evils, figures in a new Book of Revelation. The clause also employs a distinction between civilization and barbarism that is almost mapped on to the distinction between an emergent United States, representing civilization, and an established Great Britain whose present King, if not the whole country, has lapsed into barbarism. The implication is that to declare independence from a nation headed by such a King is to support civilization against barbarism and, in the context of the Declaration as a whole, this contributes to the implication that America is a new civilized nation. Such a nation, before too long, will want a literature of its own; and we can see the seeds of this in the Declaration.

The Declaration and American Literature

The Declaration was not a play, poem, or novel, but it had elements of all three. It opens as the ancient Roman poet Horace said an epic should, *in medias res*, in the middle of things. It starts with a subordinate clause of time introduced by "When"; locates itself in history, "in the Course of human events"; invokes both necessity and popular agency: "it becomes necessary for one people"; and announces an epochal event: "to dissolve the political bands which have connected them with another." "When in the Course of human events," like "Once upon a time," signals the start of a story, makes us listen up, hone our attention. Imagine this paragraph with the main clause repositioned at the beginning: "A decent respect to the opinions of mankind requires . . . ": this would be a less exciting opening, a general statement that would have to wait for the subordinate clause to give it temporal location and relate it to a specific action.

The courtroom aspect of the Declaration discussed above merges into its dramatic aspect—the law and theatre are closely related, as the French writer Jean-Paul Sartre once suggested, because both present a contest between conflicting versions of actual or fictional reality and ask the jury or audience to adjudicate between them: "The stage is the courtroom in which the case is tried" (127). The Declaration constructs, in George III, a notable villain who might feature on the stage or in the pages of a narrative poem or story; and we can easily imagine how we might, in a dramatization or novelization, distribute parts of the declaration among different characters. The Declaration also makes effective use of rhetorical techniques found in poetry and poetic prose such as alliteration, anaphora, inversion, strategic repetition, and shifts in tense.

The philosopher Alfred North Whitehead once remarked that "the European philosophical tradition [. . .] consists of a series of footnotes to Plato" (39); a provocative exaggeration but not wholly untrue. It could also be said that the American literary tradition consists of a series of variations on the Declaration of Independence; another provocative exaggeration, but again not wholly untrue.

Prior to the Declaration of Independence, many writers of fiction and nonfiction, in poetry, drama, or prose, had been concerned with national identity—perhaps most notably, and in a way that can still resonate across the globe today, Shakespeare in his history plays; but, as in those plays, this concern was often with a national identity that was already established, to some extent, and that was seen as in need of revision, development, correction, and frequently, retrieval and restoration, the recovery of a lost and supposedly better past or originary state. (This kind of restorative concern would emerge later in American history and culture, in the idea of lighting out for the territory, like Mark Twain's Huckleberry Finn, or going on the road like Jack Kerouac's Sal Paradise and Dean Moriarty in Kerouac's novel of that title.) With the Declaration of Independence, it was not only a new nation but also a new kind of writing that was coming into being. In a sense, Jefferson would be the first modern postcolonial writer, the forerunner of those authors, for example in Africa and Asia, who would, especially in the twentieth century, aim, in both fictional and nonfictional modes, to identify, create, and explore the identity of nations emerging from colonial rule into independence. Like these authors, Jefferson faced a complex negotiation between the promise of the present and the pressure of the past; between white paper and palimpsest.

White Paper and Palimpsest

In *An Essay Concerning Human Understanding* (1690), the English philosopher John Locke, whose work Jefferson knew and admired, offered an image of the mind at birth as "white Paper, void of all characters" (104, capital "P" in original), a blank sheet, a *tabula rasa* that contained no innate ideas but upon which sensory experience would, over time, give rise to inferences and concepts. At the time of the drafting of the Declaration of Independence, the blank sheet could also become an image of a new nation at birth. Crucial to the idea of America—and to what would later be called "the American Dream"—was the idea of the United States as a blank sheet, a *tabula rasa*, on which it was possible to inscribe truth and possibility free of the misleading and constraining texts of the past.

Tabula rasa, however, literally means, in Latin, "a scraped tablet," a blank surface on which to write from which earlier inscriptions have been erased. That earlier writing may, even if wholly invisible, haunt the later writing inscribed upon it, and it may be at least partly restorable to sight and interpretation. In this respect, the *tabula rasa* resembles a palimpsest, a surface on which later writing is superimposed upon effaced earlier writing that it may be possible to recover to some extent. Written in English, the language of the colonial power, by an author who had grown up under colonial rule, the Declaration was bound to bear strong linguistic traces of its former oppressor; drawing implicitly on English, Scottish, and European philosophy, it was bound to bear deep conceptual traces of the old world.

Despite these traces of the colonial past, there was one especially notable innovation in the Declaration: the phrase "the pursuit of Happiness." Its familiarity today should not obscure its radicalism and novelty. "Happiness," at least of a worldly kind, had not been universally regarded as the highest aim in western or world culture; it had been seen as fragile, transient, illusory, and a potential distraction from more exalted aims such as moral virtue, philosophic calm, or spiritual salvation (which may generate or incorporate happiness but do not have happiness as their primary goal). The *Ethics* of the ancient Greek philosopher Aristotle, for example, a text Jefferson would have read in the original language, contends that happiness [*eudaimonia*] consists of "activity in accordance with [. . .] the highest virtue, and this will be the virtue of the best part of us" (328). To make happiness a central aim, without implying or specifying what kind of happiness it should be, is a bold move.

The Declaration does not go so far as to say "happiness" in itself is a right in the same way as "life" and "liberty," coupled alliteratively in the same sentence, are; it asserts, not an "inalienable" right to happiness but to its pursuit, without any guarantee that it will be gained: and this puts the stress on movement, striving, straining, which may result in either success or fatigue or failure—perhaps a greater sense of futility and failure than would be the case if happiness had not been pursued as a central goal. Eleven years after the Declaration, in a letter from Paris of 7 February 7, 1787, to Anne Willing Bingham, Jefferson, in an outline of a typical day in the life of a fashionable Parisian lady, uses the phrase not to denote an unalienable right but to mark a futile quest: thus such a lady is "eternally in *pursuit of happiness* which keeps eternally before us" (159, italics added). This suggests that the "inalienable" right to "the pursuit of Happiness" is a right to a perhaps hopeless quest that may result in greater unhappiness. He does go on to contrast this with the supposedly full life of the American wife and mother at that time, but she seems to find fulfilment less in pursuing happiness than in performing her duties to her husband, her children, and their house and its grounds. Almost 150 years after the Declaration of Independence, F. Scott Fitzgerald's *The Great Gatsby* (1925) appeared, a novel that might partly stand as a particularly penetrating updating and revision of that founding American document, especially of its assertion of the right to "the pursuit of Happiness" and its conclusion is skeptical about such a pursuit, whose aim is figured in the ever-elusive "green light": "It eluded us then, but that's no matter—tomorrow we will run faster, stretch out our arms farther. . . . And one fine morning—" (141, ellipsis in original).

Nonetheless, Jefferson remained keen, a quarter of a century after the Declaration and after many national vicissitudes, to affirm the novelty of the American enterprise. On March 21, 1801, he wrote to the English scientist Joseph Priestley: "We can no longer say there is nothing new under the sun. For this whole chapter in the history of man is new." Here Jefferson weaves into his own prose a potent declaration of pessimism adapted from the Old Testament Book of Ecclesiastes: "*there is* no new *thing* under the sun" (AV 1.9, italics in original); but he does so in order to negate it, boldly contradicting a key Biblical text by asserting that, whatever may have been the case in the past, the new example of the United States now shows that Ecclesiastes is wrong. "The great extent of our republic is new. Its sparse habitation is new. The mighty wave of public opinion which has rolled over it is new." Allowances must be made for the context of this affirmation; Jefferson is writing in the first month of office as the third President of the United States, having defeated, for the moment, those Federalists who seemed to him to threaten a possible return to monarchical rule, and the addressee of his letter is a prominent progressive member of the English and European enlightenment. Even if he did feel any doubts about the newness of America, it is unlikely that he would have disclosed them to such a recipient; but it demonstrates his continued concern to reinforce the idea of America as a new and, by that newness, optimistic nation.

What was not new in America, however, was its negative stereotyping of ethnic otherness, although it was given distinctive and complex dimensions by the particular social mix of the United States of America. It is the contribution of Jefferson's words to this stereotyping and his uneasy wrestling with it, in regard to both Native Americans and African Americans, that we now turn.

Words about Native Americans

The ethnic other explicitly mentioned in the Declaration is a generalized idea of the Native American, woven into the eighteenth and last clause of those "Facts" indicting George III. The final charge is that the British king "has endeavoured to bring on the inhabitants of our frontiers, the merciless Indian Savages, whose known rule of warfare, is an undistinguished destruction of all ages, sexes and conditions." To use the term "savages" reinforces the link between George III's Great Britain and barbarism but also categorizes the Native Americans as an outside civilization and the adjective "merciless" and the definition of their "rule of warfare" as "an undistinguished destruction of all ages, sexes and conditions" reinforces this (though the attribution of a "rule of warfare" to the "savages" acknowledges that they are not wholly without rules, which clearly modifies the idea of their supposed savagery). Jefferson could hardly have failed to be aware, on some level, that Native Americans might have other reasons to attack the white inhabitants of the frontier lands—whom they might see as invaders of lands of which they themselves were the rightful possessors—but he confines himself to the attacks that can be seen as incited by the British, thus strengthening his case against the latter but also depriving the Native Americans of any independent agency of their own.

The deployment of such a negative stereotype in this context, however, signals a problem for American identity after independence. The British could, in principle, be driven out of the United States or deprived of sovereign power so they could no longer try to dominate and control American affairs; the Native Americans were already there and could only be eliminated by deportation or genocide; otherwise, however contained and diminished, they had in some way to be assimilated into the identity of the emergent nation. This is an issue to which Jefferson—and the United States—will return.

Words about African Americans

The most notable ethnic others absent from the Declaration are African Americans and mixed race Americans living in slavery (members of Jefferson's household among them). Interestingly, Jefferson did mention them in his original draft; and it is at this point that the language in which George III is condemned grows particularly strong. The English king "has waged cruel war against human nature itself, violating its most sacred rights of life and liberty in the persons of a distant people who never offended him." He has done this by capturing these "persons of a distant people" and "carrying them into slavery in another hemisphere, or to incur miserable death in their transportation thither." This,

Jefferson asserts, is the kind of warfare practiced by pirates, but it is now being pursued by "the CHRISTIAN king of Great Britain, determined to keep open a market where MEN should be bought and sold." The English king has vetoed every attempt to pass laws banning or curtailing "this execrable commerce." (capitals in original, punctuation modified).

Moreover, as he allegedly did with the Native Americans, George III is now inciting the slaves in America "to rise in arms" against its white inhabitants, thus "paying off former crimes committed against the liberties of one people, with crimes which he urges them to commit against the lives of another."

In a distinction not unfamiliar at this time, Jefferson deplores the slave trade as a fundamental violation of a human nature that has a right to life and liberty while not engaging directly with the continued existence of slavery in the emergent United States (or indeed in his own household and estate), and he attributes armed resistance by slaves in America to incitement by the English king rather than as in any sense a response to present injustice perpetrated by the white inhabitants of the emergent country—a response that could be seen as structurally akin to that of the American rebels taking up arms against the British. The peculiar vehemence of Jefferson's denunciation of George III at this point might be seen, at least in part, as a form of displacement and projection, whereby one's own responsibility for behavior one condemns is displaced from oneself and projected on to another person, who is judged even more harshly than he might seem to deserve in order to shift any blame from oneself.

In his *Autobiography*, Jefferson contends that this clause "reprobating the enslaving the inhabitants of Africa" was excised in deference to the states of South Carolina and Georgia because they had never tried to control importing slaves and, indeed, wanted to go on doing so (loc 299). Jefferson suggests that the northern states might have been sensitive to such reprobation as well because while they "had very few slaves themselves" they had transported them to other states (loc 301). Despite the eloquence of his denunciation of the slave trade in his draft Declaration, Jefferson did not insist upon its inclusion in the final version, even in a compressed and moderated form. There were pragmatic reasons for this—to try to do so could have risked fracturing the fragile unity of the revolutionaries by alienating the slave states—but it is, nonetheless, an intriguing counterfactual speculation to ask what difference it might have made to American identity at its emergence and in its later manifestations if the final Declaration had included some reference to slavery of the kind contained in Jefferson's draft, however displaced and projected. It might well, for example, have been alluded to and cited in the civil rights struggles of the 1950s and 1960s, in the speeches and writings of Martin Luther King.

In *Notes on the State of Virginia*, Jefferson records that 126 new acts were to be passed after independence and identifies seven of these as "the most remarkable": two of these, the second and the last, mention slaves. The second is "To make slaves distributable among the next of kin, as other moveables" (94); in law, a "moveable" is that which has the nature of a chattel, an item of property other than freehold land. The casual, automatic categorization of slaves as "moveables" in Jefferson's description of this act sits oddly with the emphasis in the Declaration on the axiom that "all men are created equal" and have inalienable rights to "Liberty" and "the pursuit of Happiness" that are difficult for an item of property to exercise.

The seventh act, as Jefferson presents it, is the shortest and clearest: "To emancipate all slaves born after passing the act" (94–95). But some rather convoluted backtracking immediately follows. This was not itself an act but an amendment to be proposed at an opportune moment; and it had a further element, which Jefferson sets out in some detail: the babies in question "should continue with their parents to a certain age, then be brought up, at the public expence, to tillage, arts or sciences, according to their geniusses [*sic*], till the females should be eighteen, and the males twenty-one years of age, when they should be colonized to such place as the circumstances of the time should render most proper" (94). The idea of educating such children in agriculture, arts or sciences "at the public expence" sounds quite benign; but the wording also implies that they will be removed from their parents without asking permission and then "colonized"—which means, here, that they will be established in a colony where they will eventually be declared "a free and independant people" (94)—but only after their compulsory deportation from their native land.

Jefferson is aware of a possible objection to his plan and includes it in his discussion at this point: "It will probably be asked, Why not retain and incorporate the blacks into the state, and thus save the expence of supplying, by importation of white settlers, the vacancies they will leave?" (94). We should note, however, that the question is couched in economic terms, as an issue of avoiding public expense; another way of putting it, rephrasing the second part of the question and drawing on the Declaration of Independence, would be: "Why not retain and incorporate the blacks into the state, and thus save the shame of violating their inalienable rights, as equal human beings, to 'Life, Liberty and the pursuit of Happiness' by making them leave their native land?" Jefferson answers the question he allows to emerge in a periodic sentence that moves from a reasoned assessment to an apocalyptic future scenario:

> Deep rooted prejudices entertained by the whites; ten thousand recollections, by the blacks, of the injuries they have sustained; new provocations; the real distinctions which nature has made; and many other circumstances, will divide us into parties, and produce convulsions which will probably never end but in the extermination of the one or the other race. (94)

This starts by acknowledging "Deep rooted prejudices entertained by the whites"—and in Jefferson's Enlightenment perspective, prejudices are negatively coded, pre-judgements in the literal sense of the term, unsupported by evidence or rational argument, that the light of reason can, in principle, dispel. He then goes on to recognize the injuries the blacks have sustained and, moreover, to identify them both as retained in collective memory and as numerous: the "ten thousand" is not a precise figure and while in certain contexts such a number might sound like hyperbole, an exaggeration, in regard to the actual though largely unrecorded tally of injuries, it is an example of litotes, of understatement; but it does hint at the enormous scale of those injuries. The next phrase, "new provocations," is ambiguous concerning the source of those provocations—whites, blacks, historical events?—but the next phrase is the killer: "the real distinctions which nature has made." Here Jefferson makes it clear that he believes there are real distinctions between blacks and whites—and, as we shall see shortly, he elaborates these to denigrate the former. He then looks forward, apocalyptically, to "convulsions" that will end in the "extermination" of one race or the other. In other words, he forecasts the likelihood of a lethal race war.

Jefferson goes on to enumerate what he sees as "the physical and moral" differences between blacks and whites, (94) and for him they clearly reinforce the idea that the former are inferior to the latter, though he does not commit himself to a definite assertion: "I advance it therefore as a suspicion only, that the blacks, whether originally a distinct race, or made distinct by time and circumstances, are inferior to the whites in the endowments both of body and mind" (97–8). Here the appearance of reasonableness, of putting forward a tentative hypothesis, could seem more dubious than making a dogmatic assertion by implying that the "suspicion" is an acceptable subject for discussion and investigation. For Jefferson, this posited inferiority poses a problem for freeing the slaves: the "unfortunate difference of color, and perhaps of faculty, is a powerful obstacle to the emancipation of these people." Whereas slaves in ancient Rome could be freed and subsequently integrate without difficulty because they were white, America could not stop there but must take a second, unprecedented action, "unknown to history": "When freed, he [the slave] is to be removed beyond the reach of mixture" (98). In other words, deported.

In his *Autobiography*, he returns to this topic, recognizing the eventual inevitability of the emancipation of the slaves in America to avoid violence but insisting that it cannot mean integration or even peaceful coexistence:

> Nothing is more certainly written in the book of fate, than that these people are to be free; nor is it less certain that the two races, equally free, cannot live in the same government. Nature, habit, opinion have drawn indelible lines of distinction between them. It is still in

our power to direct the process of emancipation and deportation, peaceably, and in such slow degree, as that the evil will wear off insensibly, and their place be, *pari passu* [equivalently] filled up by free white laborers. (loc 772)

Once more, hints of apocalypse follow. There can be no getting away from this aspect of Jefferson's discourse, partly because of the clarity and eloquence with which it is expressed. His words for a nation, taken as a whole, endorse both liberation and oppression, unity and division, equality and discrimination.

Conclusion

Jefferson falls under that "universal law" identified in the novel *Cancer Ward* (1968), by the Russian writer Aleksandr Solzhenitsyn: "everyone who *acts* breeds both good and evil. With some it's more good, with others more evil" (102, italics in original). The balance of good and evil in any individual case is difficult to determine, particularly in a figure as eminent as Jefferson, whose personal and political power gave him a freedom of action that was bound to breed quite a bit of both. Each person, and the court of history, can make their own judgment; close attention to the actual words he spoke or wrote can help us to do so.

Works Cited

Aristotle. *The Ethics: The Nicomachean Ethics.* Translated by J. A. K. Thomson. Revised with Notes and Appendices by Hugh Tredennick. Introduction and Bibliography by Jonathan Barnes. Penguin Classics. Penguin, 1986.

Fitzgerald, F. Scott. *The Great Gatsby.* Edited by Matthew J. Bruccoli. The Cambridge Edition of the Works of F. Scott Fitzgerald. Cambridge U P, 1995.

Jefferson, Thomas. *Autobiography.* 1821. Madison & Adams P, 2018.

_____. Declaration of Independence, "Original Rough Draught" June 1776. www.pbs.org/jefferson/archives/documents/ih198038. htm.

_____. *The Essential Jefferson.* Edited with an introduction by Jean M. Yarbrough. Hackett Publishing, 2006.

_____. *Notes on the State of Virginia*. 1785. Digireads.com, 2010.

_____. "We can no longer say." "From Thomas Jefferson to Joseph Priestley, 21 Mar. 1801," *Founders Online,* National Archives. founders.archives.gov/documents/Jefferson/01-33-02-0336. [Original source: *The Papers of Thomas Jefferson*, vol. 33, *17 February–30 April 1801*, ed. Barbara B. Oberg.] Princeton: Princeton U P, 2006, pp. 393–95.]

Jefferson, Thomas, et al. The Declaration of Independence: A Transcription. National Archives. https://linkprotect.cudasvc.com/url?a=https%3a%2f%2f%2f%2fwww.archives.gov%2ffounding-docs%2fdeclaration-transcript&c=E,1,mHSI-GZy7L7OJk2clyF1v3j DLOLI8ZEfGj0ppqguJJPbLAXBrpTvRzqJYZg34TV1H9ThXLBp Tgxyked5hBxKa7J_Op2N_TJEFmQsUQNs&typo=1.

Kennedy, John F. "Remarks at a Dinner Honoring Nobel Prize Winners of the Western Hemisphere." Online by Gerhard Peters and John T. Woolley. The American Presidency Project. www.presidency.ucsb.edu/documents/remarks-dinner-honoring-nobel-prize-winners-the-western-hemisphere.

Locke, John. *An Essay Concerning Human Understanding*. Oxford U P, 1975.

Meacham, Jon. *Thomas Jefferson: The Art of Power*. Kindle edition Random House, 2012.

Sartre, Jean-Paul. "Interview with Kenneth Tynan (1961)." In *Sartre on Theater*: Documents assembled, edited, introduced, and annotated by Michel Contat and Michel Rybalka. Translated by Frank Jellinek. Quartet Books, 1976, pp. 121–34.

Solzhenitsyn, Aleksandr. *Cancer Ward*. 1968. Penguin, 1971.

Whitehead, Alfred North. *Process and Reality*. Free P, 1979.

Whitman, Walt. *Song of Myself*. The Text from the First Edition of *Leaves of Grass* (1855). In *The Complete Poems*. Edited by Francis Murphy. Penguin English Poets. Penguin, 1982, pp. 673–738.

Thomas Jefferson, Lord Kames, and the Declaration of Independence_____

Robert C. Evans

Thomas Jefferson is remembered today less as a President than as a writer. In particular, he is recalled as the author of the Declaration of Independence, which is not only the founding document of the United States but also one of the most famous calls for—and defenses of—freedom in world history. The Declaration, however, is remembered not simply for its ideas but for its powerful phrasing. Jefferson's style, as much as his thought, has made the Declaration one of the most memorable and consequential pieces of writing of all time.

How did Jefferson learn to write so well? The simplest answer is that he read very widely and thoughtfully. This, after all, is how most great writers learn to write. What did he read? We have evidence relevant to this question in a letter he wrote on August 3, 1771—just a few years before he composed the Declaration—to Robert Skipwith. Skipwith had asked Jefferson to send him a list of books worth owning. Skipwith had specified that he wanted (or was only able) to spend £30 on such books. Jefferson, however, like any good book lover, could not resist sending a list much longer than Skipwith would be able to purchase with only thirty pounds:

> I sat down with a design of executing your request to form a catalogue of books amounting to about 30. lib. sterl. but could by no means satisfy myself with any partial choice I could make. Thinking therefore it might be as agreeable to you, I have framed such a general collection as I think you would wish, and might in time find convenient, to procure. Out of this you will chuse for yourself to the amount you mentioned for the present year, and may hereafter as shall be convenient proceed in completing the whole. (Jefferson, *Writings* 740)

In other words: here are the books I love and recommend; purchase first the ones that appeal to you most, and then later you can purchase even more of them!

What kinds of books did Jefferson list? The simple answer is "all kinds" (see Jefferson, *Writings* [740–45]). Interestingly enough, the first items on his list fell under the category of "Fine Arts" and included many names that might also be considered essential today, such as Homer, Virgil, Shakespeare, Dryden, Addison, Tasso, Molière, Terence, and so on (*Writings* 743–44). Usually the works of these writers came in multiple volumes, so the sheer number of actual, physical books Skipwith would have added to his library would have been even longer than Jefferson's list suggests. His total list of literary works amounts to 75 different items, and many of those items were printed in more than one volume—often in two but ranging, in one case, up to nine. Skipwith would have needed many bookshelves to accommodate just the "Fine Arts" books Jefferson recommended, not to mention the many other books listed under such other categories as "Politicks [and] Trade" (eight distinct works), "Religion" (fifteen separate works), "Law" (three distinct titles), "History. Antient [sic]" (twelve works, including the Bible), "History. Modern" (eight titles), "Natural Philosophy, Natural History &c." (thirteen titles), and "Miscellaneous" (five titles).

Many of the titles Jefferson listed under these categories, especially those dealing with ancient history, would often today be classified as literature or would at least be valued as much for their artful phrasing as for their factual contents. And if we total up the number of titles listed for *all* the many categories just mentioned, we discover that they amount to 65 titles—less than the 75 listed just for the Fine Arts. This is a somewhat remarkable finding: who would have expected that Jefferson would have taken such a strong interest in literature when he himself is not known as a writer of literature but rather as a political theorist and practical statesman?

There is, however, one category from Jefferson's list that I have so far failed to mention. That category is "*Criticism* on the Fine Arts" (my emphasis). Jefferson, in other words, was interested not only in the fine arts themselves but in what had been written *about* them.

How many books did he list under this category? Only seven—one of which (Samuel Johnson's famous *Dictionary*) would not today be classified as criticism *per se*). Here is Jefferson's list:

> Ld. Kaim's elements of criticism 2 v. 8vo. 10/
> Burke on the sublime and beautiful. 8vo. 5/
> Hogarth's analysis of beauty. 4to. £1.1
> Reid on the human mind. 8vo. 5/
> Smith's theory of moral sentiments. 8vo. 5/
> Johnson's dictionary. 2 v. fol. £3
> Capell's prolusions. 12mo. 3/ (*Writings* 744)

Why did Jefferson mention "Ld. [i.e., "Lord"] Kaim" first in this list—even before the great and still well-known Edmund Burke? Why did Jefferson, almost a quarter century later, again place "Ld. Kaim" high on his list of authors worth reading by anyone interested in understanding literature? (see Berman 207). Why did "Ld. Kaim's" name, in fact, appear three different times among all the writers Jefferson recommended to Skipwith?

Who, exactly, was "Ld. Kaim"?

Lord Kames

"Ld. Kaim" is best known today as Henry Home, Lord Kames. He was born in 1696 in Scotland and died in 1792, less than twenty years after the American Revolution. During his long life, Kames (as I will now refer to him), rapidly rose to become a prominent jurist, a well-known writer, and a key figure in the so-called "Scottish Enlightenment" (see Rahmatian, *Lord Kames*, and also Lehmann). He played a major role in outlawing slavery in Scotland, wrote frequently about the law, and published numerous influential works. These included *Remarkable Decisions of the Court of Session* (1728); *Essays upon Several Subjects in Law* (1732); *Essay Upon Several Subjects Concerning British Antiquities* (c. 1745); *Essays on the Principles of Morality and Natural Religion* (1751); *Historical Law-Tracts* (1758); *Principles of Equity* (1760); *Introduction to the Art of Thinking* (1761); *Elements of Criticism* (1762); *Sketches of the History of Man* (1774); *Gentleman Farmer*

(1776); and *Loose Thoughts on Education* (1781). Of these works, Jefferson recommended three to Skipwith: "*Natural Religion*" (as he abbreviated the title), *Principles of Equity*, and *Elements of Criticism*. Kames has long been recognized as a key influence on Jefferson's own thinking (see, for example, Berman 292), but scholars have mostly paid attention to Jefferson's interest in Kames's views of morality, philosophy, and the law (see, for example, Holowchak; Jayne; and Rahmatian, "The Influence"). Much less attention has been paid to Jefferson's enthusiasm for the *Elements of Criticism* (see, for example, Berman [passim] and Golden and Golden, 344–45). But it was in the latter work, especially in its stunningly detailed second volume, that Jefferson would have found an extraordinary amount of specific advice about the art of writing.

The first volume of Kames's *Elements* is mainly concerned with aesthetics in a very broad sense, as one branch of philosophy. In the second volume, however, Kames offers voluminous point-by-point advice both about how to write and why to write as he suggests. Sometimes his advice is directed specifically at poets, but initially he offers counsel that would have been just as useful to writers of prose. Many of his ideas are the sort that would be found today in books dealing with rhetoric and composition. And, in fact, much of his specific advice is *exactly* the sort that today is *still* found in such books. Jefferson would have learned, from Kames, many of the standard rules still taught by composition teachers. And he would also have learned, from Kames, the logic behind those rules.

What, exactly, did Kames advise writers to do? What kind of phrasing did he most admire and recommend, and why?[1]

First, he argued that the best kind of writing occurs when an idea is expressed with **clarity and vividness**—or, as he puts it, with "perspicuity and sprightliness" (2:5). As we will see, this stress on **clarity** is his key emphasis: clarity should never be sacrificed for any other kind of linguistic effect. But Kames was definitely interested in beauties of language in addition to the key beauty of clarity, and, in fact, he thought that these additional beauties could enhance the impact of a clear idea.

Critical Insights

Kames discusses, in far more detail than I have space for here, practically every matter imaginable. Such topics include the nature of vowels and consonants, the kinds of syllables that are "agreeable to the ear" (2:5), the differences between harsh sounds and appealing sounds, the right ways to combine sounds for best effect, and the ways sounds can best be combined. In discussing the sounds of individual words, as well as the sounds of words in combination, he hits upon another of his key themes: **the importance of variety**. Monotony of any kind should be avoided unless there is a specific reason to employ it (such as to reinforce, through the sounds of words, the very idea of monotony). Kames especially recommended words that involved alternating stressed and unstressed syllables, such as "*alternative, longevity,* [and] *pusillanimous.*" He disliked words of insufficient variety, such as "*petitioner, fruiterer,* [and] *dizziness.*" On the other hand, he felt that "the intermixture of long and short syllables is remarkably agreeable; for example, *degree, repent, wonderful, altitude, rapidity, independent, impetuosity*" (2:7). But Kames did not think he was merely offering a personal opinion; he thought, for reasons he was quite willing to explain, that he was dealing with laws of human nature. All people of good taste, he believed, would agree with his claims. So far, **his key claims were that effective language must be clear, vivid, and varied.**

Kames's emphasis on variety meant that **he preferred phrasing that alternated between smooth and rough sounds**:

A smooth gliding sound is agreeable, by calming the mind, and lulling it to rest: a rough bold sound, on the contrary, animates the mind; the effort perceived in pronouncing, is communicated to the hearers, who feel in their own minds a similar effort, rousing their attention, and disposing them to action. I add another consideration: the agreeableness of contrast in the rougher language, for which the great variety of sounds gives ample opportunity, must, even in an effeminate ear, prevail over the more uniform sounds of the smoother language. (2:8)

Phrasing that was uniformly smooth, or uniformly rough, would be monotonous and thus boring. Here, then, as always, Kames preferred variety, and he thought most other humans naturally did as well.

But variety, in Kames's view, should also be well organized. Disorganized variety might merely seem chaotic. For example, he thought that when writers offered a list, they should arrange words or phrases from shortest to longest. To illustrate this rule, he quoted several examples from Cicero, one of which can be translated as follows:

> "The office to which I seek election;
> the ambition that I cherish in my heart;
> the reputation for which I have risen early and toiled in the heat to gain." (2:9, 264)

This kind of "order of words or members gradually increasing in length, may," Kames wrote, be called "*a climax in sound*" (2:10; his italics). By definition, a climax involves order imposed upon variety, and so Kames once again emphasized his key rule of the need for variety: "to avoid a tedious uniformity of sound and cadence, the arrangement, the cadence, and the length of the members, ought to be diversified as much as possible: and if the members of different periods [i.e., sentences or lengthy parts of sentences] be sufficiently diversified, the periods themselves will be equally so" (2:10).

Kames quoted, in fact (from a "noted writer" named J. Scot), a sentence that illustrated many of the features he most admired: ". . . by means of speech we can divert our sorrows, mingle our mirth, impart our secrets, communicate our counsels, and make mutual compacts and agreements to supply and assist each other" (2:10). Here is the kind of well-composed variety Kames always commended. He believed that when one examined a sentence, two matters should "be regarded: first, the words of which it is composed; next, the arrangement of these words; the former resembling the stones that compose a building, and the latter resembling the order in which they are placed" (2:10). Good writers would carefully choose both their words and their arrangements of those words.

Concerning the *choice of words*, Kames returned to his chief criterion: the need for clarity. Such clarity, he wrote,

> ought not to be sacrificed to any other beauty whatever: if it should be doubted whether perspicuity be a positive beauty, it cannot be doubted that the want of it is the greatest defect. Nothing therefore in language ought more to be studied, than to prevent all obscurity in the expression; for to have no meaning, is but one degree worse, than to have a meaning that is not understood. (2:11)

Therefore, an effective writer must, first and foremost, choose clear words and clear phrasing. Kames then quoted numerous examples (from Latin writers) of phrasing he considered unclear and explained why he considered some of them, in particular, lacking in clarity. Even the "slightest ambiguity in [the] construction" of a sentence could make the sentence unclear, such as illogical shifts in cases (say, from nominative to accusative) and illogical shifts of many other kinds (2:12). Thus Kames, like many current teachers of composition, advocated for logical consistency in phrasing and structure. He rejected any illogical, ambiguous shift of meaning. Clarity, he reiterated, "ought never to be sacrificed to any other beauty" (2:13).

Kames's emphasis on the *logic* and *consistency* of *clear writing* can be seen in several more of his rules:

> . . . the language ought to correspond to the subject. Heroic actions or sentiments require elevated language; tender sentiments ought to be expressed in words soft and flowing; and plain language void of ornament, is adapted to subjects grave and didactic. Language may be considered as the dress of thought; and where the one is not suited to the other, we are sensible of incongruity, in the same manner as where a judge is dressed like a fop, or a peasant like a man of quality. Where the impression made by the words resembles the impression made by the thought, the similar emotions mix sweetly in the mind, and double the pleasure; but where the impressions made by the thought and the words are dissimilar, the unnatural union they are forced into is disagreeable. In a thought of any extent, we commonly find some parts intimately united, some slightly, some disjoined, and

some directly opposed to each other. To find these conjunctions and disjunctions imitated in the expression, is a beauty; because such imitation makes the words concordant with the sense.

Kames continued,

This doctrine may be illustrated by a familiar example. When we have occasion to mention the intimate connection that the soul hath with the body, the expression ought to be, *the soul and body;* because the particle *the,* relative to both, makes a connection in the expression, resembling in some degree the connection in the thought: but when the soul is distinguished from the body, it is better to say *the soul and the body*; because the disjunction in the words resembles the disjunction in the thought. (2:13)

Kames then offered many more examples to illustrate this point, but his larger argument is always in favor of words and phrases being logically connected to thought. Illogical connections and illogical shifts of any kind should be avoided. For example, Kames cited a flawed sentence and then immediately offered a correction that struck him as more logical: "'He did not mention Leonora, nor that her father was dead.' Better thus: 'He did not mention Leonora, nor her father's death'" (2:14). Kames also endorsed balanced sentence structures and alliteration (as long as it was not overdone), as in this example from John Dryden's translation of Virgil's *Aeneid*: "My life's companion, and my bosom-friend, / One faith, one fame, one fate shall both attend" (2:14). As always, Kames offered numerous examples—both of successful sentences and of unsuccessful sentences—to illustrate his point.

Balanced sentence structure was always important to Kames, even or especially when it involved *antithesis*, the placement of opposites. Thus he quoted a sentence describing the Roman general Coriolanus: "With a proud heart he wore his humble weeds." He then quoted Coriolanus himself, speaking in Shakespeare's play concerning that figure: "Had you rather Caesar were living, and die all slaves, / than that Caesar were dead, to live all free men?" And Kames also quoted from Shakespeare's *Julius Caesar*: "He hath cool'd my friends and heated mine enemies" (2:15). Kames cautioned, however, that where there is no logical connection between a thought and the word used to express it, artificial balances and connections should be avoided. Interestingly, almost all the examples he cited to support this rule involved puns made by Shakespeare—puns that most critics today would find genuinely witty (2:16–17). Kames, however, considered them forced and unnatural and, therefore, definite stylistic defects.

In line with his insistence on logical consistency, Kames objected to the inconsistent or illogical use of verb tenses, just as he also objected to uniting contrasting ideas unless when trying to be funny. In general, though, he insisted on logic, appropriateness, and consistency. Thus he advised that a

> sentence or period ought to express one entire thought or mental proposition; and different thoughts ought to be separated in the expression by placing them in different sentences or periods. It is therefore offending against neatness, to crowd into one period entire thoughts requiring more than one; which is joining in language things that are separated in reality. (2:17)

Two examples Kames cited to illustrate this point do definitely sound illogical: "Behold, thou art fair, my beloved, yea pleasant; also our bed is green"; and "His own notions were always good; but he was a man of great expence" (2:17). In both sentences, the thoughts that come at the end seem to have no logical connections to the thoughts that come at the beginning. Kames offered many more examples to underscore this argument.

Again, emphasizing his interest in logical consistency, Kames insisted (as do many composition books today) that only similar things should be compared, especially when using similes. For example, he cited this illogical sentence, written by Jonathan Swift: "I have observed of late, the style of some great *ministers* very much to exceed that of any other *productions*" (Kames's italics). Kames commented that instead "of *productions,* which resemble not ministers great nor small, the proper word is *writers* or *authors*" (2:18). Kames then proceeded to list many other examples of illogical thought expressed in illogical phrasing. Logical phrasing, he believed, should express and contribute to logical thought.

Now, however, he proceeded

> to a rule of a different kind. During the course of a period, the scene ought to be continued without variation: the changing from person to person, from subject to subject, or from person to subject, within the bounds of a single period, distracts the mind, and affords no time for a solid impression. (2:21)

Of the many examples Kames cited to illustrate this point, one seems especially noteworthy: "After a short time *he* came to himself; and the next day, *they* put him on board his ship, *which* conveyed him first to Corinth, and thence to the island of Aegina" (2:21). Here the grammatical subject of the sentence shifts three different times—from "he" to "they" to the "ship." A longer example of the same sort of illogic (from Jonathan Swift) appears in the following example, where Kames italicized the shifting subjects:

> The *Britons,* daily harassed by cruel inroads from the Picts, were forced to call in the Saxons for their defence, *who* consequently reduced the greatest part of the island to their own power, drove the Britons into the most remote and mountainous parts, and *the rest of the country,* in customs, religion, and language, became wholly Saxon. (2:22).

Kames could (and often did) go on citing example after example of this kind of illogic. But the simple point is obvious: he insisted that clear logic would help create clear writing and that clear writing would help emphasize clear logic.

But Kames was also very much interested in the sounds of syllables, words, and sentences and the contributions such sounds could make to the meaning and effectiveness of writing. He followed Longinus, for instance, in noting that sometimes "it animates a period to drop the copulatives," citing the following example from Xenophon: "Closing their shields together, they were push'd, they fought, they slew, they were slain" (2:23). Instead of using "and" after all but the first comma, Xenophon put maximum emphasis on the verbs and thus enhanced the sentence's speed. The sentence's rhythm reinforces the rhythm of what it describes. If Xenophon had wanted to slow down the sentence's speed and emphasize each particular action, he would have inserted three "ands." "It follows," Kames continued, "that a plurality of copulatives in the same period ought to be avoided: for if the laying aside copulatives give force and liveliness, a redundancy of them must render the period languid" (2:23). He was perfectly prepared, however, to admit multiple copulatives when doing so reinforced the sense, mood, and/or meaning of the sentence or the personality of the speaker or when many copulatives were used "to give an impression of a great multitude consisting of many divisions; for example: 'The army was composed of Grecians, and Carians, and Lycians, and Pamphylians, and Phrygians'" (2:24). In discussing copulatives, as in discussing so much else, Kames typically deduced rules but then also explained logical exceptions to them. Logic and clarity, however, are always his chief criteria for assessing effective writing.

Kames next discussed what he called the "second kind of beauty; which consists in a due arrangement of the words or materials" (2:24). His general rule in this case was that in

> a complete thought or mental proposition, all the members and parts are mutually related, some slightly, some intimately. To put such a thought in words, it is not sufficient that the component ideas be clearly expressed; it is also necessary, that all the relations contained in the thought be expressed according to their different degrees of intimacy. (2:24)

Nature itself had helped generate the specific consequences of this general rule. As before, Kames argued that every particular part of a sentence must make sense in relation to all the other parts. For example, in English, "adjectives accompany their substantives; an adverb accompanies the word it qualifies; and the verb occupies the middle place between the active and passive subjects to which it relates" (2:25). But along with these inflexible rules of grammar, "variety in the expression . . . enriches language" (2:26). Inversion of standard sentence structure, for example, could sometimes be used, but not to any extreme degree. (**Avoiding extremes** is another central criterion of Kames's thoughts about writing.) In general, the normal order of a sentence should be preferred, but

> this arrangement may be varied, when a different order is more beautiful: a circumstance may be placed before the word with which it is connected by a preposition; and may be interjected even between a relative word and that to which it relates. When such liberties are frequently taken, the style becomes inverted or transposed. (2:26)

But excessive inversion soon sounds unnatural; in good writing, nothing should be overdone or should become monotonously predictable. Sometimes, for example, a subordinate clause can precede the independent clause: "In the sincerity of my heart, I profess, &c." is as acceptable and even as natural as "I profess in the sincerity of my heart" (2:26). Kames actually admired many kinds of inversion precisely because they kept phrasing from becoming stale, and he several times quoted Milton as a master of the technique (as in the famous opening sentence of *Paradise Lost*). "Language," Kames wrote, "would have no great power, were it *confined* to the natural order of ideas" (my italics). He thought, in fact, that "by inversion a thousand beauties may be compassed, which must be relinquished in a natural arrangement." In fact, "the mind of man is happily so constituted as to relish inversion, tho' in one respect unnatural; and to relish it so much, as in many cases to admit a separation between words the most intimately connected" (2:28). The human mind is so constituted that variety is as important as the normal, "natural" order of syntax.

Kames now proceeded to discuss what he called "the rules of arrangement; beginning with a natural style, and proceeding gradually to what is the most inverted" (2:28). As usual, "perspicuity" or clarity was his chief demand. Indeed, "perspicuity ought not to be sacrificed to any other [kind of] beauty" (7:28). The unnatural arrangement of words could create confusion about meaning, and confusion should always be avoided. Kames cited many examples of such confusion created by odd syntax. For instance, he cited this sentence as an example of faulty sentence structure creating confused meaning: "If he was not the greatest king, he was the best actor of majesty at least, that ever filled a throne." This sentence, he thought, would be clearer if rewritten as follows: "If he was not the greatest king, he was at least the best actor of majesty, &c." (2:29).

Kames could—and often did—go on for page after page citing faulty phrasing and then offering his corrections. And his corrections almost always resulted in clearer, more logical sentences. Sometimes the corrections involved rearranging words or clauses; sometimes they involved inserting or deleting punctuation; but in nearly every case Kames improved the sentences he censured. He cautioned, however, that while punctuation alone could sometimes make writing clearer, it was best not to over-rely on punctuation to clarify a faulty sentence structure. It was best to choose, from the beginning, as clear a sentence structure as possible. Well-structured sentences were not only clearer than ambiguously structured ones; they were also more "musical" (2:33).

Kames argued, in general, that "human nature" is

> prone in every instance to place together things in any manner connected: where things are arranged according to their connections, we have a sense of order; otherwise we have a sense of disorder, as of things placed by chance: and we naturally place words in the same order in which we would place the things they signify. (2:33)

He then, in his typical fashion, offered many examples of the "bad effect of a violent separation of words or members thus intimately connected" (2:33). Pronouns should follow as closely as possible the nouns they echo; subordinate clauses should come earlier in sentences rather than later; and key words should come last in a sentence, since that position gives them maximum impact. The next best position for emphasizing a key word comes at the beginning of a sentence, not the middle. In fact, the start of a sentence is the best place to mention the name of a person being addressed. In general, however, the "order of words in a period will always be the most agreeable, where, without obscuring the sense, the most important images, the most sonorous words, and the longest members, bring up the rear" (2:39).

Having discussed the general structure of entire sentences, Kames now turned to the issue of how to handle lists of words within those sentences. He argued that where each item in a list was equal to the others, their precise arrangement did not matter. But if they were unequal, they should be arranged in "an increasing series," for the movement from least to most or smallest to largest gives "a very sensible pleasure," creating "*a climax in sense*" (2:39). Kames thought, however, that when arranging people in order of rank, this natural sequence could be reversed, with the most important person being mentioned first. Similarly, sentences themselves should be arranged so that they moved from shorter to longer, but they should also exhibit variety in their arrangement. Finally, in discussing the use of inversion in sentences, where the "natural" sentence structure is significantly altered, Kames showed that although he admired plain, straightforward sentence structures because they are so clear, he could also admire inverted syntax if it was clear and not overdone. Or, as he put it in an important passage that closes a major section of his treatise:

> the beauty of a plain or natural style . . . [results when] the order of the words corresponds precisely to the order of the ideas. Nor is this the single beauty of a natural style: it is also agreeable by its simplicity and perspicuity. . . . [However], language, by means of inversion, is susceptible of many beauties that are totally excluded in a natural arrangement. From these premises it clearly follows, that inversion ought not to be indulged, unless in order to reach some beauty superior to those of a natural style. It may with great certainty be pronounced, that every inversion which is not governed by this rule, will appear harsh and strained, and be disrelished by every one of taste. Hence the beauty of inversion when happily conducted; the beauty, not of an end, but of means, as furnishing opportunity for numberless ornaments that find no place in a natural style: hence the force, the elevation, the harmony, the cadence, of some compositions: hence the manifold beauties of the Greek and Roman tongues, of which living languages afford but faint imitations. (2:42–43)

The Relevance of Kames to the Declaration of Independence

Kames, who is never anything less than detailed, next went on to discuss how language could achieve beauty "from a resemblance between sound and signification"—that is, how the very sounds of certain words (as in onomatopoeia) could enhance their effectiveness (2:43). He also discussed many other details of effective phrasing, such as the actual rhythm of words and sentences. But to follow him down these paths would result in an essay far longer than this one already is. Instead, it seems worthwhile to ask, at this point, precisely why and how Kames's ideas about writing may have affected the actual writing Thomas Jefferson did—especially the writing he did in the Declaration of Independence. Kames, after all, seems to have been one of the main theorists of rhetoric Jefferson read in the years *before* writing the Declaration. (He would mention other theorists of rhetoric, such as Hugh Blair, *after* writing his most famous composition; see Berman 189–91.) If we look back over the preceding survey of Kames's ideas, twenty seem especially significant:

1. good writing should be clear, vivid, and varied
2. although varied, it should also be well organized
3. words and phrases should move from shortest to longest
4. words, and their arrangement, should be carefully chosen
5. phrasing and structure should be logical and consistent
6. good writers should reject illogical, confusing shifts of meaning
7. balanced sentence structures are often valuable
8. only similar things should be compared, especially in similes
9. clear logic helps create clear writing
10. clear writing helps emphasize clear logic
11. good writers should avoid extremes of all kinds
12. nothing should be overdone or monotonously predictable
13. confusion should always be avoided
14. pronouns should follow as closely as possible the nouns they echo
15. subordinate clauses should come earlier rather than later
16. key words should come last, where they have maximum impact
17. the next best position for key words is at a sentence's beginning, not the middle

18. movement from least to most or from smallest to largest creates a pleasurable "climax in sense"
19. sentences themselves should move from shorter to longer
20. sentences, like words, should also exhibit varied arrangement

If we use these twenty criteria to evaluate the Declaration, what do we find? Consider that document's opening sentence, which consists of many clauses that exhibit both variety and a certain degree of progression in their length:

> When in the Course of human events, it becomes necessary for one people to dissolve the political bands which have connected them with another, **[24 words]** and to assume among the powers of the earth, the separate and equal station to which the Laws of Nature and of Nature's God entitle them, **[26 words]** a decent respect to the opinions of mankind requires that they should declare the causes which impel them to the separation. **[21 words]**[2]

Here the three clauses are of relatively equal length. The structure of the sentence is thus well balanced, partly to reinforce the sense of a well-balanced, rational statement of abstract principles. The language itself is somewhat abstract; even the one obvious metaphor—"dissolve the political bands"—is not especially concrete. And the clauses are balanced not only in length but in internal structure. Thus "to dissolve the political bands" is balanced by "to assume among the powers," as are the references to "the Laws of Nature" and "of Nature's God." Ironically, although Kames had taught that it was best to begin with short sentences and then move gradually to longer ones, Jefferson chose to begin with quite a long sentence indeed. It consists of 71 words altogether, but each word and clause fits perfectly into the larger structure. It is as if Jefferson wanted to begin with a long and commanding statement of general purpose before moving into particulars.

It is the next sentence, of course, that may be the most famous sentence Jefferson ever composed—one of the most famous sentences in all human history: "We hold these truths to be self-evident **[7 words]**, that all men are created equal, **[6 words]** that they are endowed by their Creator with certain unalienable Rights [**11 words**], that among these are Life, Liberty and the pursuit of Happiness." [**11 words**] Kames could hardly have asked for a better illustration of his teachings than this sentence. The first two relatively short clauses balance one another, as do the two longer clauses that follow. A further sense of balance both in logic and in phrasing comes from the repeated "that . . . that . . . that" structure. The word "created" foreshadows the word "Creator," and the sentence evolves logically from a focus on human beings to a focus on their creator and then to a focus on the rights he has created for them. When introducing the three basic rights enumerated—"Life, Liberty and the pursuit of Happiness"—Jefferson lists them as Kames would have wished: first a single word of one syllable, then a single word of three syllables, then a phrase of four words consisting of six syllables. And, of course, "Life" and "Liberty" are effectively linked by alliteration—another trait of style Kames admired, but which I did not discuss earlier. In the first two clauses, the key words—"equal" and "Rights"—come at the end of each clause, while the end of the final clause consists of the emphatic list of very particular rights. It is hard to imagine a better-constructed sentence. Any attempt to rearrange the words seems flawed by comparison. ("Life, Liberty and the pursuit of happiness are among certain unalienable Rights . . . etc."—a complete mess of a sentence.)

Jefferson's sentence seems all the more effective the more closely it is examined. It begins with "We," not with "I" (too specific) nor with "Humans" (too broad), but with "We"—the particular people who will later sign the declaration and thereby put their very lives, liberty, and potential to pursue happiness at genuine risk. (Jefferson knew that if the Revolution failed, he and his comrades would probably be hanged as traitors.) "We hold these truths": at first this might seem to mean "we embrace these truths," "we affirm these truths." Only later do we realize the full meaning of the verb: "We hold these truths *to be self-evident.*" And they are "truths," not opinions or ideas. And, furthermore, they are "self-evident"— so obviously true that they hardly need to be defended, merely explained and elaborated upon. The phrase "that all men are created equal" shifts the focus from the earlier, somewhat narrow "we" to the much broader, far more comprehensive "all men." The "we" here presume to speak on behalf of the "all," but they only speak a truth that "all men" are likely to consider "self-evident." This next part of the sentence nicely moves from four brief monosyllables—"that all men are"—to two words of greater length—"created equal." Kames definitely would have admired this progression from shorter words to longer ones. In fact, it is hard to imagine how even someone as nit-picky as Kames could fault anything in this entire sentence.

Jefferson next proceeds to a list of further "that's"—the first one very short, the next two considerably longer, and all three exhibiting the kind of balance and logic Kames so admired. Thus, the first "that" clause immediately looks back to the preceding reference to "these rights" and then balances the word "Governments" with the word "governed." In this initial "that" clause, the words that precede the first comma amount to five; the words that precede the second comma also amount to five, and the words that precede the period amount to ten, giving the sentence this kind of mathematically precise structure: $5 + 5 + 10$. It seems unlikely that Jefferson designed this structure consciously or deliberately. Instead, he probably simply trusted his ear and his preference for putting short clauses at the beginnings of sentences and long clauses at the end.

The very next "that" clause exhibits the kind of variety—especially in the lengths of its clauses—that Kames endorsed. The first portion of the sentence consists of eleven words; the second consists of thirteen words; the third contains five words; the fourth contains thirteen words; the fifth also contains thirteen words. The over-all structure of the sentence, then, looks something like this: $11 + 13 + 5 + 13 + 13$. Four of the five sections are roughly equal in length, with one very short section included in the middle for variety. But the sentence contains other kinds of balance as well, as when Jefferson mentions the right of people "to alter or to abolish" a destructive government and "to institute" a new one; and when he balances such verb phrases as "laying its foundation" and "organizing its powers"; and then, finally, when he closes by mentioning the people's dual "Safety and Happiness." Safety comes first (one might argue) because safety is *the* key value a government provides. Once they are confident in their safety, people can then pursue their happiness, however they choose as individuals to define that very broad-brush term. Later examples of balance in the ensuing sentence involve the words "suffer" and "sufferable"; "abuses and usurpations"; "it is their right, it is their duty"; and the link between "to throw off" and "to provide."

Jefferson is also very skilled in constantly looking back over his shoulder and logically linking new points with preceding points, as when he refers to "these Rights" and "these Ends," and when he balances "Such has been" with "such is now." He even works in a bit of a paradox: "necessity . . . constrains [the colonists] to alter" their government. Their *choice* of freedom is *dictated* by necessity! They have no other choice but to choose freedom. But as the Declaration proceeds, one notices especially how often and how well Jefferson chooses balanced phrasing: "The history . . . is a history"; "injuries *and* usurpations" (my italics); "absolute Tyranny" (singular) "over these States" (plural).

Next comes one of the most rhetorically effective of all the parts of the Declaration—the ever-lengthening list of the King's abuses. Here Jefferson uses the technique known as *anaphora*, in which each new clause begins with similar phrasing. Here are the first few words of each item in Jefferson's list—a list that puts maximum emphasis on the initial verbs: "He has refused"; "He has forbidden"; "He has refused"; "He has called together"; "He has dissolved"; "He has refused for a long time"; "He has endeavoured"; "He has obstructed"; "He has made"; "He has erected"; "He has kept among us"; "He has affected"; and "He has combined." These thirteen separate clauses make a powerful impact. They accuse George III of just about every conceivable abuse of power one could easily imagine. He comes across sounding like a very inventive tyrant, constantly thinking up new ways to abuse the colonists. Meanwhile, the list itself is richly varied in structure and content. The first clause contains sixteen words; the second clause (of thirty-six words) more than doubles the first; the very next clause contains thirty-seven words; the clause after that shrinks a bit (to thirty-one words); and the clause after that shrinks even further (to nineteen words). Jefferson thus employs the variety in sentence structure that Kames so heartily recommended.

But Jefferson also employs, in these clauses, the kind of balanced phrasing to which his logical, rational mind seems to have been naturally drawn. Examples include "wholesome and necessary"; "immediate and pressing"; "unless suspended" and "when suspended"; "invasion from without, and convulsions within"; "amount and payment"; and even a long, nicely balanced conclusion: "a right *inestimable to them* and *formidable to tyrants* only" (my italics). Sometimes Jefferson effectively uses lists, as when he mentions "places unusual, uncomfortable, and distant," where each adjective gets strong emphasis. Sometimes he even balances, through antithesis, the beginnings of adjacent clauses, as when he writes "He has called together" and next writes "He has dissolved." And, in one case, Jefferson combines balanced structure with a verb that almost sounds like a metaphor comparing the King's troops to locusts: he has "sent hither swarms of Officers to harrass our people, and eat out their substance." All in all, this section of the Declaration is a very impressive rhetorical performance.

But the next section is, if anything, even *more* impressive. Here again Jefferson uses anaphora, but now the items in the lists are much shorter than before. The king has assented to laws "For Quartering large bodies of armed troops among us"; "For protecting them . . ."; "For cutting off our Trade . . ."; "For imposing Taxes . . ."; "For depriving us . . .; "For transporting us . . ."; "For abolishing . . ."; "For taking away . . ."; and "For suspending." These nine accusations are then followed by five more that echo the earlier use of anaphora: "He has abdicated . . ."; "He has plundered . . ."; "He is at this time . . ."; "He has constrained . . ."; and "He has excited . . .". It is hard to think of another public document that so effectively uses lists, verbs, and indeed lists *of* verbs. Sometimes, in fact, he uses lists within lists, as in "abolishing," "establishing," and "enlarging" and in "taking away," "abolishing" and "altering"; and in "plundered," "ravaged," "burnt," and "destroyed." The king stands accused of imposing "death, desolation and tyranny" and of engaging in "Cruelty & perfidy" by forcing Americans to fight against their "friends and Brethren." He has set Indians against the colonists—Indians who routinely destroy people of "all ages, sexes and conditions." Jefferson often makes George III, not the colonists, sound like the innovative revolutionary who is overturning traditional, established rights and practices. In this Declaration, the main emphasis is on the many tyrannical *actions* of the king—actions that make the *reactions* of the colonists seem not only justified but also inevitable.

The Declaration continues for another 326 words (out of a total word count of 1333), but by now enough has been said to suggest why and how Kames might have admired the document purely as a piece of writing. Its phrasing is clear, vivid, and varied but also very well organized. Its diction, syntax, and overall structure are logical and consistent, with a forcefully developing argument and no confusing shifts. It frequently uses all kinds of balanced structures of words, phrases, sentences, and paragraphs. Moreover, it makes extraordinarily effective use of lists, with especially effective emphasis on verbs. In short, the Declaration is not only a clear product of its own historical era, but it is also a work that exhibits the kinds of traits rhetoricians have emphasized for centuries, both before Kames and since.

Notes

1. To make Kames's key thoughts as visible and easy to find as possible, they are highlighted in bold.

2. Quotes from the Declaration of Independence were taken from the online version found at: www.archives.gov/founding-docs/declaration-transcript.

Works Cited

Berman, Eleanor. *Thomas Jefferson among the Arts: An Essay in Early American Esthetics*. Philosophical Library, 1947.

Golden, James E., and Alan L. Golden. *Thomas Jefferson and the Rhetoric of Virtue*. Rowman and Littlefield, 2002.

Holowchak, M. Andrew. *Thomas Jefferson: Moralist*. McFarland, 2017.

Jayne, Allen. *Jefferson's Declaration of Independence: Origins, Philosophy, and Theology*. U of Kentucky P, 2015.

Jefferson, Thomas. "Declaration of Independence: A Transcription." *National Archives*. www.archives.gov/founding-docs/declaration-transcript.

_____. *Writings*, edited by Merrill D. Peterson. Library of America, 1984.

Kames, Henry Home, Lord. *The Elements of Criticism*, [1762] edited by Peter Jones. Liberty Fund, 2005, 2 vols., oll.libertyfund.org/titles/kames-elements-of-criticism-2-vols.

Lehmann, William C. *Henry Home, Lord Kames and the Scottish Enlightenment: A Study in National Character and in the History of Ideas*. Springer, 2013.

Rahmatian, Andreas. *Lord Kames: Legal and Social Theorist*. Edinburgh U P, 2015.

_____. "The Influence of Lord Kames (Henry Home) on Some of the Founders of the United States." *Historia et Ius*, 7, 2015, pp. 1–48, eprints.gla.ac.uk/107289/1/107289.pdf.

CRITICAL READINGS

My Life with Thomas Jefferson

John B. Boles

How and why did you first become interested in Jefferson?
As a child I found Jefferson fascinating especially because of his curiosity about so many aspects of his world and because of the range of his accomplishments. Then, in the first semester of my final undergraduate year at Rice University, I took a history course offered by Sanford W. Higginbotham entitled "Jeffersonian and Jacksonian Democracy." As part of that course we read Merrill D. Peterson's masterpiece, *The Jefferson Image in the American Mind,* along with a compilation of Jefferson's essential writings edited by Adrienne Koch and William Peden. The Koch and Peden volume, some 700 pages, contained many of Jefferson's most important public writings and a healthy sampling of his letters. I found the letters absolutely fascinating—I wished the book contained more— and was amazed by Jefferson's evident learning and literary ability. The Peterson book impressed me even more; I had never read a book like it. Not a biography of Jefferson at all, it was rather, as its very first sentence stated, "not a book on the history Thomas Jefferson made but a book on what history made of Thomas Jefferson." Here was what Americans had thought about Jefferson over time, how they had refashioned him to fit their era, how he had been a living intellectual construct continually evolving. It was an intellectually exciting book, my first real dive into the complexity of what we in graduate school called historiography—history as written, not lived. I had already decided to go to graduate school; after all, this was 1965, and a war was raging in Vietnam, and I knew about scholarly deferments. But I had truly become devoted to history; I just hadn't yet decided what area or topic to specialize in. The Peterson book, and Jefferson's writings, persuaded me to study the age of Jefferson, and knowing Peterson taught at the University of Virginia (and quickly learning that two other eminent Jefferson scholars, Bernard Mayo and Dumas Malone, were there), I decided to apply to U.Va.

When I arrived at U.Va. in the fall of 1965, I fully expected to write on Jefferson. Mr. Jefferson suffused the air in Charlottesville, and there resided Bernie Mayo, a wonderfully effective teacher; [Merrill] Peterson, exuding an aura of incomparable learning; and, in an upper suite of the Alderman Library, the great [Dumas] Malone laboring away at his multi-volume biography, *Jefferson and His Time*, with volume III having recently been published (with three more yet to come). Within the first day or so the dean of the graduate school spoke to the incoming graduate students and urged upon us the importance of quickly nailing down a dissertation topic. Now I think he meant within a semester or year or two, but being a literalist of sorts, I thought he meant like within a few weeks. My final semester at Rice I had loved an anthropology course entitled "Primitive Religion" taught by Edward Norbeck, and both in the course and in his textbook he discussed a religious revival that occurred in Kentucky in 1800 that featured unusual responses to evangelical preaching including uncontrollable shaking, falling unconscious, and so on. Having grown up in rural East Texas and witnessed present-day examples of such religious exercises, I was surprised to read about what apparently were the origins of such religious expression in the South of 1800. So, feeling pressed with the need to quickly come up with a dissertation topic, I decided upon the general topic of religion in the age of Jefferson and more specifically the so-called Great Revival in the West.

That became my dissertation topic and the subject of my first book, *The Great Revival, 1787–1805*, and that book more or less typecast my work for the next decade. I followed up my first book with a study of religion in Kentucky from frontier days to the Civil War, and this book contained a chapter on slave religion. This interest led to reading and eventually a short history of slavery, *Black Southerners: 1619–1869*, that became widely assigned in college classes, and to an edited work on slave religion. During this time I moved from Tulane University back to Rice in 1981, both to teach and to edit the *Journal of Southern History*. I became very active in training graduate students (eventually directing sixty-two dissertations) and editing and writing books on a variety of subjects.

Finally, in 2013, I retired from editing the *Journal of Southern History*, which, though immensely fulfilling, had been immensely time consuming. At this point it occurred to me that although I had gone to Charlottesville almost fifty years before explicitly to study Jefferson, I had, in fact, not yet done so. I realized that if I wanted to get anything done on Jefferson, it was past time to get started. But it occurred to me also that I may have waited too long.

In the fall of 1965, Jefferson was at the apex of his favorability rating in America. He was understood as the Renaissance Man (everyone knew how President Kennedy, addressing a room filled with Nobel prize winners, had said "I think this is the most extraordinary collection of talent, of human knowledge, that has ever been gathered at the White House—with the possible exception of when Thomas Jefferson dined alone.") and the consummate spokesman of liberty in the midst of the Cold War. But the South was in the process of being rediscovered and remade in the 1960s. The Civil Rights Movement was underway, and every thinking American was reconsidering the role of race in the nation's history. How had slavery survived so long in the reputed land of liberty? In the midst of this intellectual moment the history of slavery in the United States was being revolutionized: already Kenneth M. Stampp (1956) and Stanley M. Elkins (1959) had written provocative books, soon to be followed with an avalanche of brilliant books by authors such as [John W.] Blassingame, [Edmund] Morgan, [Timothy H.] Breen, [Winthrop D.] Jordan, [Eugene] Genovese, [Lawrence W.] Levine, [Richard C.]Wade, [Gordon S.] Wood, [Herbert G.] Gutman, and [Charles] Joyner—to mention just a few in no particular order. Slavery studies represented perhaps the most remarkable outpouring of historical scholarship in the nation for several decades after the late 1950s. Never again was southern history seen as it had been before; and amid this intellectual and historiographical revolution, the reputation of Jefferson took a terrible tumble. Now he was seen primarily as nothing more than a racist, a hypocrite who wrote "all men are created equal" but was a life-long slaveholder and the keeper of a black mistress, Sally Hemings.

In the 1980s and afterwards Jefferson was demonized; he became the stand-in for all southern slaveholders, guilty of the national sin of slavery. In article after article and book after book, he was attacked; for most Americans, almost everything in Jefferson's life was expunged except for his having been a slaveholder. In popular culture he was denigrated, and people spoke of wishing they could dynamite his likeness off Mount Rushmore. The mythical man-on-the-street, and to a surprising degree the typical student, had now an understanding of Jefferson that was only bumper-sticker deep: he was seen as no more than a hypocritical racist and rapist, neither one to admire nor examine. If I had pursued Jefferson as a topic of research and writing in the 1960s, I would have approached him in one way, but this was 2013! Was Jefferson still worth study? Was he only to be attacked? Had by delay I missed the opportunity to write about Jefferson? Especially after the completion of Malone's six volumes and Peterson's magisterial 1970 study, *Thomas Jefferson and the New Nation: A Biography*, was Jefferson finished as a potential topic?

But I remembered Peterson's first book, *The Jefferson Image in the American Mind*. Jefferson's reputation had always been changing, and we were now in only a later phase of it. Was there not a place even today, I wondered, for a new biography, one that covered the entirety of his career and accomplishments, good and bad, not just narrowly and simplistically focused on slavery? Jefferson should, I believed—as should any historical figure—be portrayed in the context not just of his time, but of his gender, race, and region. That gave me a reason to proceed. Moreover, I had the benefit of fifty years of penetrating scholarship on a whole range of relevant issues that Malone and Peterson did not have. And when Peterson wrote his major biography, he had only seventeen volumes of the *Papers of Thomas Jefferson* (edited by Julian Boyd and others) available to him; when Malone had begun, he had none. Now I had available more than fifty volumes, and the modern published letters of the Founders and others have been a monumental accomplishment of modern scholarship. I wondered, could one person (who, as editor of the *Journal of Southern History,* had been forced to stay abreast of southern history scholarship and much of the writing on Jefferson) master the entire corpus of Jefferson's writings and a reasonable portion of the secondary scholarship on him and write a modern, up-to-date, and interpretative biography that addressed all (or most) of Jefferson's interests and accomplishments, seeing him whole and fully in context, admittedly appreciative but critical when appropriate, and do so in about half the space of Peterson's biography and less than one-fifth of the pages Malone had filled? That was the task I put to myself, realizing what a very different book I would be writing now than if I had done it in the 1960s or so. The result is *Jefferson: Architect of American Liberty*, published in 2017.

In what ways do you think Jefferson is still relevant today?

Jefferson was the most eloquent of the Founders, especially upon the topics of liberty and freedom, but also on topics like education, religious freedom, nature, and governance. No one wrote more inspiringly about liberty and freedom even though, like all humans, he could not live up to the highest principles of his ideals. This is most evident on the issue of slavery, but Jefferson can also disappoint us on issues like education for women. Perhaps this is because, as he was so advanced on many topics that we care about, we expect him to have been advanced on every topic. Alas, on many issues he was very much a man of his time. We do not expect more of most Founders, but we do of Jefferson. No doubt this is because of the power of his writings and the idealism he expressed in such memorable language. Yet Jefferson provided us with the words with which to advance the cause of human rights, including expanding the rights and roles of women and people of all races, even though he did not see the way to achieve the values of which he wrote. On topics like the value of learning and the importance of religious freedom, Jefferson wrote in ways that pointed toward the future. We should not approach him expecting perfection, but if we consider him within the context of his time, race, gender, and position, he remains a thoughtful spokesperson for this nation's highest aspirations. His failure on race, combined with his eloquence on liberty, present him as the central paradox of our history.

Which works—especially any lesser-known works—by Jefferson would you particularly recommend, and why?

In addition to his book *Notes on the State of Virginia*, which has both wonderful and deeply disturbing passages, I would suggest his "Summary View of the Rights of British America," of course the Declaration of Independence, his first inaugural address, his text for the "Virginia Statute of Religious Freedom," and a good sampling of his thousands of letters. The *Notes* contains many of the most famous Jefferson quotes on a variety of topics along with an attack on slavery and a problematical discussion of the inferiority of blacks. His first inaugural address reveals Jefferson as the effective political leader, and his language on behalf of religious freedom is central to the tradition of separation of church and state in this country. Jefferson's many letters on every topic imaginable reveal his literary skill, the breadth of his learning, his humanity, and his curiosity about everything.

What are your thoughts on Jefferson and slavery and particularly on the matter of Sally Hemings?

These are two complicated matters that dominate present-day discussion of Jefferson. I believe that Jefferson was an authentic opponent of slavery who, paradoxically, never freed his own slaves or, as president, tried to free the nation's slaves as if by fiat. Let me try to state my view on this before moving on to the Sally Hemings issue, and here I am summarizing topics I discuss in more detail in my biography of Jefferson. Clearly, Jefferson early in his career spoke out against slavery and made moves to limit or end it. One of his first acts as a member of the Virginia colonial assembly was to try to make it easier for slaveholders to free (or manumit) their slaves, but this failed. He inserted a long paragraph attacking slavery in the Declaration of Independence, though the Second Continental Congress excised it; he had also attacked slavery in his 1774 "Summary View of the Rights of British America." He prepared a new constitution for Virginia in 1783 that called for the ending of slavery in 1800, but no convention was called to draft a new constitution for the state. As a member of the Congress of the Articles of Confederation, in 1784, he drafted a proposal for how to deal with the new territory between the Appalachian Mountains and the Mississippi (gained as a result of the American Revolution) that called for the end of slavery in the entire region after 1800—this proposal failed in the Congress by one vote. He spoke and tried to act against slavery more than any of the other prominent Founders, and on every occasion he failed. His final effort was his urging of Congress in 1806 that when it met in the new session in 1807, it pass legislation ending the Trans-Atlantic Slave trade to the United States in 1808 as the Constitution allowed but did not require. Congress did follow Jefferson's admonition and banned the international slave trade in 1808.

He continued to speak against slavery his entire life. But he never acted to free his own slaves. Why not? The answer should not be just that he was a racist white Virginian—end of story. That is too lazy and incomplete an analysis. Jefferson was extremely conflicted on this issue, and we should try to understand what kept him from moving on an issue that he obviously cared about. Of course anything approaching abolition was an extremely controversial issue and would have hurt him politically, but this was probably not the central reason. Jefferson was greatly in debt after his wife's father, John Wayles, died in 1774. Upon his death she, and legally Jefferson himself, inherited thousands of acres of land, and 135 slaves, and a huge amount of debt. Jefferson was never able to escape from this debt; and in 1792, the Virginia Assembly passed legislation allowing creditors to seize the freed slaves of anyone who owed them money. In other words, had Jefferson freed any of his slaves, his creditors could have seized them in repayment. This restricted Jefferson's freedom of action. He also believed that if one freed one's slaves, then one should provide them with land, tools, draft animals, and make it possible for them to prosper in life. But Jefferson was essentially broke most of his life, his land became almost worthless in the severe Virginia depression of the early nineteenth century, and he could not free his slaves and distribute his Monticello lands to them because an 1806 Virginia law required that slaves who were freed had to leave the state within a year or face re-enslavement. These two laws shaped what Jefferson could do. He also always had a large number of biological dependents living with him whom he felt a moral obligation to support—widowed sisters, nephews and nieces, later his daughter Martha and her large number of children. Laws and family moral obligations deprived Jefferson, he believed, of the freedom to free his slaves. Those like George Washington, who were not in debt and who died before 1806 (and had no biological dependents) were much freer to emancipate their slaves. Men like Edward Coles and John Randolph who freed their slaves also had ample funds and no dependents to support. We might imagine that if we were in Jefferson's position we would "have done the right thing" whatever the cost to our children and grandchildren, but realistically such a heroic action is rare in life.

Jefferson had plenty of evidence that achieving emancipation through legislation would be difficult, if not impossible. Every attempt he made failed. And just as he returned from his ambassadorship to France and became secretary of state, a huge controversy broke out in the Congress over two petitions to free slaves. Congressmen from South Carolina and Georgia went practically berserk in their opposition, threatening to destroy the union. This frightened every single Congressmen, all of whom believed the union was a fragile experiment and likely to fail. At the same time, most of them—Jefferson included—believed that slavery was an outmoded institution and was near extinction. They didn't know the exact process by which this was to happen, but it was commonly believed that slavery was a dying institution. Believing this, why risk destroying the union to attack an institution already on the way out? Of course they were wrong; the union was strong (until finally disrupted by the slavery issue in 1861), and the invention of the cotton gin and the rise of cotton invigorated slavery after the early 1790s. But the Founders did not foresee these events.

Jefferson was an avowed foe of monarchy and believed that governmental decisions in the United States should be made as the result of legislative actions, not the proclamation of a dictatorial monarch. Even could he have ended slavery by such action, he thought that was not how a democratic government should work. If the votes were not presently there to effect emancipation, the role of education and moral protest was to create the sentiment sufficient to solve the dilemma of slavery although it would take time. And Jefferson, as a free white man, was patient, expecting somehow, sometime, Providence would effect the end of slavery. On democratic principle he thought it inappropriate for a president to end the evil—even could he do so—without an electoral decision. His commitment to democracy in the face of the perceived fragility of the union trumped his commitment to quick emancipation. He hoped his words, his principles, his support of education, absorbed by the coming generations, would ultimately make possible the desired change. It was all in the hands of Providence, he came to believe. And living as he did in a pre-Darwinian world that did not expect change to be as common or as rapid and pliable as we do, he was content to await the work of Providence. No doubt his race and class allowed such a willingness to be quiescent, if not fatalistic. Nothing else about Jefferson so disappoints us, and we find it difficult to accept his reasoning. He did not have the value of our hindsight.

I believe that without foreseeing it, Jefferson and Sally Hemings, when she was a teenager serving in his home in Paris, developed attitudes approaching mutual affection. Jefferson treated Sally and her brother James as servants in Paris (slavery was illegal in France), paid them wages, and paid for them to take French lessons (and James lessons in French cooking). When it was time for Jefferson to return to the United States, both James and Sally knew they could, simply by approaching the authorities, remain in Paris. Jefferson persuaded James to return to Monticello to teach his younger brother how to do French cooking, and then he would give him his freedom. James accepted this proposal, and Jefferson did free James. Sally could have remained in Paris, could easily have gotten a position as a ladies' maid, but she, too, apparently agreed to return and more or less live with Jefferson, understanding that in so doing she would remain his slave no matter how "well" treated.

Jefferson had promised his wife upon her deathbed that he would never remarry; by law Jefferson could not marry Sally because she was a slave (Sally was very light skinned and bore a family resemblance to Martha, but slavery was a matter of law, not skin color); and by Virginia law, a man could not marry the sister of his deceased wife, and Sally was the half-sister of Martha Jefferson. Sally did not move to New York, Philadelphia, or later Washington, DC, but always stayed at Monticello, where she apparently bore her first child by Jefferson in 1795; subsequently she had other children, and within a few years moved from a cabin near Monticello to a room underneath the south terrace near the kitchen. She bore no children after 1809, when Jefferson retired from the presidency and returned permanently to Monticello; by then his daughter Martha had moved into the house, with her children, and became the manager of his household. Probably Sally continued to look after Jefferson's laundry and his private rooms, but their relationship was extraordinarily discrete. Visitors later reported seeing a young enslaved man about the place who looked like Jefferson, but nothing was said publicly about this. Jefferson in his will emancipated Sally's children (asking legislative approval for their remaining in the state) and unofficially freed Sally by asking his daughter Martha to allow her her time, that is, to live as though free, and giving her a small house. In all this I follow the research and conclusions of Annette Gordon-Reed.

What traits do you most admire about Jefferson "as a writer"?

Jefferson had the ability to write aphoristically about a variety of topics: he can be carefully analytical, thoughtful, vividly descriptive, and simply eloquent. His personal letters are obviously individualized to fit the background, gender, and interests of his correspondent, so he writes in a different tone to different people. Many of his letters are succinct essays about important topics, and most of them have a literary quality that make reading them pleasurable.

Are there any scholarly works you particularly recommend, especially to novice readers of Jefferson?
Risking self-promotion, I would suggest my biography of Jefferson (*Jefferson: Architect of American Liberty*) and the collection of Jefferson's writings edited by Merrill D. Peterson, along with the essays in Peter S. Onuf's *Jeffersonian Legacies*, particularly the chapters by Paul K. Conkin, Jan Lewis, Lucia C. Stanton, and Gordon S. Wood. On the important issue of Jefferson and slavery, I would suggest Lucia Stanton, *"Those Who Labor for My Happiness": Slavery at Thomas Jefferson's Monticello* and Annette Gordon-Reed, *The Hemingses of Monticello: An American Family.*

Are there any general scholarly approaches that you find particularly helpful and/or unhelpful?
One must immerse oneself in the primary sources, and luckily for those interested in Jefferson, practically all his correspondence and that of his notable contemporaries has been published in modern, annotated editions. One must read the background literature on the politics, culture, and society for the era that encompasses the individual whose life one is examining. It is important to try to understand a person's life holistically, not just one slice of it, and to place the person as completely as possible in the entirety of his or her context. One should remember that understanding a person in the past does not mean justifying that person, and that easy moralizing about a person in the past betrays a condescending attitude about the past. The point of historical understanding is not to magnify our sense of moral superiority to those in the past but to try to grasp why men and women acted as they did, given their range of alternatives as they saw them. We can and should make clear how they failed in terms of our current values, but we should avoid lazy condemnation of those who came before us even when they made decisions that we consider terribly wrong today.

Are there any kinds of approaches to Jefferson that remain undeveloped and seem worth pursuing?

The intellectual riches of his book *Notes on the State of Virginia*, especially the changes it went through in its various drafts, need to be better understood. A forthcoming book by Cara Rogers will significantly illuminate the writing and influence of this Jefferson work. I would like to see a detailed analysis of Jefferson the farmer and an examination of the operation of Monticello as a farming enterprise, worked by slaves. I think there needs to be a very careful, in-depth analysis of Jefferson's evolving religious views, and this should also relate to his concerns for religious freedom. There needs to be a new biography of William Short that carefully analyzes his relationship with Jefferson. I would like to see a full-scale analysis of Jefferson and slavery, written with nuance and fully contextualized, not a presentist attack on him like the works of Wiencek and Finkelman. I would also like to see a diplomatic history/foreign policy analysis of Jefferson's political career as well as a history of Jefferson as husband, father, and grandfather contextualized in the scholarship on marriage, child rearing, etc.

What do you think of the various films, especially documentaries, that have been made about Jefferson?

I haven't been impressed by the several movies about Jefferson, but I do think the Ken Burns documentary entitled *Thomas Jefferson* does a good job of capturing the essence of Jefferson, though it needs to be updated. For those who have never visited Monticello, the film wonderfully reveals the natural beauty of the site and the architectural beauty of the house, inside and out.

How, if at all, has your own thinking about Jefferson evolved over the years?

I believe I now have a better sense of how Jefferson's ideas about religion evolved over time, from basic orthodoxy to profound questioning to ultimately accepting a minimalist version of Christianity that sees Jesus as the most profound moral thinker but not divine; Jefferson rejected miracles but accepted the idea of a supreme God who could and did intervene in history, and he believed in life of some sort in the hereafter when the dead would be rejoined with loved ones. By no means did he become an orthodox Christian, but he valued the principles that Jesus advocated. Still, he insisted on editing the New Testament to carve out only the authentic words of Jesus, although he never explained the exact process by which he believed he could determine those words other than by remarking that they were as evident as diamonds in a dung heap.

I also now sense more than earlier the dilemma that Jefferson faced regarding slavery, the contradiction presented by his genuinely believing slavery was wrong but never having the courage, or imagination, or lack of felt obligation toward his biological dependents to end the institution for himself, constrained as he was by law. And I think I understand better than earlier why he did not act unilaterally as president to abolish slavery. Also, my views on his relationship with Sally Hemings have evolved. As a student in the 1960s, I—without any independent research—simply accepted what the major biographers at that time said, that it was "unthinkable" that Jefferson would have had a black mistress. Now because of such books as those by Annette Gordon-Reed, Joshua D. Rothman, Eva Sheppard Wolf, Andrew S. Curran, and Lucia Stanton, I believe the evidence points pretty convincingly toward Jefferson and Hemings having had a long, consensual, monogamous relationship based on real affection if not something very close to love. Certainly such relationships were common in the South, and in Albemarle County—and even in the household of Jefferson's father-in-law. This issue begets much controversy even today, with some condemning Jefferson for it and others condemning scholars for suggesting it existed. But the fullness of Jefferson's contribution to American history and culture transcends this controversy.

Works Cited

Boles, John B. *Black Southerners, 1619–1869*. U P of Kentucky, 1983.

_____. *The Great Revival, 1787–1805: The Origins of the Southern Evangelical Mind*. U P of Kentucky, 1972.

_____. *Jefferson: Architect of American Liberty*. Basic Books, 2017.

Curran, Andrew S. *The Anatomy of Blackness: Science and Slavery in the Age of Enlightenment*. Johns Hopkins U P, 2011.

Finkelman, Paul. *Slavery and the Founders: Race and Liberty in the Age of Jefferson*. 3rd ed. M. E. Sharpe, 2014.

Gordon-Reed, Annette. *The Hemingses of Monticello: An American Family*. Norton, 2008.

_____. *Thomas Jefferson and Sally Hemings: An American Controversy*. U P of Virginia, 1997.

Koch, Adrienne, and William Peden, editors. *The Life and Selected Writings of Thomas Jefferson* The Modern Library, 1944.

Onuf, Peter S., editor. *Jeffersonian Legacies*. U P of Virginia, 1993.

Peterson, Merrill D. *The Jefferson Image in the American Mind*. Oxford U P, 1960.

_____. *Thomas Jefferson: Writings*. Library of America, 1984.

Rothman Joshua D. *Notorious in the Neighborhood: Sex and Families Across the Color Line in Virginia, 1787–1861*. U of North Carolina P, 2003.

Stanton, Lucia. *"Those Who Labor for My Happiness": Slavery at Thomas Jefferson's Monticello*. U of Virginia P, 2012.

Wiencek, Henry. *Master of the Mountain: Thomas Jefferson and His Slaves*. Farrar, Straus and Giroux, 2012.

Wolf, Eva Sheppard. *Race and Liberty in the New Nation: Emancipation in Virginia from the Revolution to Nat Turner's Rebellion*. Louisiana State U P, 2006.

Jefferson and the Long Eighteenth Century_____

Nicolas Tredell

Thomas Jefferson became the third President of the United States just after the start of the nineteenth century, taking the oath of office on March 4, 1801, at the age of 57; he went on to serve two terms, leaving the White House in 1809, and lived to be 83, dying on July 4, 1826, the fiftieth anniversary of the Declaration of Independence. His years of greatest eminence were thus in the early nineteenth century; but he had been born in 1743 and his formation was an eighteenth-century one, first under British colonial rule and then in the brightening but sometimes storm-crossed dawn of American independence. This essay draws on the perspective of those modern historians, most notably Frank O'Gorman in his pioneering 1997 book *The Long Eighteenth Century: British Political and Social History 1688–1832,* who have argued, in respect of British history, that a century, judged in terms of its major social, cultural, and political movements does not start at year zero and end at year ninety-nine but begins sometime in the previous century and persists in key respects for a while into the following century.

We shall not attempt to determine whether and how the idea of "the long eighteenth century" might apply in general to the course of American history; or to speculate on what its dates and duration might have been; we shall, rather, use it as a kind of cursor to hover over and, where appropriate, home in on the eighteenth-century elements in Jefferson's thought and language that he carried through into the nineteenth century. We shall focus especially on his relationship to eighteenth-century culture and literature and to the harbingers in that literature of the Romanticism that began to emerge near the end of the nineteenth century—partly in relation to the epochal historical changes of the era, of which the American Revolution was one of the most important, and in which Jefferson played a central role as the key drafter of the Declaration of Independence and as an active politician who would eventually hold the highest office in the

United States. We shall also consider how eighteenth-century ideas of reason, justice, equality, and interest permeated his cultural and political attitudes.

Unlike some other gifted wordsmiths who have become national leaders—Benjamin Disraeli and Sir Winston Churchill in the United Kingdom, for example—Jefferson was neither a good public speaker nor, in his lifetime, a prolific published writer. *Notes on the State of Virginia* (1785) is the only complete full-length book that appeared in his lifetime, but it contains the seeds for shelves of potential volumes. Written in poised and periodic eighteenth-century prose, it is a fascinating and very eighteenth-century book, difficult to classify because it emerged in an era when disciplinary boundaries and demarcations were less rigidly fixed: it is, among other things, a compendium, a miscellany, and an embryonic encyclopedia, assembling prose passages, tables, and lists demonstrating Jefferson's wide and intense range of interests, his concern to connect the specific and general, and his desire for knowledge that was both disinterested and intimately bound up with his concern to construct a new nation.

As the term "Notes" in its title indicates, this book does not offer a continuous argument or narrative. Its "Advertisement"— a term that, at this time, meant a notice to its readers about the nature of the text rather than, as in the modern sense, an attempt to sell it—presents it as a series of responses by its author to the queries of a generic "Foreigner of Distinction" then living in the United States of America. His *Autobiography* identifies this questioner as François Barbé-Marbois of the French legation in Philadelphia, who was gathering information about the states of the Union for his government. The "queries" are not phrased in an obviously interrogative way: they take the form of statements with a question mark at the end, such as "The constitution of the state, and its several charters?" (77). But they are sufficient to give a sense that the *Notes* began as an attempt to explain America, as manifested in one of its key states, to Europe: and among the many aspects of the new country it tried to encompass were culture and literature.

Culture and Literature

Jefferson had a well-stocked mind and a well-stocked library; the latter, eventually and appropriately, became the bibliographical foundation stone of the Library of Congress. Like later postcolonial writers, he recognized that a nation, especially a new nation distancing and differentiating itself from Europe, needed to be well-stocked culturally; that culture was part of, though not subordinate to, political power. He was, therefore, concerned to affirm the high quality of American culture in thought and art even though he realized it was only at its beginning.

In this concern, he knew what he was up against; as a cultivated man of the eighteenth century, he enjoyed an easy cultural commerce, through reading, correspondence, and personal encounter, with the British and French intelligentsia. Like Benjamin Franklin, he was at home in Paris; and if, like John Adams, he had spent almost three years in England, he would have been equally at home in the literary and cultural London of the period (he only paid one short visit to the British capital, for five weeks in March to April 1786). He appreciated the formidable cultural heft of Britain and Europe and wanted to assume some of its gravitas; but he also wanted to help fashion a distinctively American cultural presence on the world stage of the time.

Like most eighteenth-century Western intellectuals, Jefferson could read both ancient Greek and Latin and regarded Homer and Virgil as the poets who transcended national boundaries:

> An Englishman, only, reads Milton with delight, an Italian Tasso, a Frenchman the Henriade [by Voltaire], a Portuguese Camões : but Homer and Virgil have been the rapture of every age and nation: they are read with enthusiasm in their originals by those who can read the originals, and in translations by those who cannot. (44)

Even though Milton, Tasso, Voltaire, and Camões have, in this perspective, a narrower appeal than Homer and Virgil, their quality, at least for readers who share their respective nationalities, is implicitly acknowledged. As Jefferson was well aware, however, this posed a problem in the new nation whose founding document, the Declaration of Independence, he had largely composed: what could an American read (apart from the Declaration itself) that would be both distinctively American and of the same quality as those English and European literary texts? He was also well aware that the same question applied to other kinds of creative and intellectual production.

In tackling this question in the *Notes*, Jefferson takes issue with a claim by the French encyclopedist and polymath Georges-Louis Leclerc, the Comte de Buffon, whose writings are an important reference point in the book, cited 22 times, and quoted in the original French (thus demonstrating Jefferson's own familiarity with that language, one of the credentials of his cultivation). Buffon expresses surprise that America "n'ait pas encore produit un bon poëte, un habile mathematician, un homme de genie dans un seul art, ou une seule science [has not yet produced a good poet, a skillful mathematician, a man of genius in a single art or science]" (qtd 43). Jefferson seems to concede the first charge, that America has not yet produced a good poet, but attributes this to the newness of the country, pointing out that it was a long time before the Greeks "produced a Homer, the Romans a Virgil, the French a Racine and Voltaire, the English a Shakespeare and Milton" (43).

Addressing Buffon's charge that America has not produced "one able mathematician, one man of genius in a single art or a single science," Jefferson points to specific counterexamples: "In war we have produced a Washington"; "In physics we have produced a Franklin"; and in astronomy, practical mechanics, surveying and other fields, America has produced the multi-skilled David Rittenhouse, who, for Jefferson, combined natural intelligence, craft skills, and aesthetic creativity: a "self-taught" man who, "[a]s an artist," "has exhibited as great a proof of mechanical genius as the world has ever produced" and who "has not indeed made a world" but "has by imitation approached nearer its Maker than any man who has lived from the creation to this day" (43). This almost makes Rittenhouse a kind of Romantic demiurge, in the Gnostic sense of a celestial being who is secondary to God but controls the material world. Here Jefferson permits himself a certain hyperbole (a favorite trope); this befits his rhetorical purpose in combating a patronizing and ill-informed European assumption of American intellectual and artistic inferiority; but, hyperbole aside, the range and depth of Rittenhouse's skills and achievements were undoubtedly impressive and fit an eighteenth-century ideal of the all-round man who partakes of and contributes to art and science, combines intellectual and practical ability; a man, as it happens, not unlike Jefferson himself.

The examples of Washington, Franklin, and Rittenhouse lead up to Jefferson's ringing affirmation of American cultural equality and his implication that it might, in the fullness of time, achieve superiority:

> As in philosophy and war, so in government, in oratory, in painting, in the plastic art, we might shew that America, though but a child of yesterday, has already given hopeful proofs of genius, as well of the nobler kinds, which arouse the best feelings of man, which call him into action, which substantiate his freedom, and conduct him to happiness, as of the subordinate, which serve to amuse him only. (43–4)

It is significant in this passage that Jefferson uses a term that features so strongly in the Declaration of Independence: "happiness" The Declaration includes, among man's "unalienable rights," "Life, Liberty and the pursuit of Happiness" without saying more about the nature of the happiness that human beings have an unalienable right to pursue. Here Jefferson is more specific: he distinguishes between "happiness" and "amusement," seeing the latter as subordinate to and more limited than the former. It is "the nobler kinds" of "genius" that "arouse the best feelings of man," "call him into action" and "conduct him to happiness." This places happiness on an elevated, ennobled plane and sees it as a product of culture.

One of the arts that Jefferson identifies as already giving "hopeful" proofs of American genius is that of oratory, and the example of this he gives in *Notes* is particularly striking since its source is a Native American: and we shall turn now to consider some examples of his response to cultural productions by ethnicities other than white ones.

Oratory and Writing

In his praise of an oration by Logan, a war leader of the Cayuga people, Jefferson invokes two great orators of ancient Greece and Rome, Demosthenes and Cicero, respectively:

> I may challenge the whole orations of Demosthenes and Cicero, and of any more eminent orator, if Europe has furnished more eminent, to produce a single passage, superior to the speech of Logan, a Mingo chief, to Lord Dunmore, when governor of this state. (41)

This places Logan in the most exalted company. As Edward D. Seeber points out in his essay "Critical Views on Logan's Speech" (1947), Logan's oration was and remained controversial, receiving both wide praise and censure, and doubts were raised about its authenticity; but Jefferson's backing of it carried great weight and demonstrates his readiness to acknowledge the possibility that a Native American might make a major contribution to American and world culture.

Jefferson was much more grudging in his response to writings by eighteenth-century African Americans and mixed-race Americans. In *Notes on the State of Virginia*, he offers a magisterial putdown of Phyllis Wheatley's poetry: "Religion indeed has produced a Phyllis Whately [*sic*]; but it could not produce a poet. The compositions published under her name are below the dignity of criticism" (96). This is a familiar move in critical rhetoric—to assert that the supposed literary texts under consideration do not truly belong to literature and, therefore, do not merit critical analysis and assessment; and it has the advantage that it absolves the critic from close engagement with the text. But Jefferson goes further: to drive home his denigration, he instances Alexander Pope's biting mock-epic satire on London literary life, *The Dunciad* (1743), thereby displaying his own knowledge of English high culture; but he suggests that Wheatley would not even feature as a target in this and that, indeed, Pope's satirized scribblers, the hacks of London's Grub Street, are truly heroic compared to her, as the mythological hero Hercules was to Pope himself (there is perhaps an implied sneer here at the English poet's physical disabilities). "The heroes of the *Dunciad* are to her, as Hercules to the author of that poem" (96). Jefferson has already provided a pithy well-phrased criticism of Wheatley, and this last simile seems like overkill: if Wheatley were truly such a negligible poet, it would hardly seem necessary to invoke Pope and Hercules to drive the point home; it looks as though Jefferson might be fending off a cultural threat arising from the very possibility that a female poet of color might exist.

Turning to a male writer of color, the British African Ignatius Sancho, whose *Letters* appeared in 1782, two years after his death, Jefferson is willing to concede some stylistic merit, though with qualifications. His letters "breathe the purest effusions of friendship and general philanthropy, and shew how great a degree of the latter may be compounded with strong religious zeal" (96). If religious zeal was somewhat more suspect for proponents of reason, even for those among them who still believed in some form of God, it was acceptable if tempered by such key eighteenth-century virtues as friendship and general philanthropy. Jefferson goes on to praise Sancho's prose—"He is often happy in the turn of his compliments, and his stile is easy and familiar"—but makes a key exception: those moments "when he affects a Shandean fabrication of words" (96). The adjective "Shandean" here derives from the eighteenth-century novel *The Life and Opinions of Tristram Shandy, Gentleman* (1759–67) by the Irish writer Laurence Sterne, with whom Sancho engaged in a famous correspondence about the slave trade. Jefferson's allusion to Sterne's novel in an adverse judgement on an aspect of Sancho's prose, is an index of Jefferson's eighteenth-century mainstream aesthetic. Sterne's novel was the object of a famous dismissal by the most dominant Anglophone critic of the eighteenth century, Dr Johnson: "Nothing odd will do long. 'Tristram Shandy' did not last" (Boswell, 1.649).

Oddity, or eccentricity, is one of the major targets of Jefferson's censures of Sancho; he can exceed rational bounds and lose measure and balance: "his imagination is wild and extravagant, escapes incessantly from every restraint of reason and taste, and, in the course of its vagaries, leaves a tract of thought as incoherent and eccentric, as is the course of a meteor through the sky." From a different aesthetic viewpoint, prose with this meteoric quality might seem rather exciting; indeed, we could see it as a herald of the Romanticism that would start to rise towards the end of the eighteenth century. Jefferson's reprobation of it shows his eighteenth-century aesthetics: Sancho is "always substituting sentiment for demonstration" (96).

Jefferson then comes back to Sancho's ethnicity, admitting him "to the first place among those of his own color who have presented themselves to the public judgment" but placing him "at the bottom of the column" when compared to his fellow English authors, particularly those known for their letters (96). But, as with Phyllis Wheatley, he goes into overkill mode by concluding that it is very difficult to determine whether another (implicitly white) hand might have amended his *Letters*—thus imparting by innuendo, as Jefferson, the lawyer, might have done in a courtroom whose codes forbade unfounded direct accusation, a suspicion that the *Letters* were not all Sancho's own work (similar suspicions had been cast upon Logan's oration, but Jefferson does not address these). While his criticisms of Sancho's style were couched in aesthetic terms and might have been made of a white writer, this last aspersion may relate to an inability on Jefferson's part to accept that a person of color could write as well as Jefferson grudgingly concedes that Sancho sometimes did.

Jefferson's aesthetics, as they emerge in his assessment of Sancho, are in the eighteenth-century mainstream. But one area where his aesthetics start to shift and merge into more Romantic currents in the later eighteenth century is in poetry and prose that evokes landscapes. We can also find this in Jefferson's descriptions of American landscapes and riverscapes in *Notes*.

American Landscapes: The Sublime and the Beautiful

Jefferson's topographical descriptions in *Notes* are sometimes practically focused but can move into lyrical mode. In his inventory of the rivers of Virginia, for instance, he calls the Illinois "a fine river, clear, gentle and without rapids" but relates these elements, within the same sentence, to its practical use: "it is navigable for bateaux [flat-bottomed shallow-draft boats] to its source" (6). The approbatory adjectives in this sentence could be seen to arise from and primarily apply to the practical use of the river, its navigability, rather than its aesthetic qualities; but elsewhere Jefferson's laudation of Virginia rivers is pitched unequivocally in aesthetic terms: for example, he calls the Wabash "a very beautiful river" (8) but makes the highest aesthetic claims for the Ohio river, the adjective becoming a superlative: it "is the most beautiful river on earth. Its current gentle, waters clear, and bosom smooth and unbroken by rocks and rapids, a single instance only excepted" (6). The flowing rhythm of the prose here conveys the sense of gentleness, clarity and smoothness; the plosives (*b, d, k, p*) of "un*b*ro*k*en," "ro*ck*s" and "ra*pid*s" inject a slight aural abrasiveness that ultimately contributes to the overall impression of smoothness as they occur in words invoking potential obstructions that are almost wholly absent; "rocks and rapids" slightly perturb the prose but hardly break up the actual surface it denotes.

Though Jefferson is describing water rather than land here, the imagery of the "smooth bosom," with its erotic and maternal intimations, anticipates F. Scott Fitzgerald's evocation at the end of *The Great Gatsby* (1925) of the "fresh, green breast of the new world" that the original Dutch sailors who made landfall in America supposedly encountered. To call the Ohio "the most beautiful river on earth" is to employ hyperbole; like any human being in the late eighteenth century, Jefferson had not seen all the rivers on earth, even in representations, as we could in principle do today by searching the Internet; he had not even seen all the rivers in America, having travelled no further into the interior than Hot Springs in Arkansas; but his claim retains its validity as an index of his subjective response and as an assertion of state and national pride. Virginia is a core part of America, and America has features that surpass in beauty anything else on the globe.

Jefferson's claims for the visual spectacle of the passage of the Potomac River through the Blue Ridge are introduced in a more tentative fashion—"*perhaps one of* the most stupendous scenes in nature" (12, italics added), rather than an unequivocal and unique superlative (as it would be in the expression "the most stupendous scene in nature"); but he develops the description more fully, using the second person rather than the first or third in order, as it were, to put the bodies and minds of his readers, imaginatively, in the picture:

> You stand on a very high point of land. On your right comes up the Shenandoah, having ranged along the foot of the mountain an hundred miles to seek a vent. On your left approaches the Patowmac, in quest of a passage also. In the moment of their junction they rush together against the mountain, rend it asunder, and pass off to the sea. (12)

We are no longer in the realm of the beautiful here but of a different aesthetic experience theorized by Edmund Burke, supporter of the American and opponent of the French Revolution, in *A Philosophical Enquiry into the Origin of Our Ideas of the Sublime and Beautiful* (1757): the sublime is an experience of awe, fear and terror, produced here by a sense of the power of a mobile natural force, water, to rend asunder a monumental natural phenomenon, a mountain.

Jefferson does not stop, however, with this dramatic vista; rather, he goes on to say how its sensory impact generates a geological history: "The first glance of this scene hurries our senses into the opinion, that this earth has been created in time" (12). The verb "hurries" here echoes Burke's analysis, in his *Philosophical Inquiry*, of "the great power of the sublime": "far from being produced by them [our reasonings], it anticipates our reasonings, and *hurries* us on by an irresistible force" (63, italics added). Here sublime experience anticipates and accelerates ratiocination, speeding up the intellectual production of an empirically based hypothesis: this basing of a hypothesis on sensory experience, in a specific situation, is a characteristic eighteenth-century philosophical position, deriving from Locke and Hume. But it also anticipates the nineteenth-century emphasis on geological time, most notably in Sir Charles Lyell's *Principles of Geology* (1830–33), which would challenge the implied chronology of the Biblical account of earth's creation and development.

It is notable as well that Jefferson, extrapolating and extending the immediate sensory experience of witnessing the confluence of the Potomac and Shenandoah rivers, travels back through geological time to encompass a process in which the rivers formed an inland ocean whose waters eventually broke over and "have torn the mountain down from its summit to its base" (12). He then returns to what he judges to be immediate empirical evidence: "The piles of rock on each hand," especially "on the Shenandoah," and "the evident marks of their disrupture and avulsion from their beds by the most powerful agents of nature, corroborate the impression" (12).

Jefferson then moves into the aesthetic dimension again, describing the landscape as if it were a painting combining a scene of geological violence with an ultimately peaceful prospect: "the distant finishing which nature has given to the picture is of a very different character. It is a true contrast to the fore-ground. It is as placid and delightful, as that is wild and tremendous" (12). Once again, he uses the second person pronoun "you" to position the reader in the scene:

> For the mountain being cloven asunder, she presents to your eye, through the cleft, a small catch of smooth blue horizon, at an infinite distance in the plain country, inviting you, as it were, from the riot and tumult roaring around, to pass through the breach and participate of the calm below. (12)

Jefferson does not, however, stay with the static peaceful pleasure offered to the contemplative eye: he points out that it is possible to travel, along an actual road, through the prospect that eye contemplates. He continues to use the second person pronoun "You" but now sets the reader in motion, as an active agent, as he takes them across the Potomac and moves into the realm of sensory, emotional, and aesthetic experience: "through the base of the mountain for three miles, its terrible precipices hanging in fragments over you" (12). We are again in the zone of the sublime, the experience of awe, fear and terror caused here by perceiving such phenomena as "terrible precipices hanging in fragments over you."

The height of sublimity is, for Jefferson in *Notes on the State of Virginia*, the geological formation called the Natural Bridge, which calls for a superlative: it is "the most sublime of Nature's works" (15). As with his account of the passage of the Potomac River through the Blue Ridge mountains, he envisages its cause to be that of a huge past natural upheaval: "It is on the ascent of a hill, which seems to have been cloven through its length by some great convulsion" (15). Characteristically, he moves from this sense of past cataclysm to a calm enumeration of calculable dimensions, acknowledging their uncertainty where appropriate—for instance, "[t]he fissure, just at the bridge, is, by some admeasurements, 270 feet deep, by others only 205" (15). He then proceeds, however, to bring readers, in their sensory imaginations, directly and vertiginously into the scene and also then relates his own physical response:

> Though the sides of this bridge are provided in some parts with a parapet of fixed rocks, yet few men have resolution to walk to them and look over into the abyss. You involuntarily fall on your hands and feet, creep to the parapet and peep over it. Looking down from this height about a minute, gave me a violent head ach [sic]. (15)

Jefferson then contrasts this "painful and intolerable" view from the top with a view from below that is "delightful in an equal extreme":

> It is impossible for the emotions arising from the sublime, to be felt beyond what they are here: so beautiful an arch, so elevated, so light, and springing as it were up to heaven, the rapture of the spectator is really indescribable! (15)

Here sublime and beautiful are combined, with the arch both graceful and awesome. There is an intertextual trace here of the line from the Books of Psalms in the Old Testament, "Truth shall spring out of the earth" (85.11), but rather than the evanescence of a rainbow that as Wordsworth puts it in his "Ode on Intimations of Immortality," "comes and goes" (463, 2.1), it has a mineral hardness and durability.

The sublime threatens the rational. In a sense it is not surprising that its chief theorist, Edmund Burke, became a prominent conservative philosopher, challenging the claims of reason in his *Reflections on the Revolution in France* (1790) and affirming the value of prejudice. Jefferson, in the prose poetry of his evocations of American landscape, moves towards the sublime and an embrace of the irrational that anticipates the Romantic poets. But, formed and fused by the eighteenth century, he ultimately takes his stand on the apparently firm ground of reason.

Reason and Interest

Whatever the many causes and subsequent course of the American Revolution, it was, like the French Revolution, significantly driven by the eighteenth-century Enlightenment ideal of reason—and this was an ideal that Jefferson upheld throughout his life and writing. As he put it in his plea for religious tolerance in the *Notes*: "Reason and free enquiry are the only effectual agents against error. Give a loose to them, they will support the true religion, by bringing every false one to their tribunal, to the test of their investigation. They are the natural enemies of error, and of error only" (107). In other words, reason is never the enemy of truth.

In the *Notes*, Jefferson goes on to affirm: "Difference of opinion is advantageous in religion" (107). He then poses the question: "Is uniformity attainable?" (107) His answer encapsulates centuries of human suffering and persecution: "Millions of innocent men, women, and children, since the introduction of Christianity, have been burnt, tortured, fined, imprisoned; yet we have not advanced one inch towards uniformity" (107). The term "Millions" signals a scale of mass destruction and coercion more associated with the twentieth than the eighteenth century; but a strong awareness of such massacres, and the desire to obviate them was a strong driver of eighteenth-century Enlightenment.

It should be stressed that the culprit here is not Christianity *per se* but the vain goal of attaining an impossible uniformity of religious or political belief (as in Communism and Fascism). Jefferson makes a plea for an acknowledgement of plurality: the world's people "profess probably a thousand different systems of religion," of which "ours is but one": "if there be but one right, and ours that one, we should wish to see the 999 wandering sects gathered into the fold of truth. But against such a majority we cannot effect this by force. Reason and persuasion are the only practicable instruments" (107). For Jefferson, this clearly also applies in politics and in other fields of life.

Jefferson was also, however, aware of the limits of reason, not least because of the intense, sometimes bitter political struggles in which he had been embroiled. As he said over three decades later in his *Autobiography* (begun 1821): "Reason, justice and equity never had weight enough on the face of the earth, to govern the councils of men. It is interest alone which does it, and it is interest alone which can be trusted" (loc 523–24). We should understand "interest" here not simply in a selfish or pecuniary sense but in the broader sense of "[t]hat which is to or for the advantage of any one; good, benefit, profit, advantage"; the sense in which Edmund Burke uses it in a letter of April 26, 1846 when he speaks of "One who has our interest at heart" (qtd online *Oxford English Dictionary*, "interest," noun, sense 2b). Burke's connection here of "interest" with the "heart," traditionally the seat of emotion, is significant in relation to Jefferson's use of the term, as it acknowledges the crucial importance of feeling in human action and interaction. For Jefferson, reason, justice, and equity are necessary but not sufficient regulators of worldly conduct.

Conclusion
In the final years of the eighteenth century, between 1797 and 1799, the Spanish artist Francisco Goya produced an etching famously entitled "El sueño de la razón produce monstruos" ["The Sleep of Reason Produces Monsters"]. By 1826, however, when Jefferson died, the American, French, Romantic, and industrial revolutions had transformed the world; and feeling had displaced reason in literature, art, culture, politics, and even in science and technology, where a huge excitement, as well as rational procedures of hypothesis, calculation, and experiment, drove discovery, invention,

and innovation. But the long eighteenth century was still in progress and reason persisted in various forms, not least in the person and pen of Thomas Jefferson.

Reason suffered a series of further assaults in the later nineteenth and in the twentieth century; indeed, by the later twentieth century, powerful postmodernist and poststructuralist attacks effectively reinterpreted Goya's title to mean: Reason is the sleep that brings forth monsters. Such attacks condemned the Enlightenment project as an agent of oppression that had helped to generate and mask the subjugation and exclusion of those who, on gender, ethnic, ableist, or other grounds did not conform to its schematizations.

Effective attacks on reason, however, usually appeal to rationality on some level, even if fueled from those other sources, libidinal and emotional ones, for example, that such attacks tend to emphasize. In the name of reason itself it is necessary to recognize the rational force of anti-Enlightenment arguments in their many forms, while also acknowledging, as that very recognition demonstrated, the endurance of reason. If we want to encounter its operations in their full weight and complexity (including their complicity with racism and sexism), we can go to a vital source that both upholds reason and engages deeply with the unreason of the world: the prose of Thomas Jefferson, which captures key elements of eighteenth-century Enlightenment ideas and attitudes at their finest and most fraught.

Works Cited

Boswell, James. *The Life of Samuel Johnson, LL.D.* 1791. 2 vols. Odhams P, n.d.

Burke, Edmund. *A Philosophical [E]nquiry into the Origin of Our Ideas of the Sublime and Beautiful with an Introductory Discourse Concerning Taste, and Several Other Additions.* 1757. Cassell's National Library series. Cassell, 1891.

Fitzgerald, F. Scott. *The Great Gatsby.* Edited by Matthew J. Bruccoli. The Cambridge Edition of the Works of F. Scott Fitzgerald. Cambridge U P, 1995.

Jefferson, Thomas. *Autobiography.* 1821. Madison & Adams P, 2018.

_____. *Notes on the State of Virginia*. 1785. Digireads.com, 2010.

Jefferson, Thomas, et al. The Declaration of Independence: A Transcription. National Archives. www.archives.gov/founding-docs/declaration-transcript.

O'Gorman, Frank. *The Long Eighteenth Century: British Political and Social History 1688–1832*. Arnold History of Britain series. Bloomsbury, 1997.

Seeber, Edward D. "Critical Views on Logan's Speech." *The Journal of American Folklore*, vol. 60, no. 236, Apr.–June 1947, pp. 130–46. JSTOR. www.jstor.org/stable/i223565.

Wordsworth, William. "Ode: Intimations of Immortality from Recollections of Early Childhood." *The Poetical Works of William Wordsworth*. With Introduction by Edward Dowden. Ward, Lock, n.d., pp. 463–65. www.poetryfoundation.org/poems/45536/ode-intimations-of-immortality-from-recollections-of-early-childhood.

Jefferson the Dramatist: His "Dialogue between the Head and the Heart" (with a Complete, Numbered Text)

Robert C. Evans

While serving as the American ambassador to France from 1785 to 1789, Thomas Jefferson enjoyed the mixed blessing of meeting and falling in love with a beautiful, talented English painter named Maria Cosway (1760–1838). Jefferson, a widower, found Maria profoundly attractive, but the blessing of meeting her was mixed for at least two reasons. First, he had once promised his dying wife, Martha, that he would never remarry. Second and more important, Maria herself was already married to another talented English painter—Richard Cosway (1742–1821). When the Cosways decided to return to England in 1786, Jefferson was heartbroken and depressed. His pain, however, led him to write a long, intriguing, and extremely well-crafted letter to Maria commonly referred to as his "Dialogue between the Head and the Heart." This text (reprinted, with line numbers, at the end of this essay) has usually been discussed biographically and/or philosophically—that is, in relation to Jefferson's life and his feelings for Maria Cosway and/or in relation to his larger thinking about reason and the emotions. The "Dialogue," however, has been examined far less often as a *literary text*—that is, as a piece of writing interesting *as a piece of writing*. In the "Dialogue," Jefferson shows real skills as a creative author. In fact, he demonstrates real talent as a *dramatist*. The "Dialogue" is worth reading as much for its phrasing as for what it actually says.

Jefferson's "Dialogue" really deserves to be included in the standard anthologies of early American literature, but it is absent from almost all of them. This omission is seriously unfortunate, because this text strongly displays Jefferson's sense of humor, his talent for recreating credible speech, and his shrewd psychological insight. As a piece of writing, the "Dialogue" is variously fascinating, especially in its complexities and ambiguities and in the complicated responses it can elicit from readers. It is definitely one of Jefferson's most compelling texts and reveals his personality in many intriguing ways.

My purpose in the present essay is to highlight the *literary* features of the "Dialogue," which can be considered one of the best examples of early American drama.[1]

"The Dialogue" Itself

Jefferson's letter, dated October 12, 1786, displays effective phrasing right from the start. Here are its first few sentences:

> [MY DEAR] MADAM
> Having performed the last sad office of handing you into your carriage at the Pavillon de St. Denis, and seen the wheels get actually into motion, I turned on my heel and walked, more dead than alive, to the opposite door, where my own [carriage] was awaiting me. Mr. Danquerville was missing. He was sought for, found, and dragged down stairs. [We] were crammed into the carriage, like recruits for the Bastille, and not having [sou]l enough to give orders to the coachman, he presumed Paris our destination, [and] drove off. (1–8)[1]

Jefferson already begins to display the humor, varied syntax, and engaging sound effects employed throughout the text. The word "heel" echoes "wheels"; the phrase "sought for, found, and dragged down the stairs" effectively lists and emphatically emphasizes strong verbs; and the phrase "recruits for the Bastille" (the famously hellish French prison) turns pain into humor—a technique Jefferson repeatedly uses later. In this "Dialogue," Jefferson must often tread a very fine line: he knows that his words will be read not only by Maria but also by her husband. The letter suggests Jefferson's real suffering but—for many reasons—he had to present that suffering light-heartedly. With Richard as the letter's second reader, Jefferson could not afford to be too open about his actual passion for Richard's wife. But his humor may also have been psychologically self-protective: "I will joke about my feelings because being emotionally vulnerable is painful and may in fact seem weak."

Thus, Jefferson goes out of his way to emphasize that both he *and* Mr. Danquerville miss both Maria *and* Richard. Later the letter more clearly focuses on Maria, but at first Jefferson pretends to a kind of impersonality and impartiality. With effective alliteration he describes how, upon arriving home, he found himself "[s]eated by my fire side, solitary and sad" before next launching into the dialogue itself, which begins as follows:

> *Head.* Well, friend, you seem to be in a pretty trim.
> *Heart.* I am indeed the most wretched of all earthly beings. Overwhelmed with grief, every fibre of my frame distended beyond it's natural powers to bear, I would willingly meet whatever catastrophe should leave me no more to feel or to fear. (19–23)

Already Jefferson creates the distinctive speech and tones of his two speakers. Head's first sentence is very brief and already a bit sarcastic, as if Head really *can* separate himself from Heart's sufferings and be amused by them. Head's brevity makes him seem cool, calm, and in control. But his words are followed by a flood of language four times as long: Heart answers Head's ten words with 41 of his own. Throughout the "Dialogue," Jefferson effectively uses varying sentence length as well as varying word choice to help characterize his speakers, and that process begins immediately. Heart already seems more voluble and emotional than Head. Heart's thoughts and speech seem both uncontrolled and uncontrollable. His language is typically extreme ("*most* wretched"; "*all* earthly beings"; "*every* fibre"; "*whatever catastrophe*"; my italics). He already seems comically over-emotional.

Head, in contrast, seems far more rational. Thus, he answers Heart by saying "These are the eternal consequences of your warmth and precipitation" (24–25)—nicely abstract-sounding language (especially in that reference to "precipitation"). Here and throughout the "Dialogue," one is reminded Oliver Hardy's memorably line to Stan Laurel: "Well, this is another nice mess you've gotten me into." But Hardy's words are far simpler and blunter than Head's, a fact that reinforces our sense of Head as supremely intellectual. Head, however, *can* sound exasperated; neither he nor Heart is a simplistic caricature. Instead, both become increasingly complex personalities as the dialogue proceeds. Thus, Head's next sentence really does foreshadow Hardy's rebuke of Laurel: "This is one of the scrapes into which you are ever leading us" (25–26). We can *hear* Head's frustration: Heart's foolishness, far from being unique, is part of a large, long pattern.

But when Head rebukes Heart, Jefferson is also, of course, rebuking himself. The "Dialogue" is an *internal* debate, which Jefferson cleverly allows us to over-hear. And, since almost everyone has experienced precisely this kind of internal conflict between reason and emotion, Jefferson is dealing not simply with a purely personal situation but with an archetypal human conflict—a conflict to which almost everyone can relate. The Dialogue, although rooted in Jefferson's complex feelings for Maria, instantly transcends its personal source. In fact, this sort of discussion will remain relevant to all humans for as long as all humans feel torn between emotions and rationality.

But this text's effectiveness depends as much on its particular choices of phrasing as on its archetypal relevance. Thus, in his very next sentence, the super-rational Head uses various kinds of vivid and memorable language, including emphatic verbs, effective repetition of ideas, nicely balanced sentence structure, and striking sound effects: "You confess your follies indeed: but still you *hug* and *cherish* them, and *no reformation* can be hoped, where there is *no repentance*" (26–28; my italics). Heart, responding to this lengthy sentence, replies with emphatic brevity and also with his favorite kind of punctuation: an exclamation mark: "Oh my friend!" (29). Half the fun of reading the "Dialogue" comes from the contrast between the hyper-emotional Heart and the super-rational Head. Sometimes their exchanges sound like ones between "Bones" and Spock on *Star Trek*. "Heart" often sounds comically melodramatic, as when he protests, with his typical emphasis on alliteration and other sound effects, "I am *rent* into *fragments* by the *force* of my *grief*!" (29–30; my italics). Heart's phrasing is often comically hyperbolic: "If you have any balm, pour it into my wounds: if none, do not harrow them by new torments" (30–32). Heart often shifts the lengths of his exclamations: "Spare me in this awful moment!" (32). One can easily imagine how a talented actor could comically "overplay" these lines, making them even funnier on stage than they already are on the page. But sometimes Heart also starts to sound a bit like Head, who prefers abstract diction: "At any other [moment]," Heart says, "I will attend with patience to your admonitions" (32–33). Later, Head will also sometimes sound like Heart, a fact suggesting both their complexity and also Jefferson's.

There You Go Again

Much of the fun of the "Dialogue" comes from our sense that this is just the latest instance of a long-running dispute. Henri Bergson long ago suggested that comedy is funny partly because people sometimes behave like automatons and repeatedly do stupid things, as Heart does here. Thus, an exasperated Head, in his typically abstract language, replies to Heart's promise to behave better by saying, "I never found that the moment of triumph with you was the moment of attention to my admonitions" (32–33). Apparently they have had many previous conversations just like this one. Head continues: "While suffering under your follies you may perhaps be made sensible of them, but, the paroxysm over, you fancy it can never return. Harsh therefore as the medecine may be, it is my office to administer it" (36–38). Here again is all the abstract, complicated language we expect from Head (especially in such phrases and words as "attention to my admonitions," "paroxysm," and "office to administer"). But there is also, at the end here, a nice suggestion of reluctance: if Head is causing Heart pain, it is only, he implies, for Heart's own good.

Heart, in a typically human way, soon tries to shift the blame:

"Sir, this acquaintance [with the Cosways] was not the consequence of my doings. It was one of your projects which threw us in the way of it. It was you, remember, and not I, who desired the meeting. . . . I never trouble myself with domes nor arches. The Halle aux bleds" [an impressive Parisian building] might have rotted down before I should have gone to see it." (45–50)

Heart's exaggeration and exasperation are quite funny, but then he turns the tables on Head: he recalls Head's earlier words in the "Dialogue" while adding some very specific and memorable phrasing of his own: "But you, forsooth, who are *eternally getting us to sleep* with your *diagrams* and *crotchets*, must go and examine this wonderful piece of architecture" (50–52). Heart, with nice sarcasm, even makes Head sound like Heart himself by making him sound overly emotional: "And when you had seen it, oh! it was the most superb thing on earth! What you had seen there was worth all you had yet seen in Paris!" (53–54). Now it is *Head* who, supposedly, uses exclamations and exclamation marks. No sooner does Heart mock Head's enthusiasm for the impressive Hall, however, than he seems to admit sharing Head's feelings: "I thought so too" (54). For one brief moment Head and Heart seem to be on the same page, until Heart admits that *his* enthusiasm was provoked by "the lady" (whom he mentions first) "and gentleman to whom we had been presented, and not [by] a *parcel of sticks and chips put together in pens*" (55–56; my italics). The characters' apparent moment of concord is like a rug suddenly pulled out from under us. Their seemingly shared opinion collapses. Jefferson has fun at his own expense by mocking *both* parts of his own personality. But this ability to mock himself, in fact, makes him seem all the more appealing. An arrogant man would never have exposed himself to such satire or inflicted such satire on himself. The more Jefferson lampoons himself, the more engaging he seems. As an extended exercise in self-mockery, this "Dialogue" is actually one of the most winning things Jefferson ever wrote. It reveals a sense of humor not often apparent in many of his more famous writings.

Other aspects of the "Dialogue" make it immensely attractive. Jefferson gives each speaker his due. In other words, he lets each aspect of his own personality score effective points, both rhetorically and philosophically. The exchanges never seem "rigged": both characters make persuasive arguments. Unlike Plato's dialogues, where the outcome is often foreshadowed right from the start (as in the *Ion*), in Jefferson's little play each character is given effective moments. Like any skilled dramatist, Jefferson knew how to sustain interest and generate suspense. Not until the very end—and not even then—can we be sure who has "won" the debate, or how.

In the meantime, there is plenty of clever humor and sarcasm, as when Head says, "It would have been happy for you if my diagrams and crotchets had gotten you to sleep on that day, as you are pleased to say they eternally do" (58–60). Although there is often an edge to such comments, there also seems to be a more than a bit of good-natured joshing. Head and Heart have been debating one another for years; this "Dialogue" is just their latest comic dispute. Each character tries to make his case as fully and variously as possible. Thus, Head implicitly accuses Heart of self-centeredness and implicitly commends his own public-spiritedness (61). But Head, anticipating possible building projects he hopes to undertake when he returns to America, sounds almost as swept away by enthusiasm as Heart is when contemplating Maria Cosway (61–68). Head even imagines how his plans to improve Philadelphia could help "warm and feed the poor of that city"—an especially interesting comment in light of Heart's later extended claim that Head neglects the needy (68; 291–309). Paradoxically, Head is often most imaginative and emotional when envisioning how he can use practical reason to benefit the public at large. And, since the entire "Dialogue" helps variously delineate different aspects of Jefferson's *own* character, Head's desire to help others (rather than merely benefit himself) benefits Jefferson's own image. Everything Head says about Heart reflects back on Jefferson, and the same is true in reverse. While outlining the protagonists' personalities, he illuminates some of his own complexity.

Interestingly, Head even manages to blame the Cosways themselves, in part, not only for starting the friendship but also for lying to their other friends so they could pursue it: "Every soul of you had an engagement for the day. Yet all these were to be sacrificed, that you might dine together. Lying messengers were to be dispatched into every quarter of the city with apologies for your breach of engagement" (71–74). Jefferson thus mocks not only his Heart but also the Cosways—as well as his own complete self, since *he*—including his Head—assented to the scheme. No one escapes this "Dialogue" without being made fun of, including the Cosways, who are several times subjected to good-natured teasing (81–82). The "Dialogue" not only recounts their first meeting with Jefferson but, through this kind of clever leg-pulling, helps cement the friendship even further.

In a particularly funny moment, Heart responds in an unexpected way to Head's sarcasm. Instead of being chastened by Head's mockery, Heart enthuses over the memory: "Oh! my dear friend, how you have revived me by recalling to my mind the transactions of that day!" (83–84). Once again, Bergson's idea that comedy results from mechanical behavior seems relevant: Heart, so to speak, has a one-track mind. Everything said to him provokes a passionate response. He is obsessed, and obsessed people are often funny (or annoying) precisely because they lack self-control. They literally can't be reasoned with, and thus Heart's obsessions especially—and appropriately—help reinforce our sense of his emotional personality.

Head had earlier dryly listed a few of the places Jefferson had visited with the Cosways, recalling that they had travelled "to St. Cloud, [and then] from St. Cloud to Ruggieri's, [and] from Ruggieri to Krumfoltz" (79–80). Heart, typically full of enthusiasm, now passionately offers a much more vivid list of his own:

> paint to me the day we went to St. Germains. How beautiful was every object! the Port de Neuilly, the hills along the Seine, the rainbows of the machine of Marly, the terras of St. Germains, the chateaux, the gardens, the [statues] of Marly, the pavillon of Lucienne. Recollect too Madrid, Bagatelle, the King's garden, the Dessert. How grand the idea excited by the remains of such a column! The spiral staircase too was beautiful. (87–92)

Not only is Heart's list longer than Head's, but it is also far more literally picturesque. Heart doesn't just enumerate places he has been; he recreates them in his (and our) mind's eye. His list overflows: it stops, restarts, and then zooms off in an entirely new direction. It even ends by contradicting his earlier assertion that he has no interest in architecture. Jefferson's characterizations of Heart are especially funny, partly because Heart so comically compulsive. He often shifts abruptly from one mood to another and thus adds greatly to the suspense and interest of the piece. We can never quite predict what he will say or how he will say it. Thus he quickly shifts from his enthusiastic list to a tone of calm good-humor: "Retrace all those scenes to me, my good companion, and I will forgive the unkindness with which you were chiding me. The day we went to St. Germains was a little too warm, I think, was not it?" (97–100).

But no sooner does Heart settle down into a spirit of genuine good will than Head himself impatiently explodes: "Thou art the most incorrigible of all the beings that ever sinned!" (101). Part of the fun of the "Dialogue" arises from this kind of abrupt shift from one mood to another: sometimes Head will seem passionate while Heart sounds perfectly rational, and sometimes *vice versa*. Perhaps Jefferson is subtly implying that human personalities are less divided, and more complicated, than we often imagine; perhaps there *is* no easy separation between our heads and our hearts. In any case, he manages to create characters of fascinating (and often hilarious) complexity. Head, while urging Heart to control himself, often loses control *him*self; Heart, while urging Head to sanction emotion, often makes persuasively logical arguments. The "Dialogue" provokes serious thought about the relationship between reason and passion while also arousing much amusement and laughter. But the "Dialogue" can also encourage real self-examination: as we sympathize now with Head and now with Heart, we realize how complicated our own personalities can be, how difficult it is to adjudicate, in any simple way, between logic and emotion. In a sense, then, Jefferson recreates *in us* the very kind of tension he explores within himself and between his two interlocutors.

Pervasive Techniques

As the "Dialogue" develops, Jefferson uses language that is variously intriguing in its own right. This includes diction and syntax that are sometimes full of vivid imagery (e.g., 144–45; 161–63; 191;), sometimes appropriately abstract (e.g., 107–08), sometimes obviously humorous (e.g., 194–96), and sometimes brimming with effective, often rhythmical lists (e.g. 109–11; 113; 136–37; 141; 143; 166–70; 175–79; 193; 247–50; 256; 276–78; 280–81; 346–50). Sometimes the phrasing is deliberately and memorably repetitive (e.g., 109–10), sometimes rich in alliteration and/or assonance (e.g., 110; 145; 160; 196–97), and sometimes well-crafted in its balanced sentence structure (e.g. 118–19; 238–40; 251–52; 258; 260–65; 268–73; 275–76; 276–78). Often the "Dialogue" features quick changes from one kind of sentence length to another (e.g., contrast 114–20 with 121; contrast 156–57 with the single-word sentence in 158; contrast 186–88 with 189; contrast 198–200 with 201; contrast 256 with 257; contrast 293–97 with 297–98). Sometimes the tone sounds comically desperate (e.g., 121); sometimes humorously self-pitiful (e.g., 126, 130); sometimes proudly nationalistic (e.g., 132–33; 136–37; 159–61, 182–83); and sometimes stingingly sarcastic (e.g., 320–24).

Sometimes, paradoxically, Head speaks in strongly emotional terms whereas Heart sounds eminently rational (e.g., 161–63; 166–70; 172–74); sometimes the syntax mimics the behavior or feelings it describes (e.g., "No sleep, no rest" [191–92]; see also 193); sometimes the "Dialogue" employs striking metaphors (e.g., 142–43; 158); sometimes it uses memorable similes or even extended similes (e.g., 201–04). Sometimes it tries to play subtly on *Maria*'s emotions (e.g., such as by tempting her desire for fame in 137–39 or by arousing pity—both in Maria and in us—for Jefferson's own genuine suffering in 151–55); and, in one rather daring sentence, it even suggests that Monticello would make a good refuge for Maria is ever she needed an "asylum from grief" (such the grief of widowhood? [146–47]). Jefferson instantly tones down this startling implication by quickly emphasizing his potential compassion for any future suffering by *both* Cosways (148–49). He quickly adds a touch of exaggerated humor (149–51), hopes that heaven will forbid any suffering by the Cosways, in general, or by Maria, in particular, (156–57), and makes it sound as if *Heart* is the character most preoccupied with Maria, thus safely distancing Head from any inappropriate attraction (e.g., 171). Maria, however, surely could not have missed the idea that if her husband ever *did* die, there was a widower in Virginia ready to comfort her (see Brodie 211).

As the "Dialogue" advances, it becomes increasingly thought-provoking. This is especially true when Head, warning against the dangers of making friends too easily, asserts that "Everything in this world is matter of calculation" (201). How should we take this? Does it express sensible prudence or self-centered self-concern? In a sentence whose very imagery and structure mimic the actions and results it describes, Head advises Heart to "Advance then with caution, the balance in your hand. Put into one scale the pleasures which any object may offer; but put fairly into the other the pains which are to follow, and see which preponderates" (201–04). In the first quoted sentence, six syllables appear to the left of the comma and six to the right. Thus, a sentence advising balance is itself nicely balanced in sound. Similarly, in the second quoted sentence, sixteen syllables precede the semicolon, and then sixteen follow it until the comma arrives: another well-balanced sentence. But then, in the final clause, six syllables tip the sentence's balance in favor of the second part, just as scales tip when one scale finally outweighs the other. Whether Jefferson deliberately and consciously constructed this sentence in this intriguing fashion, the fact remains that its very design mimics balance followed by a slight tip in one direction— exactly as a scale itself would operate.

"The making an acquaintance," Head continues,

> is not a matter of indifference. When a new one is proposed to you, view it all round. Consider what advantages it presents, and to what inconveniencies it may expose you. Do not bite at the bait of pleasure till you know there is no hook beneath it. The art of life is the art of avoiding pain: and he is the best pilot who steers clearest of the rocks and shoals with which it is beset. Pleasure is always before us; but misfortune is at our side: while running after that, this arrests us. The most effectual means of being secure against pain is to retire within ourselves, and to suffice for our own happiness. (204–12)

How do we—how *should* we—respond to this? Is it sensible advice, or is it too cautious, too self-centered, too self-protective?

How should we react to Head's emphasis on "advantages" and "inconveniences" when speaking of friendships? Do those words sound *too* calculating?

However we respond to this advice philosophically, it is hard *not* to admire the skill of Jefferson's phrasing, especially the vivid imagery and alliteration of "Do not bite at the bait of pleasure till you know there is no hook beneath it," or the striking metaphor referring to steering clear of rocks and shoals, or the doubly well-balanced sentence beginning "Pleasure is always before us." Head's advice may sound too self-interested, but there are probably few people, looking back on failed or painful relationships, who will not wish they had sometimes followed it. Here as so often in the "Dialogue," an interlocutor simply voices thoughts that probably all people have pondered from time to time.

The Effectiveness of the "Dialogue"

Part of the effectiveness of the "Dialogue" lies in this sort of archetypal appeal. Head, after all, merely offers the kind of advice a Stoic would offer, and there is good reason to think that Jefferson himself admired the Stoics. Head recommends the attractiveness of "intellectual pleasures"—an idea and phrase we too often neglect, because we tend to associate the word "pleasure" with sensuality. When Head describes "intellectual pleasures," he offers one of the most effective and best-balanced lists of the entire "Dialogue" (217–220). In fact, his sentences often provide the very sort of intellectual pleasures he endorses. And then his very long sentence is immediately and effectively followed by a very short one (222). No sooner, however, does Head make a fairly persuasive case for Stoicism and the pleasures of the mind than he risks sounding a bit arrogant: "Leave the bustle and tumult of society to those who have not talents to occupy themselves without them" (223–24). And then he runs the even greater risk of sounding unattractively cynical: "Friendship is but another name for an alliance with the follies and the misfortunes of others" (224–25). The comment about steering clear of others' "follies" seems persuasive, but what about the advice to steer clear of their "misfortunes"? Should we really try to ignore others' pains simply to preserve our own peace of mind? In any case, even within an apparently simple sentence, Jefferson offers some nicely balanced tension between alternatives.

As Head proceeds, we notice more and more ways in which Jefferson's phrasing is effective, as in the following sentence, with its well-balanced structure and its abrupt shift from a statement to a question: "Our own share of miseries is sufficient: why enter then as volunteers into those of another?" (226–27). But once again, what should we make of Head's advice not to share others' miseries? Is this advice selfish, prudent, or some mixture of both? By this point we realize increasingly that the "Dialogue" has evolved from a somewhat funny letter to an attractive lady into a genuinely searching and provocative philosophical debate. By asking questions rather than simply making statements, Jefferson not only crafts a dialogue between Head and Heart but also engages in a dialogue with himself and with his readers, as when Head asks, "Is there so little gall poured into our own cup that we must needs help to drink that of our neighbor?" (227–28). Here, as often, the metaphorical imagery is striking and the question itself is genuinely thought-provoking. We are no longer simply *reading* a dialogue but are being invited to participate *in* it.

Head continues: "A friend dies or leaves us: we feel as if a limb was cut off" (228–29). Here it is *Head*, with his vivid imagery, who sounds emotional, sympathetic, and capable of true suffering. He then goes on, speaking again of a hypothetical friend: "He is sick: we must watch over him, and participate of his pains" (229–30). How should we interpret the word "must" here? As reflecting a genuinely heartfelt obligation or as reflecting a kind of imposed social pressure, or both? Head then mentions another particular hypothetical example: "His [that is, the friend's] fortune is shipwrecked: ours must be laid under contribution" (230–31). Does this sound too selfish, or is it simply a genuinely prudent worry? Should a person be willing to sink his own fortune because a friend's fortune has sunk, perhaps through the friend's foolishness? Jefferson seems less interested in definitively answering such questions than in memorably raising them. Head's extended argument here ends with an effective list, effective sound effects, and effectively ambiguous use of the word "must": "He loses a child, a parent or a partner: we must mourn the loss as if it was our own" (231–32). In what senses, again, does Head mean "must"—because of our own deep and innate sympathy (in which case Head sounds like an attractive personality) or because of social pressures or a sense of imposed obligations (in which case Head sounds too selfish)? Here, as so often throughout the Dialogue, we are left to reach our own conclusions about how convincing the speakers' arguments are.

Heart, responding to Head's reasoning, reacts with alliterative emotionalism than can even seem a bit comic, as if mutual pain is a source of genuine pleasure: "And what more sublime delight than to mingle tears with one whom the hand of heaven hath smitten!" (233–34). But if this response seems a bit overblown, the next one makes more sense and sounds more obviously admirable: "To watch over the bed of sickness, and to beguile it's tedious and it's painful moments!" (234–35). The shift from somewhat foolish emotion to legitimately impressive compassion is typical of Jefferson's method throughout the "Dialogue": just when we think we've figured out one of the characters, Jefferson complicates his presentation and our reaction. Heart here may have sounded a bit foolish at first, but as each new sentence is added he sounds increasingly admirable— partly because he sounds increasingly *reasonable*: "To share our bread with one to whom misfortune has left none! This world abounds indeed with misery: to lighten it's burthen we must divide it with one another" (236–38).

Even here, however—or at least in the ensuing two sentences, with their emphatic exclamation marks (241–43; see also 246–47)— Jefferson may be having some fun with Heart, who is rarely less than completely enthusiastic. Jefferson's characterization of both speakers is typically complex, which is one reason his "Dialogue" seems more a genuine piece of literature than a simple philosophical debate. The characters are treated as real personalities rather than as merely abstract spokesmen for merely abstract ideas. Thus, Heart— making his case for helping others—himself offers a rhetorically balanced and rational idea that, in fact, involves a certain degree of calculated self-concern: "For assuredly nobody will care for him who cares for nobody" (250–51).

One especially provocative idea in the "Dialogue" is Heart's claim that "[m]orals were too essential to the happiness of man to be risked on the incertain combinations of the head" (283–84). We usually think of reason as steadier and more reliable than the emotions, but Heart makes just the opposite claim, arguing that compassionate, empathetic moral *sentiments* are more dependable than calculating, rational, individual self-interest. Heart asserts that Nature laid the foundation of morality "therefore in sentiment, not in science" (285)—a phrase exhibiting Jefferson's typically artful balance of both meaning and sound. Heart continues, arguing that moral sentiment is a trait Nature "gave to all, as necessary to all," whereas she gave reason "to a few only, as sufficing with a few" (285–86). All throughout this passage, Heart makes eminently reasonable arguments *against* an excessive reliance on reason (286–90).

Especially interesting, however, are some specific examples Heart cites to support his claims. These are particularly intriguing as they make Jefferson himself sound rather cold-hearted while at the same time implying his sense of guilt and thus the actual depth of his conscience. Heart remembers that once, in the past, a

> poor wearied souldier, whom we overtook at Chickahominy with his pack on his back, begged us to let him get up behind our chariot, … [but Head] began to calculate that the road was full of souldiers, and that if all should be taken up our horses would fail in their journey. We drove on therefore. (293–98)

What are we to make of this? Does Head deserve blame for thinking this way, or were his thoughts, in fact, simply practical and sensible? Part of the power of the "Dialogue" is that Jefferson forces us to engage in an *internal* dialog with ourselves. He pits our own heads and hearts against each other and makes us ponder what we ourselves would have done in a similar situation.

As if to add to the complexity, Heart quickly admits that Head soon became "sensible," or aware, that he had made Heart "do wrong" by driving away from the weary soldier (298–99). The phrasing here is particularly complicated: it was Head, after all, who did not think it wise to help the soldier, so how can Heart blame *himself* for having done anything "wrong"? And it is Head who apparently has enough conscience to realize and concede that *he* should have responded differently. Head himself eventually realized, rationally, that "tho we cannot relieve all the distressed we should relieve as many as we can" (299–300), thereby prompting Heart to turn back and "take up the souldier" (300). Here as well as elsewhere in the "Dialogue," Jefferson manages to create some real suspense and some real surprises. When they go back to look for the soldier, they discover that "he had entered a bye path, and was no more to be found," so that "from that moment to this I [i.e., Heart] could never find him out to ask his forgiveness" (301–02). Jefferson at first makes us think that the anecdote will have a happy ending but then reveals that it did not. In this way and others, his "Dialogue" is rarely predictable. It keeps us interested, keeps us guessing, and keeps us thinking.

Complex Characterization of All Concerned

The anecdote just described reflects both ill and well on Jefferson himself, and the mere fact that he is willing to relate it, especially *to a woman in whom he had a definite romantic interest*, speaks well both of his honesty and of his sense of his own flaws. The same kind of honesty is evident in another anecdote Heart relates:

> Again, when [a] poor woman came to ask a charity in Philadelphia, you [i.e., Head] whispered that she looked like a drunkard, and that half a dollar was enough to give her for the ale-house. Those who want the dispositions to give, easily find reasons why they ought not to give. When I sought her out afterwards, and did what I should have done at first, you know that she employed the money immediately towards placing her child at school. (303–09)

Once more, Jefferson, in a text so much characterized by balanced phrasing and balanced thinking, presents a balanced view of his own personality: initially he resisted helping the woman, but eventually he not only *did* help her but actually sought her out to do so. His willingness to criticize himself helps encourage his readers to be self-critical, too—to examine their *own* flaws and their own consciences.

Finally, in concluding his case—a case, it must be said, that sounds perfectly rational—Heart observes that "If our country, when pressed with wrongs at the point of the bayonet, had been governed by it's heads instead of it's hearts, where should we have been now? hanging on a gallows as high as Haman's" (309–12). Jefferson here raises the stakes and broadens the implications of Heart's arguments. Up until this point, Heart has rooted his assertions in specific *personal* examples; now he shows the potential social, national, and international mistakes that can result from self-centered calculation. It was Jefferson himself who, in the Declaration of Independence, had made a logical, rational (if also impassioned) case for the American Revolution, but Heart insists that logic and rationality were not enough—that ultimately the Revolution began and succeeded because people were willing to take risks and trust in Providence, "whose precept is to do always what is right, and leave the issue to him" (317–18).

But just when Heart seems to have made his case most persuasively, he perhaps mars it by engaging, again, in what might be considered irrational exaggeration: "In short, my friend, as far as my recollection serves me, I do not know that I ever did a good thing on your suggestion, *or a dirty one without it*" (318–20). How seriously should we take this claim—especially that powerful word "dirty"? Is Heart really asserting that reason corrupts everything it touches? Or is he merely maintaining that *self-interest* does? Once again, Jefferson encourages not only thought but two kinds of debate: both internally, within readers, and, perhaps, also between readers and either or both of the characters he has created.

Interestingly, no sooner does Heart condemn rational calculation than he indicates that he, himself, rationally calculates before deciding to make new friends: "I receive no one into my esteem till I know they are worthy of it" (326–27). The crucial word here is "worthy." "Worthy" in what ways? Heart quickly indicates the factors he considers unimportant: "Wealth, title, office, are no recommendations to my friendship" (327–28). Is he implying that these are the kinds of factors that *do* matter to Head? In any case, he immediately insists that the traits he has just listed are not only unimportant to him but are traits he actually disdains. In fact, he thinks "great good qualities are requisite to make amends for [potential friends] having wealth, title and office" (328–30). He defends his choice of the Cosways as friends and asserts that even Head knows they are worthy—that Head's only objection to this friendship is that both Head and Heart knew it would end so soon. Responding to Head's thinking, Heart himself sounds sensibly reasonable—just the latest example of Jefferson's tendency to complicate our initial assumptions about his characters. Heart asserts that humans themselves "are not immortal," so

> how can we expect our enjoiments to be so? We have no rose without it's thorn; no pleasure without alloy. It is the law of our existence; and we must acquiesce. It is the condition annexed to all our pleasures, not by us who receive, but by him who gives them. (332–37).

Heart sounds admirably rational here, and indeed his mere engagement in intelligent discussion shows that he is not simply or entirely emotional. Ironically, if he wins the debate at all, as most commentators assume he does, it is partly because he offers good reasons to support his views. His apparent victory is due, paradoxically, to the rational arguments he makes.

As the "Dialogue" begins to draw to a close, Heart can still sound humorously emotional (e.g., 344–45), but in general he sounds much more reasonable than he did when the "Dialogue" began. In fact, there are times when Heart can even sound shrewdly calculating, as when emphasizing his deep, abiding affection *for the couple* when his main concern is probably *with the lady* (346–50). By the end of the "Dialogue," not only Head and Heart seem more complicated personalities than they seemed at the beginning, but so does Jefferson. By allowing two parts of his own character to engage in such complicated debate, he makes his own general character seem variously attractive. He displays both his thoughts and his feelings, but he also displays his honesty (on this point see

McLaughlin 216), his sense of humor, his fallibility, and his capacity for genuine affection. In all these ways, the "Dialogue" is not only an effective piece of drama but a shrewd piece of rhetoric designed to appeal, especially, to Maria Cosway, with her husband almost as an afterthought.

Jefferson, near the very end of his letter to Maria, calls the "Dialogue" merely "a tedious sermon" (360), but of course it is anything but tedious and anything but a simple sermon. It is, instead, an example of Jefferson at his most complicated and at his most creative. The "Dialogue" deserves to be considered a true piece of *literature*—interesting not only for its ideas but especially for the quality of the writing and for the pervasive complexity of its style, tone, characterization, themes, and structure.

Note

1. Many studies of Jefferson have discussed the "Head and Heart" letter in all kinds of ways, but rarely as a work of literature. Fawn Brodie (1974) calls it Jefferson's "great love letter" and cites Julian Boyd's assessment of it as "one of the greatest love letters in the English language" (210). Brodie sees it as a considerably "important . . . window into Jefferson's inner life" and says it "has been the subject of divergent and contradictory interpretations" (210). According to Brodie, many scholars see "the letter as a debate, and insist that the head emerges triumphant over the heart." She cites Boyd and Merrill Peterson as holding this view—a view she thinks overlooks Jefferson's actual passion for Maria Cosway, which she says can be documented in his later letters to her. Brodie regards the "Dialogue" as less a debate than a searching self-examination and contends that as "a self-portrait there is nothing in the Jefferson literature to contend with it." She calls it a portrait of "a deeply tormented man" (210).

    Jack McLaughlin (1988) sees the text as an "example of a popular eighteenth-century literary genre, the dramatic dialogue" (214). After summarizing its content, McLaughlin claims that its "distinction . . . derives not from what it reveals about Thomas Jefferson, but from what it discloses about those who read it. Like most works of art," McLaughlin continues, "it is richly ambiguous, arguing with equal persuasiveness for the ascendancy of intellect and of feeling" (215). "The art of Jefferson's letter," McLaughlin maintains, "lies it its refusal to resolve the contest and declare an undisputed winner." McLaughlin thinks the letter provides a key to the essence of Jefferson's personality, especially his complex attraction to both logic and love (216).

Andrew Burstein (*Inner Jefferson*; 1995) calls Jefferson's letter "an inspiring work of tender sentiment," saying that Jefferson the "intellectual wrote in spirited, sensuous language, as one who wishes it were possible in his world to incline toward the spontaneous, artistic, and natural" (80). Burstein then discusses the eighteenth-century meanings of various words Jefferson uses (81) as well as Jefferson's concepts of time; a possible sexual allusion (82); and Heart's eventual triumph and inspiring patriotism (83–84). Burstein also comments on Jefferson's partial sympathy with Head; his attitude toward the sea and sea voyages (85–86); his previous views of friendship (88); and his concepts of pleasure and delight (89). Burstein then summarizes the rest of the letter (89–94), adding that although most commentators have called "the debate a draw or insisted that Jefferson simply obeyed his Head, . . . it seems clear that in giving Heart the last word, as well as the longest uninterrupted speech, Jefferson was attempting to convince himself that the Heart was right" (94–95). Burstein concluded that although the Heart won the debate, Jefferson would still have to follow his head in getting on with his life (96). Burstein's discussion is one of the longest and most interesting responses the letter has elicited.

Burstein (*Letters*; 2002) calls the letter a "stylish, evocative composition" that is both "a testament to sentimental friendship and a window to the inner life of the man who fashioned it" (30). He finds it both "charming" and "moralistic" (32).

Jon Kukla (2009) interestingly discusses the text's use of pronouns (99) but questions the common view of this work as an extended love letter. Instead, he sees it as typifying the kind of self-absorption Jefferson commonly displayed when thinking about women (113) and as reflecting the last time Jefferson would allow a woman to ensnare his heart (114). In an appendix, Kukla examines the Jefferson-Cosway relationship in detail and doubts that it was ever sexual or even intensely romantic (203). He reviews previous scholarship on the letter and notes various errors (203–04).

Hannah Spahn (2011) calls the letter the "longest of Jefferson's [Laurence] Sterne-inspired love letters." She thinks it may illustrate the "dualistic nature of his conception of time" (25), contrasting the "Head's rational time and the Heart's sentimental time" (27).

Kevin J. Hayes (2012) suggests Boethius's *Consolation of Philosophy* as a precedent for Jefferson's letter (336). He summarizes the letter's contents (336–39) and concludes that "Heart wins the argument and gets in the last word" (339).

Ari Helo (2014) stresses the work's emphasis on "prudence" in both the personal and broader senses; argues that the "sentimental Heart eventually wins the argument over the intellectual Head"; emphasizes Jefferson's interest in "genuine happiness" (93); and explores the work's connections with preceding kinds of philosophy (94–96).

Works Cited

Bergson, Henri. *Laughter: An Essay on the Meaning of the Comic.* Macmillan, 1911.

Brodie, Fawn MacKay. *Thomas Jefferson: An Intimate History.* Norton, 1974.

Burstein, Andrew. *The Inner Jefferson: Portrait of a Grieving Optimist.* U P of Virginia, 1995.

_____. *Letters from the Head and Heart. Founders Online.* The National Archives. https://founders.archives.gov/documents/ Jefferson/01-10-02-0309.

Hayes, Kevin J. *The Road to Monticello: The Life and Mind of Thomas Jefferson.* Oxford U P, 2012.

Helo, Ari. *Thomas Jefferson's Ethics and the Politics of Human Progress: The Morality of a Slaveholder.* Cambridge U P, 2014.

Kukla, Jon. *Mr. Jefferson's Women.* Random House, 2009.

McLaughlin, Jack. *Jefferson and Monticello: The Biography of a Builder.* Holt, 1988.

Spahn, Hannah. *Thomas Jefferson, Time, and History.* U of Virginia P, 2011.

Jefferson's Dialogue between the Head and the Heart

From Thomas Jefferson to Maria Cosway, 12 October 1786

To Maria Cosway

Paris Octob. 12. 1786.

[My dear] Madam[1]

Having performed the last sad office of handing you into your carriage at the Pavillon de St. Denis, and seen the wheels get actually into motion, I turned on my heel and walked, more dead than alive, to the opposite door, where my own was awaiting me. Mr. Danquerville was missing. He was sought for, found, and dragged down stairs. [5]

[We] were crammed into the carriage, like recruits for the Bastille, and not having [sou]l enough to give orders to the coachman, he presumed Paris our destination, [and] drove off. After a considerable interval, silence was broke with a 'je suis vraiment affligé du depart de ces bons gens.' This was the signal for a mutual confession [of dist]ress. [10]

We began immediately to talk of Mr. and Mrs. Cosway, of their goodness, their [talents], their amability, and tho we spoke of nothing else, we seemed hardly to have entered into matter when the coachman announced the rue St. Denis, and that we were opposite Mr. Danquerville's. He insisted on descending there and   [15]

traversing a short passage to his lodgings. I was carried home. Seated by my fire side, solitary and sad, the following dialogue took place between my Head and my Heart.

Head. Well, friend, you seem to be in a pretty trim.

Heart. I am indeed the most wretched of all earthly beings. [20] Overwhelmed with grief, every fibre of my frame distended beyond it's natural powers to bear, I would willingly meet whatever catastrophe should leave me no more to feel or to fear.

Head. These are the eternal consequences of your warmth and precipitation. This is one of the scrapes into which you are ever [25] leading us. You confess your follies indeed: but still you hug and cherish them, and no reformation can be hoped, where there is no repentance.

Heart. Oh my friend! This is no moment to upbraid my foibles. I am rent into fragments by the force of my grief! If you have any [30] balm, pour it into my wounds: if none, do not harrow them by new torments. Spare me in this awful moment! At any other I will attend with patience to your admonitions.

Head. On the contrary I never found that the moment of triumph with you was the moment of attention to my admonitions.   [35]
While suffering under your follies you may perhaps be made sensible of them, but, the paroxysm over, you fancy it can never return. Harsh therefore as the medecine may be, it is my office to administer it. You will be pleased to remember that when our friend Trumbull used to be telling us of the merits and talents of these good people, [40]
I never ceased whispering to you that we had no occasion for new acquaintance; that the greater their merit and talents, the more dangerous their friendship to our tranquillity, because the regret at parting would be greater.

Heart. Accordingly, Sir, this acquaintance was not the   [45]
consequence of my doings. It was one of your projects which threw us in the way of it. It was you, remember, and not I, who desired the meeting, at Legrand & Molinos. I never trouble myself with domes² nor arches. The Halle aux bleds might have rotted down before I should have gone to see it. But you, forsooth, who are eternally   [50]
getting us to sleep with your diagrams and crotchets, must go and examine this wonderful piece of architecture. And when you had seen it, oh! it was the most superb thing on earth! What you had seen there was worth all you had yet seen in Paris! I thought so too. But I meant it of the lady and gentleman to whom we had been presented,   [55]
and not of a parcel of sticks and chips put together in pens. You then, Sir, and not I, have been the cause of the present distress.

Head. It would have been happy for you if my diagrams and crotchets had gotten you to sleep on that day, as you are pleased to say they eternally do.   [60]
My visit to Legrand & Molinos had publick utility for it's object. A market is to be built in Richmond. What a commodious plan is that of Legrand & Molinos: especially if we put on it the noble dome of the Halle aux bleds. If such a bridge as they shewed us can be thrown across the Schuylkill at Philadelphia,   [65]
the floating bridges taken up, and the navigation of that river opened, what a copious resource will be added, of wood and provisions, to warm and feed the poor of that city. While I was occupied with these objects, you were dilating with your new acquaintances, and contriving how to prevent a separation from them.   [70]
Every soul of you had an engagement for the day. Yet all these were to be sacrificed, that you might dine together. Lying messengers were

to be dispatched into every quarter of the city with apologies for your breach of engagement. You particularly had the effrontery [to] send word to the Dutchess Danville that,   [75]

in the moment we were setting out to d[ine] with her, dispatches came to hand which required immediate attention. You [wanted] me to invent a more ingenious excuse; but I knew you were getting into a scrape, and I would have nothing to do with it. Well, after dinner to St. Cloud, from St. Cloud to Ruggieri's, from Ruggieri to Krumfoltz,   [80]

and if the day had been as long as a Lapland summer day, you would still have contrived means, among you, to have filled it.

Heart. Oh! my dear friend, how you have revived me by recalling to my mind the transactions of that day! How well I remember them all, and that when I came home at night and looked back   [85]

to the morning, it seemed to have been a month agone. Go on then, like a kind comforter,[3] and paint to me the day we went to St. Germains. How beautiful was every object! the Port de Neuilly, the hills along the Seine, the rainbows of the machine of Marly, the terras of St. Germains, the chateaux, the gardens, the [statues] of Marly,   [90]

the pavillon of Lucienne. Recollect too Madrid, Bagatelle, the King's garden, the Dessert. How grand the idea excited by the remains of such a column! The spiral staircase too was beautiful. Every moment was filled with something agreeable. The wheels of time moved on with a rapidity of which those of our carriage gave but a faint idea,   [95]

and yet in the evening, when one took a retrospect of the day, what a mass of happiness had we travelled over! Retrace all those scenes to me, my good companion, and I will forgive the unkindness with which you were chiding me. The day we went to St. Germains was a little too warm, I think, was not it? [100]

Head. Thou art the most incorrigible of all the beings that ever sinned! I reminded you of the follies of the first day, intending to deduce from thence some useful lessons for you, but instead of listening to these, you kindle at the recollection, you retrace the whole series with a fondness which shews you want nothing but   [105]

the opportunity to act it over again. I often told you during it's course that you were imprudently engaging your affections under circumstances that must cost you a great deal of pain: that the persons indeed were of the greatest merit, possessing good sense, good humour, honest hearts, honest manners,   [110]

and eminence in a lovely art: that the lady had moreover qualities and accomplishments, belonging to her sex, which might form a chapter apart for her: such as music, modesty, beauty, and that softness of disposition which is the ornament of her sex and charm of ours. But that all these considerations would increase the pang of separation: [115]
that their stay here was to be short: that you rack our whole system when you are parted from those you love, complaining that such a separation is worse than death, inasmuch as this ends our sufferings, whereas that only begins them: and that the separation would in this instance be the more severe as you would probably never see them again. [120]
Heart. But they told me they would come back again the next year.
Head. But in the mean time see what you suffer: and their return too depends on so many circumstances that if you had a grain of prudence you would not count upon it. Upon the whole it is improbable and therefore you should abandon the idea of ever seeing them again. [125]
Heart. May heaven abandon me if I do!
Head. Very well. Suppose then they come back. They are to stay here two months, and when these are expired, what is to follow? Perhaps you flatter yourself they may come to America?
Heart. God only knows what is to happen. [130]
I see nothing impossible in that supposition, and I see things wonderfully contrived sometimes to make us happy. Where could they find such objects as in America for the exercise of their enchanting art?, especially the lady, who paints landscape so inimitably. She wants only subjects worthy of immortality to render her pencil immortal. [135]
The Falling spring, the Cascade of Niagara, the Passage of the Potowmac thro the Blue mountains, the Natural bridge. It is worth a voiage across the Atlantic to see these objects; much more to paint, and make them, and thereby ourselves, known to all ages. And our own dear Monticello, where has nature spread so rich a mantle under the eye? [140]
mountains, forests, rocks, rivers. With what majesty do we there ride above the storms! How sublime to look down into the workhouse of nature, to see her clouds, hail, snow, rain, thunder, all fabricated at our feet! And the glorious Sun, when rising as if out of a distant water, just gilding the tops of the mountains, and giving life to all nature! [145]
—I hope in god no circumstance may ever make either seek an asylum from grief! With what sincere sympathy I would open every cell of my composition to receive the effusion of their woes! I would pour my tears

into their wounds: and if a drop of balm could be found at the top of the Cordilleras, or at the remotest sources of the Missouri, [150]
I would go thither myself to seek and to bring it. Deeply practised in the school of affliction, the human heart knows no joy which I have not lost, no sorrow of which I have not drank! Fortune can present no grief of unknown form to me! Who then can so softly bind up the wound of another as he who has felt the same wound himself? [155]
But Heaven forbid they should ever know a sorrow!—Let us turn over another leaf, for this has distracted me.[4]
Head. Well. Let us put this possibility to trial then on another point. When you consider the character which is given of our country by the lying newspapers of London, and their credulous copyers [160]
in other countries; when you reflect that all Europe is made to believe we are a lawless banditti, in a state of absolute anarchy, cutting one another's throats, and plundering without distinction, how can you expect that any reasonable creature would venture among us? [165]
Heart. But you and I know that all this is false: that there is not a country on earth where there is greater tranquillity, where the laws are milder, or better obeyed: where every one is more attentive to his own business, or meddles less with that of others: where strangers are better received, more hospitably treated, and with a more sacred respect. [170]
Head. True, you and I know this, but your friends do not know it.
Heart. But they are sensible people who think for themselves. They will ask of impartial foreigners who have been among us, whether they saw or heard on the spot any instances of anarchy. They will judge too that a people occupied as we are in opening rivers, [175]
digging navigable canals, making roads, building public schools, establishing academies, erecting busts and statues to our great men, protecting religious freedom, abolishing sanguinary punishments, reforming and improving our laws in general, they will judge I say for themselves whether these are not the occupations of a people [180]
at their ease, whether this is not better evidence of our true state than a London newspaper, hired to lie, and from which no truth can ever be extracted but by reversing everything it says.
Head. I did not begin this lecture my friend with a view to learn from you what America is doing. Let us return then to our point. [185]
I wished to make you sensible how imprudent it is to place your affections, without reserve, on objects you must so soon lose,

and whose loss when it comes must cost you such severe pangs. Remember the last night. You knew your friends were to leave Paris to-day. This was enough to throw you into agonies. [190]

All night you tossed us from one side of the bed to the other. No sleep, no rest. The poor crippled wrist too, never left one moment in the same position, now up, now down, now here, now there; was it to be wondered at if all it's pains returned? The Surgeon then was to be called, and to be rated as an ignoramus because [195]

he could not devine the cause of this extraordinary change.—In fine, my friend, you must mend your manners. This is not a world to live at random in as you do. To avoid these eternal distresses, to which you are for ever exposing us, you must learn to look forward before you take a step which may interest our peace. [200]

Everything in this world is matter of calculation. Advance then with caution, the balance in your hand. Put into one scale the pleasures which any object may offer; but put fairly into the other the pains which are to follow, and see which preponderates. The making an acquaintance is not a matter of indifference. [205]

When a new one is proposed to you, view it all round. Consider what advantages it presents, and to what inconveniencies it may expose you. Do not bite at the bait of pleasure till you know there is no hook beneath it. The art of life is the art of avoiding pain: and he is the best pilot who steers clearest of the rocks and shoals [210]

with which it is beset. Pleasure is always before us; but misfortune is at our side: while running after that, this arrests us. The most effectual means of being secure against pain is to retire within ourselves, and to suffice for our own happiness. Those, which depend on ourselves, are the only pleasures a wise man will count on: [215]

for nothing is ours which another may deprive us of. Hence the inestimable value of intellectual pleasures. Ever in our power, always leading us to something new, never cloying, we ride, serene and sublime, above the concerns of this mortal world, contemplating truth and nature, matter and motion, [220]

the laws which bind up their existence, and that eternal being who made and bound them up by these laws. Let this be our employ. Leave the bustle and tumult of society to those who have not talents to occupy themselves without them. Friendship is but another name for an alliance with the follies and the misfortunes of others. [225]

Our own share of miseries is sufficient: why enter then as volunteers into those of another? Is there so little gall poured into our own cup that we must needs help to drink that of our neighbor? A friend dies or leaves us: we feel as if a limb was cut off. He is sick: we must watch over him, and participate of his pains. His fortune is shipwrecked: [230]
ours must be laid under contribution. He loses a child, a parent or a partner: we must mourn the loss as if it was our own.

Heart. And what more sublime delight than to mingle tears with one whom the hand of heaven hath smitten! To watch over the bed of sickness, and to beguile it's tedious and it's painful moments!   [235]
To share our bread with one to whom misfortune has left none! This world abounds indeed with misery: to lighten it's burthen we must divide it with one another. But let us now try the virtues of your mathematical balance, and as you have put into one scale the burthens of friendship, let me put it's comforts into the other.   [240]
When languishing then under disease, how grateful is the solace of our friends! How are we penetrated with their assiduities and attentions! How much are we supported by their encouragements and kind offices! When Heaven has taken from us some object of our love, how sweet is it to have a bosom whereon to recline our heads,   [245]
and into which we may pour the torrent of our tears! Grief, with such a comfort, is almost a luxury! In a life where we are perpetually exposed to want and accident, yours is a wonderful proposition, to insulate ourselves, to retire from all aid, and to wrap ourselves in the mantle of self-sufficiency! For assuredly nobody will care for him   [250]
who cares for nobody. But friendship is precious not only in the shade but in the sunshine of life: and thanks to a benevolent arrangement of things, the greater part of life is sunshine. I will recur for proof to the days we have lately passed. On these indeed the sun shone brightly! How gay did the face of nature appear!   [255]
Hills, vallies, chateaux, gardens, rivers, every object wore it's liveliest hue! Whence did they borrow it? From the presence of our charming companion. They were pleasing, because she seemed pleased. Alone, the scene would have been dull and insipid: the participation of it with her gave it relish. Let the gloomy Monk,   [260]
sequestered from the world, seek unsocial pleasures in the bottom of his cell! Let the sublimated philosopher grasp visionary happiness while pursuing phantoms dressed in the garb of truth! Their supreme

wisdom is supreme folly: and they mistake for happiness the mere absence of pain.   [265]

Had they ever felt the solid pleasure of one generous spasm of the heart, they would exchange for it all the frigid speculations of their lives, which you have been vaunting in such elevated terms. Believe me then, my friend, that that is a miserable arithmetic which would estimate friendship at nothing, or at less than nothing.   [270]

Respect for you has induced me to enter into this discussion, and to hear principles uttered which I detest and abjure. Respect for myself now obliges me to recall you into the proper limits of your office. When nature assigned us the same habitation, she gave us over it a divided empire. To you she allotted the field of science,   [275]

to me that of morals. When the circle is to be squared, or the orbit of a comet to be traced; when the arch of greatest strength, or the solid of least resistance is to be investigated, take you the problem: it is yours: nature has given me no cognisance of it. In like manner in denying to you the feelings of sympathy, of benevolence, of gratitude,   [280]

of justice, of love, of friendship, she has excluded you from their controul. To these she has adapted the mechanism of the heart. Morals were too essential to the happiness of man to be risked on the incertain combinations of the head. She laid their foundation therefore in sentiment, not in science. That she gave to all,   [285]

as necessary to all: this to a few only, as sufficing with a few. I know indeed that you pretend authority to the sovereign controul of our conduct in all it's parts: and a respect for your grave saws and maxims, a desire to do what is right, has sometimes induced me to conform to your counsels.   [290]

A few facts however which I can readily recall to your memory, will suffice to prove to you that nature has not organised you for our moral direction. When the poor wearied souldier, whom we overtook at Chickahominy with his pack on his back, begged us to let him get up behind our chariot,   [295]

you began to calculate that the road was full of souldiers, and that if all should be taken up our horses would fail in their journey. We drove on therefore. But soon becoming sensible you had made me do wrong, that tho we cannot relieve all the distressed we should relieve as many as we can, I turned about to take up the souldier;   [300]

but he had entered a bye path, and was no more to be found: and from that moment to this I could never find him out to ask his forgiveness.

Again, when the poor woman came to ask a charity in Philadelphia, you whispered that she looked like a drunkard, and that half a dollar was enough to give her for the ale-house.   [305]

Those who want the dispositions to give, easily find reasons why they ought not to give. When I sought her out afterwards, and did what I should have done at first, you know that she employed the money immediately towards placing her child at school. If our country, when pressed with wrongs at the point of the bayonet,   [310]

had been governed by it's heads instead of it's hearts, where should we have been now? hanging on a gallows as high as Haman's. You began to calculate and to compare wealth and numbers: we threw up a few pulsations of our warmest blood: we supplied enthusiasm against wealth and numbers: we put our existence to the hazard,   [315]

when the hazard seemed against us, and we saved our country: justifying at the same time the ways of Providence, whose precept is to do always what is right, and leave the issue to him. In short, my friend, as far as my recollection serves me, I do not know that I ever did a good thing on your suggestion, or a dirty one without it.   [320]

I do for ever then disclaim your interference in my province. Fill paper as you please with triangles and squares: try how many ways you can hang and combine them together. I shall never envy nor controul your sublime delights. But leave me to decide when and where friendships are to be contracted. You say I contract them at random,   [325]

so you said the woman at Philadelphia was a drunkard. I receive no one into my esteem till I know they are worthy of it. Wealth, title, office, are no recommendations to my friendship. On the contrary great good qualities are requisite to make amends for their having wealth, title and office.   [330]

You confess that in the present case I could not have made a worthier choice. You only object that I was so soon to lose them. We are not immortal ourselves, my friend; how can we expect our enjoiments to be so? We have no rose without it's thorn; no pleasure without alloy. It is the law of our existence; and we must acquiesce.   [335]

It is the condition annexed to all our pleasures, not by us who receive, but by him who gives them. True, this condition is pressing cruelly on me at this moment. I feel more fit for death than life. But when I look back on the pleasures of which it is the consequence, I am conscious they were worth the price I am paying.   [340]

Notwithstanding your endeavors too to damp my hopes, I comfort myself with expectations of their promised return. Hope is sweeter than despair, and they were too good to mean to deceive me. In the summer, said the gentleman; but in the spring, said the lady: and I should love her forever, were it only for that! [345]

Know then, my friend, that I have taken these good people into my bosom: that I have lodged them in the warmest cell I could find: that I love them, and will continue to love them thro life: that if fortune should dispose them on one side the globe, and me on the other, my affections shall pervade it's whole mass to reach them. [350]

Knowing then my determination, attempt not to disturb it. If you can at any time furnish matter for their amusement, it will be the office of a good neighbor to do it. I will in like manner seize any occasion which may offer to do the like good turn for you with Condorcet, Rittenhouse, Madison, La Cretelle, [355]

or any other of those worthy sons of science whom you so justly prize.' I thought this a favorable proposition whereon to rest the issue of the dialogue. So I put an end to it by calling for my nightcap. Methinks I hear you wish to heaven I had called a little sooner, and so spared you the ennui of such a tedious sermon. [360]

I did not interrupt them sooner because I was in a mood for hearing sermons. You too were the subject; and on such a thesis I never think the theme long; not even if I am to write it, and that slowly and awkwardly, as now, with the left hand. But that you may not be discoraged from a correspondence which begins so formidably, [365]

I will promise you on my honour that my future letters shall be of a reasonable length. I will even agree to express but half my esteem for you, for fear of cloying you with too full a dose. But, on your part, no curtailing. If your letters are as long as the bible, they will appear short to me. Only let them be brim full of affection. [370]

I shall read them with the dispositions with which Arlequin in les deux billets spelt the words 'je t'aime' and wished that the whole alphabet had entered into their composition.

We have had incessant rains since your departure. These make me fear for your health, [375]

as well as that you have had an uncomfortable journey. The same cause has prevented me from being able to give you any account of your friends here. This voiage to Fontainbleau will probably send the Count de Moutier and the Marquise de Brehan to America. Danquerville promised to visit me, but has not done it as yet.   [380]

De latude comes sometimes to take family soupe with me, and entertains me with anecdotes of his five and thirty years imprisonment. How fertile is the mind of man which can make the Bastille and Dungeon of Vincennes yeild interesting anecdotes. You know this was for making four verses on Mme. de Pompadour.   [385]

But I think you told me you did not know the verses. They were these. 'Sans esprit, sans sentiment, Sans etre belle, ni neuve, En France on peut avoir le premier amant: Pompadour en est l'epreuve.' I have read the memoir of his three escapes. As to myself my health is good, except my wrist which mends slowly,   [390]

and my mind which mends not at all, but broods constantly over your departure. The lateness of the season obliges me to decline my journey into the South of France. Present me in the most friendly terms to Mr. Cosway, and receive me into your own recollection with a partiality and a warmth, proportioned,   [395]

not to my own poor merit, but to the sentiments of sincere affection and esteem with which I have the honour to be, my dear Madam, your most obedient humble servant,   [398]

TH: JEFFERSON

Notes

1. PrC mutilated; reading of salutatation taken from TJR, II, 46; see also TJ to Mrs. Cosway, 13 Oct. 1786.

2. This word appears to have been written over "vaults."

3. This word written originally as "companion," and then altered to read as above.

4. This occurs at the bottom of the fifth page.

Work Cited

"From Thomas Jefferson to Maria Cosway, 12 October 1786," *Founders Online,* National Archives, accessed April 11, 2019, https://founders. archives.gov/documents/Jefferson/01-10-02-0309. [Original source: *The Papers of Thomas Jefferson*, vol. 10, *22 June–31 December 1786*, ed. Julian P. Boyd. Princeton: Princeton University Press, 1954, pp. 443–455.]

Jefferson's Proverbial Language

Kevin J. Hayes

Shortly after he began reading law under George Wythe in late 1762 Thomas Jefferson left Williamsburg for Shadwell, his mother's plantation in the Virginia Piedmont. He brought with him the introductory lawbooks Wythe had assigned, intending to hunker down at Shadwell and spend the winter studying. Even before the Christmas holidays ended, Jefferson was busy working through the bane of all beginning law students, *Coke upon Littleton*. He read with such intensity his eyes grew sore and bloodshot, as he informed his old school chum John Page. In a late January letter he tells Page that his days now seemed identical: "All things here appear to me to trudge on in one and the same round: we rise in the morning that we may eat breakfast, dinner and supper and go to bed again that we may get up the next morning and do the same: so that you never saw two peas more alike than our yesterday and to-day" (Boyd 1:7).

Writing to friends was one diversion Jefferson permitted himself during his legal study. His pleasure shows in the tone and content of his correspondence. The proverbial comparison—like two peas in a pod, to use the current iteration—is characteristic of his early letters, which have a playful quality that makes reading them a delight. Traditional phrases suit their natural style and engaging tone.

To entertain correspondents was one reason why Jefferson used proverbs and proverbial phrases. To endear himself to his readers, to experiment with the English language, to emphasize a point, to simplify complex ideas, to give new ideas a feeling of familiarity: all these reasons and more account for Jefferson's use of proverbs. Oftentimes, he was not content to repeat proverbs in their orally circulated versions. Instead, he would alter traditional expressions to give them an aura of originality. This dual impulse—to combine the traditional and the original—marks Jefferson's finest use of proverbs and proverbial phrases.

The Growing Sophistication of Jefferson's Proverbs

Jefferson told Page he missed Williamsburg's social life, but his letter cannot mask how much he enjoyed reading law. On a trip to Richmond that October he had the opportunity to socialize while staying with James Gunn but found it unsatisfying. Before the evening ended Jefferson left the parlor for the bedchamber, as he wrote his friend William Fleming: "From a croud of disagreeable [companions] among whom I have spent three or four of the most tedious hours of my life, I retire into Gunn's bedchamber to converse in black and white with an absent friend" (Boyd 1:12).

Like the letter to Page, the letter to Fleming possesses a playful tone, which its use of another proverbial phrase—"in black and white"—reinforces. This phrase similarly contributes to the familiar tone of Jefferson's early correspondence, but it marks an increase in literary sophistication over the earlier proverbial phrase.

Jefferson was neither the first American author to use the prepositional phrase "in black and white," nor to give it literary sophistication. Credit for its first usage in American literature goes to Thomas Morton, who applied the phrase in his knee-slapping lampoon of Plymouth colony and Pilgrim culture, *New English Canaan* (Whiting 34). A century later Benjamin Franklin used it in *Experiments and Observations on Electricity*, the book that shields the world from thunderstorms. Discussing his early concept for "points"—the tapered ends of lightning rods—Franklin remarked, "These explanations of the power and operation of points, when they first occurr'd to me, and while they first floated in my mind, appeared perfectly satisfactory; but now I have wrote them, and consider'd them more closely in black and white, I must own I have some doubts about them" (59).

As he describes them, Franklin's initial ideas about points have an indefinite quality. They seem so light and evanescent that they scarcely register as they waft through the convolutions of his brain. Committed to paper—put down in black and white—his theories acquired a solidity they formerly lacked but also became more vulnerable. Recording them on the printed page, Franklin subjected his ideas to further thought on his own part, but also made them accessible to others, who could read—and judge—them.

Whereas Franklin had used this proverbial phrase to contrast thinking and writing, Jefferson used it to contrast speaking and writing. Though he complained to Page about the dearth of social interaction at Shadwell, his letter to Fleming suggests that he much preferred writing over talking, at least when he could write a close friend and kindred spirit. Writing a letter—conversing in black and white—let him exercise his thought and apply his imagination in a way party conversation could not.

To a certain extent the playfulness of Jefferson's early letters would disappear from his subsequent correspondence. Half a dozen years later his political career would begin with his election to the Virginia Houses of Burgesses. His role in the public sphere helped him understand that thoughts put down in black and white are thoughts that cannot be taken back and that private correspondence has an annoying habit of elbowing its way into the public. His letters get more guarded and sometimes lose their casual affability. He did not stop using proverbs and proverbial phrases, but he did start using them with more purpose, more rhetorical oomph.

The Ship of State

Serving as governor of Virginia during the Revolutionary War, Jefferson wrote the state's delegates to the Continental Congress in January 1781 to have them take measures to replenish Virginia's military stores. His letter says that their gunpowder reserve had been depleted because Virginia had loaned ten tons of the stuff to the Continental Congress for the Southern army. Furthermore, Virginia's supply of cartridge paper was almost exhausted. Governor Jefferson's request ends emphatically: "It is essential that a good stock should be forwarded and without a moments delay. If there be a rock on which we are to split, it is the want of Muskets, bayonets and cartouch boxes" (Boyd 4:398).

Jefferson's proverbial phrase—"the rock on which we are to split"—alludes to a shipwreck, the rock symbolizing the hidden danger a ship faces. The proverbial phrase emphasizes the harm

Virginia and the United States would suffer without enough arms and ammunition. From a literary standpoint, it shows how Jefferson could make the traditional original. He took the rock, a symbol of solidity, and used it to represent an absence, namely, the lack of military stores. In short, Jefferson strengthened his argument by giving the absence of munitions a dangerous solidity.

The proverbial rock is one of many nautical metaphors Jefferson would use in his public and private writings. He especially enjoyed ship-of-state metaphors. The month after he wrote the Virginia Congressional delegates, Governor Jefferson wrote the lieutenants of Berkeley and Frederick counties to request that they supply troops to serve in western Virginia. He reminded them that the entire state must be defended for the Revolution to succeed. Jefferson strengthened his argument with a proverb: We are all embarked in one bottom. Or, according to the more familiar variant, we are all in the same boat. The first version had been around at least since the seventeenth century. Colonial New York governor Jacob Leisler had used it in 1690 to convey the forward-thinking notion of intercolonial solidarity (Van Rensselaer 441).

This proverb would continue to serve American politics. In 1788 the Rev. Samuel Stillman, a delegate to the Massachusetts Convention to Ratify the US Constitution, reused it, combining this proverb with another one as he spoke in favor of ratification: "I have no interest to influence me to accept this Constitution of government, distinct from the interest of my countrymen, at large. We are all embarked in one bottom, and must sink or swim together." Seven years earlier when Governor Jefferson wrote the lieutenants of Berkeley and Frederick counties, he had used the proverb to help unify his state during the war. As Stillman would, he combined it with the sink-or-swim proverb, though Jefferson was more creative, setting up an elegant geographical antithesis: "We are all embarked in one bottom, the Western end of which cannot swim while the Eastern sinks" (Kaminski and Saladino 1454; Boyd 4:628).

In the fullest study of the subject Charles A. Miller identifies possible literary sources for Jefferson's ship-of-state metaphors but ignores the oral tradition. In his discussion of proverbs and the presidency Wolfgang Mieder alternatively observes that many proverbial metaphors depict the state as a ship or vessel (149). Jefferson's vast knowledge of literature is well known, but his use of proverbs shows that he drew freely upon folklore as well as book culture. Despite his self-diagnosed bibliomania, Jefferson understood that books are not the sole repositories of knowledge, that folklore—the traditional stories people tell, the traditional sayings they repeat—can preserve the wisdom of generations.

Miller rightly perceives that Jefferson displayed his literary skill with his ship-of-state comparisons. Each time he used a nautical metaphor he tried to word it differently from his previous ones, demonstrating both versatility and ingenuity. His stylistic variants show how much he enjoyed himself as he wrote (Miller 36–37). Risking an anachronism, one could say that Jefferson's nautical metaphors resemble jazz improvisation. He starts with a basic phrase and then embellishes it to enhance its intricacy and make it all his own.

The first inaugural address Jefferson presented as US President provides a good example of how he revised and expanded a traditional saying to make it original. With this address he returned to the proverb—"We are all embarked in the same bottom"—but elaborated upon it, applying the proverb to describe what the nation faced. Addressing Congress, he spoke hopefully: "I look with encouragement for that guidance and support which may enable us to steer with safety the vessel in which we are all embarked, amidst the conflicting elements of a troubled world" (Boyd 33:148–49).

Proverbs and Native American Diplomacy

As governor of Virginia, Jefferson also had the opportunity to draft the first Indian address of his political career. "Speech to Jean Baptiste Ducoigne" addresses a mixed-race chief of the Kaskaskia nation. The speech reveals how Native American diplomacy contributed to the proverbial language. As the Revolutionary War persisted, the British tried to get the Indians to help them fight the Continental army. Jefferson's speech urges Ducoigne to remain neutral: "We do not wish you to take up the hatchet" (Boyd 6:61).

"To take up the hatchet" and its opposite, "to bury the hatchet," were two phrases from Native American diplomacy that became proverbial. From the early eighteenth century, both would be used often throughout North America (Whiting 201). Earlier during the Revolutionary War George Washington, another Founding Father who mastered the language of Indian diplomacy, announced the alliance between the United States and France in "Address to the Delaware Nation": "We have till lately fought the English all alone. Now the Great King of France is become our Good Brother and Ally. He has taken up the Hatchet with us, and we have sworn never to bury it, till we have punished the English and made them sorry for All the wicked things they had in their Hearts to do against these States" (Lengel 447).

Jefferson would continue using both phrases. While minister to France, he discussed trade policy with John Adams. Considering the possibility of a trade war, Jefferson said that if Europe attempts to hinder the transatlantic trade, then it would be time for the United States "to take up the commercial hatchet" (Boyd 9:43). Once again Jefferson took a traditional saying and made it original. In this instance he extended the proverbial metaphor beyond the realm of Indian diplomacy and applied it to international economic relations. After the War of 1812 Jefferson expressed hope that the United States and Great Britain "would now bury the hatchet and join in a mutual amnesty. No two nations on earth can be so helpful to each other as friends, nor so hurtful as enemies: and, in spite of their insolence I have ever wished for an honorable and cordial amity with them as a nation" (Looney 379).

Using the phrase "to bury the hatchet," Jefferson demonstrated his enduring respect for and fascination with the English language. He saw English as a living, breathing organism, ever growing and changing. Sayings from the oral tradition, he believed, deserve the legitimacy of a standard English dictionary (Hayes 620). When a snooty Harvard professor who saw himself as a guardian of the English language criticized Jefferson's neologisms, Jefferson defended himself in a letter to John Adams:

Dictionaries are but the depositories of words already legitimated by usage. Society is the work-shop in which new ones are elaborated. When an individual uses a new word, if ill-formed it is rejected in society, if well-formed, adopted, and, after due time, laid up in the depository of dictionaries. And if, in this process of sound neologisation, our transatlantic brethren shall not choose to accompany us, we may furnish, after the Ionians, a second example of a colonial dialect improving on its primitive. (Cappon 567)

The Mother Country eventually accepted this particular Native American phrase, which remains in common usage throughout Great Britain, as one recent example demonstrates. Relating the conciliatory efforts of Scottish Conservative leader Ruth Davidson, Kieran Andrews reported in *The Times* [London]: "Ruth Davidson has compared Boris Johnson to Prince Hal, Shakespeare's wayward monarch who grew up to be a wise king, in a move to bury the hatchet."

The Hammer or the Anvil

By September 1785, after Jefferson had been serving as minister to France for a year, he wrote his friend Charles Bellini, the first professor of modern languages at the College of William and Mary. Jefferson exclaimed, "Behold me at length on the vaunted scene of Europe!" Since Bellini was from Italy, Jefferson assumed he would be curious about his American friend's impressions of Europe. Jefferson was unimpressed: "I find the general fate of humanity here most deplorable. The truth of Voltaire's observation offers itself perpetually, that every man here must be either the hammer or the anvil" (Boyd 8:568).

That Jefferson attributed this proverb to Voltaire shows he was keeping up with his reading. Voltaire makes this remark in his *Memoirs*, first published the previous year: "In France, every man must be either the hammer or the anvil, and I was born the latter" (161–62). That Jefferson attributed this proverb to a written source does not make it any less proverbial. Like Benjamin Franklin, Voltaire had the capacity to take traditional sayings and recast them in more succinct and memorable forms.

Worded one way or another, the hammer-and-anvil proverb had been around at least since the sixteenth century (Tilley 15). Before Voltaire, Franklin may have put it best:

When you're an Anvil, hold you still;
When you're a Hammer, strike your fill. (Labaree 351)

Voltaire specifically applied the proverb to France, dividing its citizenry into two categories: hammer or anvil. Jefferson added his own variation, applying what Voltaire says about France to all of Europe.

Bellini was no slouch when it came to wordplay. He replied: "It is very true, every man must be either the anvil or the hammer. I do not complain of being the anvil, but I would desire that the strokes of the hammer should hit the center, and not falsely on the edges, in order that the anvil may not be damaged, and may do better work." According to Bellini, the hammer and anvil could have a positive working relationship, provided the hammer functioned within bounds. Jefferson did not buy it. Years later he reused the proverb, omitting Voltaire but adding a parallel. He combined the proverb from the blacksmith's shop with one from the natural world. In Europe, he observed, "every man must be either pike or gudgeon, hammer or anvil" (Bergh 332).

The Bill of Rights
Though unable to attend the Constitutional Convention, Jefferson followed the news as best he could from Paris. By late September 1788 eleven states had ratified the Constitution, two more than the nine required to put it into effect. North Carolina remained a holdout. Jefferson wrote Thomas Lee Shippen, a young American on a grand tour of Europe whom he had befriended: "No news yet from North-Carolina: but in such a case no news is good news, as an unfavorable decision of the 12th state would have flown like an electrical shock through America and Europe" (Boyd 13:642).

Hearing Jefferson utter such a commonplace saying as "no news is good news" comes as a surprise, but he enjoyed this proverb and would keep using it (Boyd 30:115, 123). Writing to Shippen, he tempered its commonplace nature with an original simile that compares the effect of an unexpected news story with modern scientific discovery: "like an electrical shock."

Many of the delegates who attended the state ratification conventions and voted to ratify the US Constitution based their vote on the promise that a set of amendments would be soon forthcoming. When the US House of Representatives sat for its first session in 1789, Rep. James Madison of Virginia—the author of the Constitution—moved that the House begin considering amendments. Before making his motion, Madison had consulted Jefferson regarding the precise nature of the amendments, expressing concern that Congress would not pass all the amendments necessary to secure the rights they wished. Jefferson allayed Madison's concern with a proverb: "Half a loaf is better than no bread. If we cannot secure all our rights, let us secure what we can" (Boyd 14:660).

It seems strange to consider the Bill of Rights, one of the supreme documents in American history, as the proverbial half a loaf, but such is the case. We need not take Jefferson's word for it; he was not the only one to apply this proverb to the Bill of Rights. In late August 1789 the House forwarded seventeen Constitutional amendments to the Senate. Many senators were against them, worried that amendments protecting individual rights would make more radical changes to the federal government impossible. Senator Richard Henry Lee of Virginia took a more enlightened view and accepted the possibility of compromise. Lee described the situation to a correspondent: "I hope that if we cannot gain the whole loaf, we shall at least have some bread" (Labunski 236; Ballagh 499).

The Proverbial Feather Bed

Jefferson continued to serve as minister to France until late September 1789, when he obtained a leave of absence from his diplomatic post to return to Virginia and attend his personal affairs. Upon disembarking at Norfolk, he was surprised to learn that President Washington had appointed him secretary of state. Jefferson reluctantly accepted the position, which meant that he would not be returning to France. To serve as secretary of state he relocated to New York in late March 1790. The first week of April Jefferson undertook the melancholy task of writing his French friends to say goodbye (Hayes 392).

Having been in Paris to witness the start of the French Revolution, Jefferson kept apprised of its developments. He diminished the bloodshed and waxed philosophic. He told Madame d'Enville: "The change in your government will approximate us more to one another. You have had some checks, some horrors since I left you. But the way to heaven, you know, has always been said to be strewed with thorns." Jefferson gave the Marquis de Lafayette much the same message but worded it differently: "So far it seemed that your revolution had got along with a steady pace: meeting indeed occasional difficulties and dangers, but we are not to expect to be translated from despotism to liberty in a feather bed" (Boyd 16:291, 293).

In these two letters, both written on Friday, 2 April 1790, Jefferson applies closely related proverbs, each concerning the pathway to heaven, which symbolizes anywhere that is a better place to be. One goes like this: "The way to heaven is not spread with rushes but set with thorns." The other says, "You cannot go to heaven in a feather bed" (Tilley 712, 303). The letter to Madame d'Enville conveys the proverb as a complete sentence, which independently verifies Jefferson's point. Into this stand-alone proverb he interjected a "you know," speaking directly to his correspondent and reminding her that traditional wisdom confirms recent events. Instead of presenting Lafayette with a stand-alone proverb, Jefferson paraphrased the traditional saying, replacing heaven with the state of liberty.

By paraphrasing the proverb Jefferson created an original saying that remains pertinent as new democracies undergo brutal violence as they emerge from political and religious tyranny. In a 2011 contribution to *Middle East Policy* R. K. Ramazani recalled Jefferson's words upon observing that the transition to democracy in North Africa and the Middle East would be a complex process taking generations:

If Arab leaders fail to transfer power to civilian control by peaceful and popular means, including fair and free elections, there is every reason to believe that new types of authoritarian regimes will rise. In his letter of April 2, 1790, Jefferson told Lafayette not to expect transition "from despotism to liberty in a feather bed." I think there is no feather bed in sight at the moment in the Middle East and North Africa. (164)

France would face further turmoil and bloodshed before the French Revolution succeeded. After news of the September massacres reached the United States, Jefferson wrote his friend and protégé William Short, lamenting that innocent lives had been lost among the guilty. Ever the optimist, Jefferson took the long view, reassuring his friend: "But time and truth will rescue and embalm their memories, while their posterity will be enjoying that very liberty for which they would never have hesitated to offer up their lives" (Boyd 25:14).

Many proverbs that circulated in Jefferson's day expressed the idea that time would reveal the truth, the simplest and most well-known being "Time will tell" (Whiting 442). Once again Jefferson starts with a proverb but then embellishes it as he applies traditional wisdom to an unprecedented situation. He used the time-will-tell proverb as many people use proverbs, that is, as a philosophical refuge. It let Jefferson distance himself from the bloodshed by indulging in the comforting notion that truth will reveal itself.

Rawhead and Bloody Bones
As secretary of state, Jefferson often butted heads with Alexander Hamilton, the secretary of the treasury. The French Revolution provided one bone of contention, to use another favorite proverbial metaphor in Revolutionary America (Whiting 39). After France had declared itself a republic and executed its king, Hamilton worried about the harm to the United States that could result from honoring the treaty of alliance with France. Jefferson, on the other hand, saw no reason for the United States to renounce the treaty or even to suspend it until the new French government stabilized. Washington asked Jefferson to put his opinion in writing.

Jefferson paraphrased Hamilton's argument that the changes France was undergoing could have unexpected consequences for the United States in "Opinion on the Treaties with France." His paraphrase applies a proverbial comparison, which ridicules Hamilton by portraying him as a fear-mongering alarmist. Assuming Hamilton's voice to relate the possible outcome of honoring the treaty, Jefferson mocks his manner: "In short it may end in a Raw-head and bloody bones in the dark" (Boyd 25:610).

Raw-head and bloody bones? This seems like an odd phrase for the secretary of state to put in a report to the president. Eighteenth-century nannies and nursemaids would often keep children under control by scaring them into submission. They would say something like, "If you children don't behave, then Raw-head and Bloody Bones will come to get you!" Raw-head and Bloody Bones was a horrific boogeyman who walked around with the skin flayed off his head, leaving little but skull, sinew, and muscles. "Bloody bones" describes the rest of Raw-head. His flesh has been torn from his body, leaving a perambulatory skeleton dripping with blood.

Numerous instances of the phrase occur in the works of eighteenth-century writers. Take for example Edward Kimber, a novelist both American and British literature can claim. As a child, the eponymous hero of Kimber's *Adventures of Capt. Neville Frowde* learns from servants all about "Murder, Apparitions, Witches, and such other Matters." Left alone young Neville imagines "Raw-head and Bloody-bones stalking about [his] Garret" (16).

The phrase "Raw-head and bloody bones" became a proverbial expression, a metaphor to characterize any attempt to shape public opinion by making people think that dreadful horror is fast approaching. Though Jefferson disliked such narrow-minded and uninformed fearmongering, he did enjoy this particular proverbial phrase and used it numerous times. In one instance he applied it to contrast his open-minded support for scientific research with others' superstitious fear of science. He told Elbridge Gerry: "I am for encouraging the progress of science in all its branches; and not for raising a hue and cry against the sacred name of philosophy, for awing the human mind, by stories of rawhead and bloody bones" (Boyd 30:646-47).

To return to "Opinion on the Treaties with France": After expressing Hamilton's fear that the treaty of alliance with France would summon Raw-head and Bloody Bones, Jefferson replied:

> Very well: let Rawhead and bloody bones come, and then we shall be justified in making our peace with him, by renouncing our antient friends and his enemies. For observe, it is not the *possibility of danger*, which absolves a party from his contract: for that possibility always exists, and in every case. It existed in the present one at the moment of making the contract. If *possibilities* would avoid contracts, there never could be a valid contract. For possibilities hang over every thing. Obligation is not suspended till the danger is become real, and the moment of it so imminent, that we can no longer avoid decision without for ever losing the opportunity to do it. But can a danger which has not yet taken its shape, which does not yet exist, and never may exist, which cannot therefore be defined, can such a danger, I ask, be so imminent that if we fail to pronounce on it in this moment we can never have another opportunity of doing it? (Boyd 25:610)

Given the numerous times he used it, Jefferson obviously enjoyed the phrase "Raw-head and Bloody Bones." Besides letting him indulge his fascination with traditional sayings, it also gave him a rhetorical edge. Instead of repeating this gruesome phrase to create fear, he used it to startle his readers, to grab their attention, after which he could present a cogent argument. In the face of Jefferson's clear logic and common sense, the macabre image of Raw-head and Bloody Bones shrivels into nothingness.

Conclusion

Jefferson would use proverbs and proverbial phrases the rest of his life. Those that pepper his writings demonstrate his ear for traditional sayings and his eye for their cultural significance. He used proverbial phrases much more often than he used stand-alone proverbs. Proverbial phrases were more malleable. He could reword them or frame with his own words. Either way, he could shape proverbial phrases to suit whatever situation he or his friends or the nation faced.

Since a letter from Jefferson to John Page began this essay, let's let one from Page to Jefferson end it. After receiving a copy of the Declaration of Independence in the summer of 1776, Page wrote to congratulate Jefferson on its composition. Page's letter shows that he, too, could turn a proverb: "I am highly pleased with your Declaration. God preserve the united States. We know the Race is not to the swift nor the Battle to the strong. Do you not think an Angel rides in the Whirlwind and directs this Storm?" (Boyd 1:470). The Declaration of Independence itself deserves a place in the history of proverbs. To express the unprecedented idea of liberty and freedom he projected, Jefferson had no proverbs at hand. So, what did he do? He invented one. It would become the most meaningful and memorable proverb to emerge from the American experience: "All men are created equal."

Works Cited

Andrews, Kieran. "Ruth Davidson Paints Boris Johnson as Wayward Prince Who Grows Up." *The Times* [London], 14 Aug. 2019, p. 10. https://www.thetimes.co.uk/article/ruth-davidson-paints-boris-johnson-as-wayward-prince-who-grows-up-323zcsdjx.

Ballagh, James Curtis, editor. *The Letters of Richard Henry Lee*. Vol. 2, Macmillan, 1914.

Bellini, Charles. "To Thomas Jefferson." 29 May 1786. "Charles Bellini, First American Professor of Modern Languages in an American College." *William and Mary Quarterly*, ser. 2, vol. 5, no. 1, Jan. 1925, pp. 6–7. JSTOR. www.jstor.org/stable/1916304?seq=1#page_scan_tab_contents.

Boyd, Julian P., editor. *The Papers of Thomas Jefferson*. Princeton U P, 1950–, 43 vols. to date.

Cappon, Lester J., editor. *The Adams-Jefferson Letters: The Complete Correspondence between Thomas Jefferson and Abigail and John Adams*. 1959, U of North Carolina P, 1987.

Kaminski, John P., and Gaspare J. Saladino, editors. *The Documentary History of the Ratification of the Constitution, Volume VI: Ratification of the Constitution by the States, Massachusetts.* State Historical Society of Wisconsin, 2000.

Franklin, Benjamin. *Experiments and Observations on Electricity, Made at Philadelphia in America.* London, 1751.

Hayes, Kevin J. *The Road to Monticello: The Life and Mind of Thomas Jefferson.* Oxford U P, 2008.

Jefferson, Thomas, and Richard Holland-Johnston. *The Writings of Thomas Jefferson.* Edited by Albert Ellery Bergh. Vol. 15–16, p. 332, (1907). The Thomas Jefferson Memorial Association of the United States: Washington DC. books.google.com/books?id=EqvTAAAAMAAJ.

[Kimber, Edward.] *The Life, Extraordinary Adventures, Voyages, and Surprizing Escapes of Capt. Neville Frowde, of Cork.* London, 1708.

Labaree, Leonard W., editor. *The Papers of Benjamin Franklin.* Vol. 7, Yale U P, 1963.

Labunski, Richard. *James Madison and the Struggle for the Bill of Rights.* Oxford U P, 2006.

Lengel, Edward G., editor. *The Papers of George Washington: Revolutionary War Series*, vol. 20, U of Virginia P, 2010.

Looney, J. Jefferson, editor. *The Papers of Thomas Jefferson: Retirement Series*, vol. 15, Princeton UP, 2018.

Mieder, Wolfgang. *Proverbs Are the Best Policy: Folk Wisdom and American Politics.* Utah State U P, 2005.

Miller, Charles A. *Ship of State: The Nautical Metaphors of Thomas Jefferson with Numerous Examples by Other Writers from Classical Antiquity to the Present.* U P of America, 2003.

Morton, Thomas. *New English Canaan.* Amsterdam, 1637.

Ramazani, R. K. "Jefferson's Dialogue with the Contemporary World: Education and Diplomacy." *Middle East Policy*, vol. 18, no. 3, September 2011, pp. 161–64. www.researchgate.net/publication/230542835_Jefferson's_Dialogue_with_the_Contemporary_World_Education_and_Diplomacy.

Tilley, Morris Palmer. *A Dictionary of the Proverbs in England in the Sixteenth and Seventeenth Centuries: A Collection of the Proverbs Found in English Literature and the Dictionaries of the Period.* U of Michigan P, 1950.

Van Rensselaer, Mariana Griswold. *History of the City of New York in the Seventeenth Century*. vol. 2, Macmillan, 1909.

Voltaire. *Memoirs of the Life of Voltaire*. London, 1784.

Whiting, Bartlett Jere. *Early American Proverbs and Proverbial Phrases*. Belknap P, 1977.

Thomas Jefferson Seen through the Eyes of Robert Penn Warren_____

Steven D. Ealy

Robert Penn Warren wrote to his friend Allen Tate in the fall of 1929 saying that he had been asked to review a new biography of Thomas Jefferson (*Letters* 167). Thus, began Warren's lifelong practice of reading and reflecting on Jefferson and occasionally writing about him.

A glance at historian Merrill D. Peterson's *The Jefferson Image in the American Mind*, a study of "what history made of Thomas Jefferson" rather than "the history Thomas Jefferson made" (vii), shows that Warren was not alone in his effort to come to terms with Jefferson and his legacy. According to Peterson, as America moved into the twentieth century, it encountered new challenges both on the economic front and in terms of complicated foreign relations and defense policy. Domestically, Jefferson's model of limited government and ideal of an agrarian society was challenged by the Great Depression and the birth of the New Deal, with increased governmental involvement in every area of life and the growth of industry and urbanization in all parts of the country. On the world stage Jefferson's vision of pacific relations and limited government was challenged by the growth of totalitarian regimes grounded in the desire for world empire and American involvement in two world wars and numerous localized conflicts.

What image of Jefferson would Americans hold in such a world? As Peterson notes, scholars recognized that all sides wanted to claim Jefferson for their political views. Political scientist Clinton Rossiter, for example, identified seven different Jeffersons emerging in contemporary political debates: "Anti-Statist, States' Righter, Isolationist, Agrarian, Rationalist, Civil Libertarian, [and] Constitutional Democrat" (445). The political debate highlighted by Rossiter was also reflected at a deeper level by theologians and political theorists such as Reinhold Niebuhr, who emphasized the "irony of American history," and Hans Morgenthau, a specialist in international relations, who thought "that the Jeffersonian faith had lost contact with the vital realities upon which it was supposed to act" (452).

Brother to Dragons and American Slavery

In the epilogue of his study, Peterson turns to Robert Penn Warren's *Brother to Dragons: A Tale in Verse and Voices* as a unique portrayal of Jefferson. Earlier variations of the American image of Jefferson tended to be triumphant: Jefferson as the defender of enlightenment and prophet of the ultimate victory of man's unconquerable reason. No one before Warren had characterized Jefferson as a slave of history rather than its master, a man of sorrow rather than of triumph, a critic of human nature rather than an advocate of man's perfectibility. Warren, wrote Peterson, was "a poet, deeply aware of the tragic miscarriage of the Jeffersonian ideal in our time" who "might imagine the spiritual father of America being brought to terms with the unpleasant facts divulged to his children" (452). But Warren's initial poetic engagement with Jefferson in *Brother to Dragons*, published in 1953, did not exhaust Warren's interest in and reflection on Jefferson. In 1976, he published a stage version of the poem and, in 1979, he issued a new version of the poem that was shorter and substantially rewritten. Comparison of these different versions show that Warren's understanding of Jefferson changed the longer he studied him. In the 1953 version of the poem Warren identifies Jefferson as "the spiritual father" (xi) of America, whereas in the 1979 version Warren states that Jefferson "helped to found," not America, but "our nation" (xii).

The claim that Jefferson is "the spiritual father" of America is based on his authorship of the Declaration of Independence, the first of his three boasts contained in the epitaph he composed (*Brother* 1953, 2). Jefferson, however, offered a more modest view of his role in a late letter to Henry Lee. First, he had not stood alone against the Crown, because, "with respect to our rights, and the acts of the British government contravening those rights, there was but one opinion on this side of the water. All American Whigs thought alike on these subjects" (*Writings* 1501). Second, Jefferson was not creating new principles to prove the right to independence, but consolidating and rearticulating principles already held.

> Not to find out new principles, or new arguments, never before thought of, not merely to say things which had never been said before; but to place before mankind the common sense of the subject, in terms so plain and firm as to command their assent, and to justify ourselves in the independent stand we are compelled to take. Neither aiming at originality of principle or sentiment, nor yet copied from any particular and previous writing, it was intended to be an expression of the American mind, and to give to that expression the proper tone and spirit called for by the occasion. All its authority rests then on the harmonizing sentiments of the day, whether expressed in conversation, in letters, printed essays, or in the elementary books of public right, as Aristotle, Cicero, Locke, Sidney, &c. (1501)

As penman of the Declaration, Jefferson highlighted key ideas that would resonate throughout American history, even as the understanding of what those ideas and ideals meant changed from generation to generation. Equality, protection of life, liberty, and the pursuit of happiness have become a sacred quartet in the American mind. Americans tend to affirm all these ideas, even though they may be in constant tension with each other. This potential tension, in fact, is at the heart of *Brother to Dragons*.

The "tale" that sets *Brother to Dragons* into motion illustrates the old adage that truth can be stranger than fiction. If the events that provide the background for the poem had not actually happened, it would be difficult to convince anyone that the plot was plausible. It revolves around the family of Charles Lewis, who had married Jefferson's sister Lucy. Lewis moved his family, including Lucy, their two sons Lilburn and Isham, and his slaves, from Albemarle County, Virginia, to the western frontier of Kentucky. Shortly after this move, Lucy died, and Charles Lewis travelled back to Virginia, leaving his son Lilburn in charge of his farm. In the foreword to the stage version Warren provides a summary. "The central event of the story of the Lewis family occurred on the night of December

15, 1811, the night when the New Madrid Earthquake stuck its first blow at the Mississippi Valley. . . . It was on that night that Lilburn, with the assistance of his younger brother Isham, a sort of drifter who was there for a visit, and before the eyes of the assembled slaves, butchered with a meat-axe a boy named George, who had broken the favorite pitcher of the dead Lucy" (66). The brothers attempted to burn the remains in the smokehouse fireplace, but this plan was defeated by the earthquake that hit later that night and led to the collapse of the chimney. At some point, one of the farm dogs carried the charred skull into Smithland, and the sheriff came out to investigate. The brothers, charged with murder and released on bail to await trial, decided that they would end their lives by shooting each other while standing over the grave of their mother. However, the "arrangements miscarried, and Lilburn, with his will in his pocket, fell dying across the grave, and Isham fled to the woods" (1953, x). Isham was captured, tried, convicted, and while awaiting execution, escaped. Legend has it that Isham disappeared until some Kentucky volunteers spoke with the mortally wounded fugitive after the Battle of New Orleans, where he had fought as a member of Andrew Jackson's army.

These real-world historical events serve as backdrop for Warren's poem, but the real action in *Brother to Dragons* is the encounter of these historical characters with each other and "R. P. W.: the writer of this poem" (1953, 2). This ghostly dialogue is set in "no place" and occurs at "any time" (1953, 3). This means, Warren wrote, "that the issue that the characters discuss is, in my view at least, a human constant" (1953, xiii). That issue is Jefferson's vision of human nature, and the "action" of the play is R. P. W.'s investigation into the question of how the murder committed by Jefferson's nephews might have affected Jefferson's understanding of human nature.

In his foreword to the stage version, Warren discussed the relationship between the historical Jefferson and the Jefferson of his creation.

As for Jefferson, several eminent authorities had assured me, while I was working on the poem that, as far as records show, he never alluded to the events in Kentucky and its blot on the family blood and his dream of humanity; and one authority even declared spontaneously that he believed it impossible for Jefferson to bring himself to face the truth. This fact of Jefferson's failure to allude to the event (a fact that may be "unfacted" by further research) is convenient for the interpretation offered in my play, but is not essential to it; for what I am concerned with is the symbolic implication of the event for the Jeffersonian notion of the perfectibility of man and the good American notion of our inevitable righteousness in action and purity in motive. (66–67)

The final version of *Brother to Dragons* opens with the ghost of Jefferson bemoaning the fact that that he cannot drink from the river Lethe and forget things he would rather not acknowledge—"unknow / All my knowing"—and desiring "To defend my old definition of man" (5). He begins with an account of the Independence Congress in Philadelphia and of his role in writing the Declaration of Independence.

> When I to Philadelphia came
>   I knew what the world was. Oh, I wasn't
>   That ilk of fool! Then when I saw individual evil,
>   I rationally said, it is only provisional paradox
>   To resolve itself in Time. Oh easy,
>   Plump-bellied comfort!
> Philadelphia, yes. I knew we were only men,
> Defined in errors and interests. But I, a man too
> . . . stumbled into
> The breathless awe of vision, saw sudden
> On every face, face after face,
> Bleared, puffed, lank, lean red-fleshed or sallow, all—
> On all saw the brightness blaze,
> And knew my own days,
> Times, hopes, horsemanship, respect of peers,
> Delight, desire, and even my love, but straw
> Fit for the flame, and in that fierce combustion, I—
> Why, I was nothing, nothing but joy,

And my heart cried out:
"Oh, this is man!" (7)

However, one must pay a cost to hold on to this idealized vision of humanity. You must deny or rationalize the reality you see and the truth you know.

And so to hold joy you must deny mere Nature, and leap
Beyond man's natural bourne and constriction
To find justification in a goal
Hypothesized in Nature. (8)

In this state of self-induced optimism concerning the nature of his species, Jefferson set about drafting the Declaration of Independence.

So seized the pen, and in the upper room,
With the excited consciousness that I was somehow
Rectified, annealed, my past annulled
And fate confirmed, wrote. And far off,
In darkness, the watch called out.
Time came, we signed the document, went home.
I had not seen the eyes of that bright apparition.
I had been blind with light.
I did not know its eyes were blind. (8)

Then, the Jefferson of Warren's poem does something that the historical Jefferson never did: he alluded to his nephews' murder of a slave.

And I who once said, all liberty
Is bought with blood, must now say,
All truth is bought with blood, and the blood is ours,
But only the truth can make us free—
Free from the fool lie.
And doom is always domestic, it purrs like a cat,
And the absolute traitor lurks in some sweet corner of the blood.
Therefore I walk and wake, and cannot die. (8–9)

From this beginning, the confrontation of Jefferson's idealized view of man as the foundation of a new society and the reality of a crime committed by his nephews comes the ensuing dialogue in which R. P. W., Jefferson, and others attempt to resolve the tension. These introductory comments are enough for me to ask if Warren's assumption at the heart of this long poem—that this murder forced Jefferson so see humanity in a more realistic light than he inclined to—is correct.[1]

Jefferson did not need the example of his nephews to see the dark side of human nature. As a slave owner, he had only to look into his own heart. In *Notes on the State of Virginia* Jefferson addresses the issue of slavery in query 18, "Manners." According to Jefferson, the institution of slavery produces evil for all parties. "The whole commerce between master and slave is a perpetual exercise of the most boisterous passions, the most unremitting despotism on the one part, and degrading submissions on the other." This relationship among adults spills over into the attitudes and actions of the young.

> Our children see this, and learn to imitate it; for man is an imitative animal. This quality is the germ of all education in him. From his cradle to his grave he is learning to do what he sees others do. If a parent could find no motive either in his philanthropy or his self-love, for restraining the intemperance of passion towards his slave, it should always be a sufficient one that his child is present. But generally it is not sufficient. The parent storms, the child looks on, catches the lineaments of wrath, puts on the same airs in the circle of smaller slaves, gives a loose to his worst of passions, and thus nursed, educated, and daily exercised in tyranny, cannot but be stamped by it with odious peculiarities. (*Writings* 288)

The existence of slavery has personal and sociological consequences, but it also has fundamental political implications, for it "destroys the morals of one part" of the country, and the love of country of the other. It erodes the foundations of free government. "And can the liberties of a nation be thought secure when we have removed their only firm basis, a conviction in the minds of the people that these liberties are the gift of God?" (289)

Warren on occasion noted that Jefferson thought "that liberty is gained by inches, so you have to nag along inch by inch" (Walker 166). This phrase is taken from a letter written by Jefferson to Rev. Charles Clay in January 1790, about a decade after he composed *Notes on the State of Virginia*. He wrote, "The ground of liberty is to be gained by inches, that we must be content to secure what we can get from time to time, and eternally press forward for what is yet to get. It takes time to persuade men to do even what is for their own good" (*Papers* 129). Although this is extremely prudent political advice—a series of small, incremental gains, over time becomes a major reorientation—it appears that Jefferson never thought that this incremental approach applied to the question of slavery. This appears to be true not only in old age, when, for example, he resisted Edward Coles plea that he free his own slaves and tried to convince Coles not to free his (*Writings* 1343–46), but throughout his adult life. Even at the end of his discussion of slavery in *Notes* he seems to reject an incremental approach (*Writings* 289). Jefferson reflected on this in one of the last letters he wrote, dated June 24, 1826: "A good cause is often injured more by ill-timed efforts of its friends than by the arguments of its enemies. Persuasion, perseverance, and patience are the best advocates on questions depending on the will of others. The revolution in public opinion which this cause requires, is not to be expected in a day, or perhaps in an age; but time, which outlives all things, will outlive this evil also" (*Writings* 1516).

Chief Joseph of the Nez Perce and Native Americans

Although Thomas Jefferson is not the primary focus of Warren's poem on the Nez Perce War of 1877, he does play a minor supporting role that will help in the effort to understand his place in Warren's thought. This poem has three epigraphs, from Jefferson, General William Tecumseh Sherman, and Chief Sealth of the Duwamish. The first two appear to offer different views concerning government policy toward the Indian tribes. Chief Sealth maintains that even when White Men have totally eradicated the Red, the invisible dead will swarm over the land: "The White Man will never be alone."

Here I will focus on Jefferson and Sherman, and then discuss the link between *Chief Joseph and the Nez Perce* and *Brother to Dragons*.[2]

The first epigraph is taken from Jefferson's letter "To the Miamis, Powtewataminies, and Weeauki," and reads, "Made by the same Great Spirit, and living in the same land with our brothers, the red men, we consider ourselves as the same family; we wish to live with them as one people, and to cherish their interests as our own." The mood of a benign vision presented here seems to stand in marked contrast to Sherman's letter to his brother John: "The more we can kill this year, the less will have to be killed the next war, for the more I see of these Indians, the more convinced I am that they will all have to be killed or be maintained as a species of paupers" (ix). As critic Hugh Ruppersburg notes, "The poem's opening epigraphs reflect the conflicting perspectives of idealism and pragmatism which order Warren's vision of American history." This fits, Ruppersburg continues, with Warren's general interest in "the annihilation of Jeffersonian Idealism by the greed of those more concerned with economic gain than forging a democratic nation" (116). A consideration of Jefferson's entire letter to the Indian tribes, however, shows that Jefferson is interested in something other than mutual friendship and acceptance. After pointing to the disadvantages of war to all sides, Jefferson makes what appears to be a pledge.

> On our part, we shall endeavor in all things to be just and generous towards you, and to aid you in meeting those difficulties which a change of circumstances is bringing on. We shall, with great pleasure, see your people become disposed to cultivate the earth, to raise herds of the useful animals, and to spin and weave, for their food and clothing. These resources are certain; they will never disappoint you: while those of hunting may fail, and expose your women and children to the miseries of hunger and cold. We will with pleasure furnish you with implements for the most necessary arts, and with persons who may instruct you how to make and use them. (*Life and Selected Writings* 333)

Thus, in this letter of January 7, 1802, Jefferson is actually suggesting that the foundation of our brotherhood and the key to living together is for these tribes to give up their nomadic ways and to settle down and tend the land. This was a longstanding concern of his, for he had stated in *Notes on the State of Virginia* that dependence on hunting game led to annual famine among the Indians (*Writings* 186). Just a year after his letter to the Miami and other tribes, in private correspondence to William Henry Harrison, Governor of the Indiana Territory, Jefferson clearly lays out his plan for dealing with the Indian tribes. Jefferson first states that Governor Harrison will be receiving an official reply to his earlier letter as well as instructions from the Secretary of War concerning Indian affairs. He continues,

> These communications being for the public records, are restrained always to particular objects and occasions; but this letter being unofficial and private, I may with safety give you a more extensive view of our policy respecting the Indians, that you may better comprehend the parts dealt out to you in detail through the official channel, and observing the system of which they make a part, conduct yourself in unison with it in cases where you are obliged to act without instruction. (*Writings* 1117–118)

Jefferson then elaborates the elements of national policy toward the Indian tribes. First, the foundation and goal: "Our system is to live in perpetual peace with the Indians, to cultivate an affectionate attachment from them, by everything just and liberal which we can do for them within the bounds of reason, and by giving them effectual protection against wrongs from our own people." Next, the specifics of the government's plan: 1) Encourage agriculture, spinning, and weaving as occupations, and discourage hunting; 2) Exchange necessaries (supplies of various kinds) for Indian land that is now superfluous in the new sedentary life; 3) Encourage trade, and extend liberal debt policies that encourage increasing debt, "because we observe that when these debts get beyond what the individuals can pay, they become willing to lop them off by a cession of lands"; 4) keep prices low at government trading houses as a way to put private competition out of business and corner Indian trade. "In this way our settlements will gradually circumscribe and approach the Indians, and they will in time either incorporate with us as citizens of the United States, or remove beyond the Mississippi" (1118).

Although Jefferson believes this policy is in the best long-term interest of the Indian tribes and founded on a desire to "cultivate their love," he realizes that it may turn out otherwise. "As to their fear, we presume that our strength and their weakness is now so visible that they must see we have only to shut our hand to crush them, and that all our liberalities to them proceed from motives of pure humanity only." However, there might be an advantage for the United States if it faced resistance. "Should any tribe be fool-hardy enough to take up the hatchet at any time, the seizing the whole country of that tribe, and driving them across the Mississippi, as the only condition of peace, would be an example to others, and furtherance of our final consolidation" (1118–19). This letter concludes with specific comments and suggestions about individual tribes, leaves it up to Harrison to determine the best policy to pursue in individual cases, and encourages Harrison to keep the plan to himself.

Even if one gives Jefferson every benefit of the doubt and accepts at face value his claim to be motivated by a philanthropic interest in the welfare of the Indian tribes, it strains credulity to think that he expected all of his agents to act based on those high principles. In fact, Jefferson acknowledges the threat to the Indians "from our own people." Historian Hans Eicholz argues, "The main thrust of Jefferson's relations with the Indian tribes was to secure western settlement for the independent agriculturalists who formed his ideal of republican citizenship" (31). Thus, the seeds of "the annihilation of Jeffersonian idealism" may be rooted in Jefferson's own public and private policies in relation to the Indian tribes.

Historian Bernard Sheehan believes that Jefferson did act upon philanthropic motives and argues, "The Indian became a victim of the white man's proclivity for conceptualization and idealization" (8).This vision included a sense of the inevitable progress of mankind toward civilization and productive labor, and the willing acceptance by untutored peoples of the advantages of these changes. This inevitable movement ran counter to traditional Indian practice, however, and native resistance to change created an impasse for Jefferson. Ultimately, thwarted philanthropic intention would meet unenlightened resistance to change with force.

In reflecting on Jefferson's philanthropic approach to the Indian tribes, Sheehan concludes, "Its crime, if it committed one, could be ascribed to naïveté, perhaps even an excess of goodwill, but not the intentional inflicting of pain on a less powerful people" (12). If Sheehan is correct, from the perspective of the American Indian there is an unavoidable tragic dimension to their encounter with European settlers: whether these settlers hate the Indians or are sympathetic and motivated by philanthropic intentions, their expectations and demands will lead to the destruction of traditional native culture and tribal life.

Between the epigraphs and the body of the poem, Warren places a note that looks back to *Brother to Dragons*: "The Nez Perce entered history as the friendly hosts to the explorers Lewis and Clark . . ." (xi). Meriwether Lewis, relative of and private secretary to Thomas Jefferson, is also a character in *Brother to Dragons*. In that earlier poem, Jefferson was blinded not only by his vision of humanity, but also his vision of the American West. He calls it "my West," and is dazzled by its possibilities. The mission of exploration is so important that he appointed Meriwether Lewis to be the commander of the Corps of Discovery. "But my own blood will go / To name and chart and set the human foot" (Warren 1979, 9). As *Chief Joseph* shows, however, Warren knew that "the human foot" had already walked the open western spaces, and that Indians had walked that land before any foreign explorers. Jefferson describes the territory acquired in the Louisiana Purchase in lyrical terms:

> I saw
> My West—the land I bought and gave and never
> Saw, but like the Israelite,
> From some high pass or crazy crag of mind, saw—
> Saw all,
>
> . . . .

It was great Canaan's grander counterfeit.
Bold Louisiana,
The landfall of my soul—
Or then it seemed— (Warren 1979 10)

It appears that the Jefferson of *Brother to Dragons* was blinded three times, by his image of mankind, by his imagined West, and by his image of himself as the new Moses.

While *Chief Joseph* looks back by referencing Lewis and Clark, *Brother to Dragons* looks forward with a brief discussion of the Ghost Dance phenomenon near the end of the Indian Wars (1979 119, 139), activities intended to keep native culture alive that were forcibly outlawed by government troops. Thus, we see the unfortunate results of Jefferson's philanthropic policy toward the Indian tribes.

Thomas Jefferson as American Hero

Just as the American image of Jefferson, as documented by Merrill Peterson, has changed through the centuries, so did Warren's view of Jefferson. In an early book review, Warren wrote that Jefferson's "principles were philosophical. But . . . he was not inferior to Franklin as a practical man of affairs" (*French View* 196). Warren argued, "The fundamental principles of that philosophy were never violated." In the same review, however, Warren acknowledged that Jefferson's argument "for a strict and rigorous construction of the Constitution" was undercut by the assumption of "a prerogative in the purchase of the Louisiana Territory which exceeded Hamilton's wildest audacities." In this early view of Jefferson Warren argues, "America was a unique experiment, one in which he had perfect faith, but it was also an experiment which could not be safely undertaken in other lands" (197). Warren found irony in the fact that American isolationism closely followed Jefferson's principles but that "the domestic development, on which his most passionate hopes were centered, should have diverged so far in both economic and social aspects." For Warren, the "fact, not the conclusion, of the Civil War meant the real defeat of those hopes."

In the first version of *Brother to Dragons*, Warren calls Jefferson "the spiritual father" of America (xi), but in the revised version he became one who "helped to found" [xii] the nation. Perhaps American ideas recreated themselves in new forms too quickly for any member of the founding generation to be a "spiritual father" to the nation for long. In *Democracy and Poetry* Warren notes briefly that Emerson and Whitman had already started to think beyond Jefferson's understanding of democracy (4–5). In "A Dearth of Heroes," Warren reflects on Benjamin Franklin, George Washington, and Jefferson as "the trio who became our first national heroes" (7). He spent more time on Franklin and Washington in this essay but provides a comment on each in his summation. "Franklin might tell you how to live and get rich. Washington might, if need be, teach you how to die. As for Jefferson, he . . . could teach you neither how to live nor how to die; but he could teach you how to envision a world worth living in or dying for" (96). Even in this essay, Warren notes a paradox in Jefferson's contributions to the nation: "Once Americans were made, especially after Jefferson had set the flag on the Pacific—against all his political principles as well as his agrarian sense of locality—the dream of distance, like the dream of the future, fed the national ego" (6). It may be Warren's judgment that Jefferson's two greatest contributions to the founding of the nation we would become almost 250 years later were: 1) drafting our national dream in the form of the Declaration of Independence and 2) setting us on the course of Manifest Destiny by the purchase of the Louisiana Territory from France in 1803.

The irony embedded in these two contributions to the nation's founding is that both the Declaration and the Louisiana Purchase had consequences never imagined by Jefferson but that helped undermine the Republic he thought he was helping to create. This, I think, is one of the reasons Warren was so fascinated with Jefferson. As C. Vann Woodward noted, "Warren was a master of the ironic and the oxymoronic. He is constantly reminding us of the contrast between the intent and the result of human motives and plans, between expectation and the outcome" (284). As the Declaration's statement of self-evident truths has morphed from a summary of basic principles of political philosophy into an aspirational declaration of self-fulfillment and government guarantee of our individual happiness, Jefferson's ideal of a minimal state has been one of its major casualties. Jefferson's use of his executive power in concluding the purchase of Louisiana has provided more guidance to later presidents wishing to expand presidential authority than did any of his writings on the limited nature of national power.

Warren hoped to salvage two elements of Jefferson's thought. First, the idea of a natural aristocracy that is not in opposition to democracy but is the outcome of a vibrant democracy (Purdy 214). In *Democracy and Poetry,* this takes the form of a discussion of "the common man." Warren argues that there are two ways to understand this concept, and that they are diametrically opposed. The first, in religious terms, sees every individual as equal in the sight of God. Warren translates this notion into secular terms: "the individual soul is precious in the eyes of democracy, but that what is glorified is the *potentiality* in man to become more fully man, more distinctly and strongly a self in fruitful relation to other selves" (79). He illustrates this idea by discussing the life of Washington.

> The will to change: this is one of the most precious heritages of American democracy. We have the story of the young Washington, who studied surveying and could, by the exercise of his skill, buy "Bullskin planation," his first one, at the age of sixteen. Thus far he had merely changed his condition. But he had the will to change himself as well, and with the same furious energy, he studied the Roman Stoics that he might achieve the admirable character he desired. (79)

This Jeffersonian vision of the common man is challenged by "the notion that the mere fact of commonness in itself constitutes an ideal—and a blessed world it would be in which the actual condition of the self, not the potential, was taken as fulfillment . . ." (80).

Second, Warren argued in "The Use of the Past" that Jefferson had a robust recognition of the importance of the past.

Thomas Jefferson did say that "The land belongs to the living generation," but he also said, in his *Notes on the State of Virginia*, that history should be the basis for the education of the free citizen. A sense of the past, according to Jefferson, was necessary to nurture a self capable of exercising judgment concerning the present and the future, a self, that is, with a feeling for destiny. (31)

This view certainly fits well with Warren's own understanding of the relationship between past, present, and future, best expressed by Jack Burden, narrator of Warren's novel *All the King's Men*: "I tried to tell her how if you could not accept the past and its burden there was no future, for without one there cannot be the other, and how if you could accept the past you might hope for the future, for only out of the past can you make the future" (435).

I am unsure how strong Warren thinks Jefferson's commitment to the study of history is. In one interview, Warren distanced himself from Jefferson by stating, "I have no romantic dreams about quick improvements, no romantic dreams about quick improvement of human nature or of human society" (Watkins 346). In addition, as I noted above, Warren suggests in *Brother to Dragons* that Jefferson was led by his vision of the new man and the new west rather than by an understanding of the dynamics of historical development.

At times Jefferson seems to denigrate the value of understanding history. In response to John Adams's description of a four-volume history of the Jesuits that he had been reading, Jefferson first noted that he is not familiar with the work and recommended "education and free discussion as the antidotes" to bigotry and religious enthusiasm. He concluded, "I like the dreams of the future better than the history of the past. So good night. I will dream on . . ." (Capon 485). In 1956, Warren offered one of his strongest critiques of Jefferson without identifying his target:

The past is always a rebuke to the present; it's bound to be, one way or another: it's your great rebuke. It's a better rebuke than any dream of the future. It's a better rebuke because you can see what some of the costs were, what frail virtues were achieved in the past by frail men. And it's there, and you can see it, and see what it cost them, and how they had to go at it. And that is a much better rebuke than any dream of a golden age to come, because historians will correct, and imagination will correct, any notion of a simplistic and, well, childish notion of a golden age. The drama of the past that corrects us is the drama of our struggles to be human, or our struggles to define the values of our forebears in the face of their difficulties. (qtd in Purdy 210)

From 1929 until the end of his active career, Robert Penn Warren read, argued with, and learned from Thomas Jefferson. C. Vann Woodward provides a simple explanation: "Jefferson remains a great man at the conclusion of *Brother to Dragons*" (286). A great man and, as Warren himself might add, a frail man, as all men are frail.

Lewis P. Simpson concludes his comparative study of the early and late versions of *Brother to Dragons* with a reflection and a prediction. "Whatever else we may learn from Warren's long pursuit of his relationship to Thomas Jefferson, we discover that we are not done with Jefferson and that Jefferson most assuredly has not finished with us" (69). Were Warren able to respond to that thought he might, in the spirit of his meditation on diminishing selfhood found in *Poetry and Democracy*, wonder if contemporary Americans have the patience to listen to, and the courage to learn from, a flawed hero.

Notes

1. For a detailed discussion of *Brother to Dragons*, New Version, see Ealy, "Robert Penn Warren's Encounter." For a comparison of the 1953 and 1979 versions, see Simpson.

2. For an overview of *Chief Joseph of the Nez Perce*, see Ealy, "Past and Present."

Works Cited

Cappon, Lester J., editor. *The Adams-Jefferson Letters*. Simon and Schuster, 1971.

Ealy, Steven D. "Past and Present in Robert Penn Warren's *Chief Joseph of the Nez Perce*." *Modern Age*, vol. 56, no. 2, Spring (2014), pp. 33–40.   library.laredo.edu/eds/detail?db=lfh&an=95733717&isbn=00267457.

_____. "Robert Penn Warren's Encounter with Thomas Jefferson in *Brother to Dragons*." *Mississippi Quarterly*, vol. 62, no. 1, 2009, pp. 95–115. *JSTOR*, www.jstor.org/stable/26476684.

Eicholz, Hans. "Thomas Jefferson (1801–1809)." *U. S. Presidents and Foreign Policy: From 1789 to the Present*, edited by Carl C. Hodge, and Cathal J. Nolan, ABC CLIO, 2007, pp. 25–33.

Jefferson, Thomas. *The Life and Selected Writings of Thomas Jefferson*, edited by Adrienne Koch, and William Peden. The Modern Library, 1944.

_____. *The Papers of Thomas Jefferson, Volume 16: 30 November 1789 to 4 July 1790*. Edited by Julian P. Boyd. Princeton U P, 1961.

_____. *Writings*. Edited by Merrill D. Peterson. The Library of America, 1984.

Peterson, Merrill D. *The Jeffersonian Image in the American Mind*. Oxford U P, 1960.

Purdy, Rob Roy, ed. *Fugitives' Reunion: Conversations at Vanderbilt*. Vanderbilt U P, 1959.

Ruppersburg, Hugh. *Robert Penn Warren and the American Imagination*. U of Georgia P, 1990.

Sheehan, Bernard W. *Seeds of Extinction: Jeffersonian Philanthropy and the American Indian*. U of North Carolina P, 1973.

Simpson, Lewis P. "The Poet and the Father: Robert Penn Warren and Thomas Jefferson." *The Sewanee Review*, vol. 104, no. 1, 1996, pp. 46–69. *JSTOR*, www.jstor.org/stable/27547142.

Walker, Marshall. "Robert Penn Warren: An Interview." In *Talking with Robert Penn Warren*, edited by Floyd C. Watkins, John T. Hiers, and Mary Louise Weaks, U of Georgia P, 1990, pp. 147–69.

Warren, Robert Penn. *All the King's Men*. Harcourt Brace, 1982.

_____. *Brother to Dragons: A Tale in Verse and Voices*. Random House, 1953.

_____. "Brother to Dragons: A Play in Two Acts." *The Georgia Review*, vol. XXX, no. 1 (1976), pp. 65–138.

_____. *Brother to Dragons: A Tale in Verse and Voices. A New Version*. Random House, 1979.

_____. "A Dearth of Heroes." *American Heritage*, vol. XXIII, no. 6, pp. 47-7, 95–99. (Oct. 1972) www.americanheritage.com/dearth-heroes.

_____. *Chief Joseph and the Nez Perce*. Random House, 1982.

_____. *Democracy and Poetry*. Harvard U P, 1975.

_____. "A French View of Jefferson." *The New Republic*, vol. 62, no. 800 (2 Apr. 1930), pp. 196–97.

_____. *Selected Letters of Robert Penn Warren, Volume I: The Apprentice Years, 1924–1934*. Edited by William Bedford Clark, Louisiana State U P, 2000.

_____. "The Use of the Past." In *New and Selected Essays*, Random House, 1989, pp. 29–53.

Woodward, C. Vann. "The Burden for Robert Penn Warren." In *The Burden of Southern History*. Updated Third Edition. Louisiana State U P, 2008.

Watkins, Floyd C. "A Dialog with Robert Penn Warren on *Brother to Dragons*." In *Talking with Robert Penn Warren*, edited by Floyd C. Watkins, John T. Hiers, and Mary Louise Weaks, U of Georgia P, 1990, pp. 336–56.

Recent Poems Inspired by Thomas Jefferson___
Robert C. Evans

Of all the "founding fathers" of the United States, Thomas Jefferson was, for a long time, the most inspiring. Now he is without doubt the most controversial. Many people among earlier generations of Americans were uplifted by Jefferson's high ideals concerning freedom and human dignity. These ideals were encapsulated in the Declaration of Independence, especially in the beliefs that "all men are created equal" and that people should be able to decide for themselves how to freely conduct their lives while pursuing whatever happiness they independently chose. More recently, however, Jefferson is usually criticized not only for *being* a slave-owner—a fact that contradicted his lofty rhetoric about freedom—but also for failing to *free* most of his slaves, even after his death.

Both aspects of Jefferson's reputation and legacy—his high ideals and his disappointing practice—are reflected in a recent volume of poetry edited by Lisa Russ Spaar. Entitled *Monticello in Mind: Fifty Contemporary Poems on Jefferson*, this collection offers an unusually diverse kaleidoscope of different perceptions of the nation's third President. Some of the poems are especially worth examining *as* poems—that is, as pieces of language interesting *as* pieces of language. The purpose of this essay, then, is to survey some of the texts included in Spaar's collection and discuss them, for the most part, not so much as pieces of political rhetoric but as works of art. (In fact, the better they are as art, the more effective they are as rhetoric.) But the second half of the essay will explore, in detail, an even more impressive achievement: a long poem titled "The Hand of Thomas Jefferson," by the distinguished poet Mary Jo Salter. Salter's work is one of the most important poetic text Jefferson has ever inspired, at least in recent times. The fact that her poem exists, and that fifty others have been collected by Spaar, shows that Jefferson is not just a historical or political figure but also a continuing source of artistic inspiration of one kind or another.

Spaar's Volume: I

Spaar's book opens with an impressive poem by Debra Allbery—
"An Ordinary Portion of Life: *Jefferson to Adams, 1822*"—that
manages convincingly to imitate Jefferson's own styles of thinking
and writing. The poem's opening stanza reads as follows:

> The life of the feeder, my dear Sir, is better
> than that of the fighter. But I reach only my garden now,
> and that with sensible fatigue. *With laboring step*
> *to tread our former footsteps, to beat and beat*
> *the beaten track*—it is surely not worth a wish. (1)

Here and throughout the poem, Allbery manages to weave words
quoted or adapted from Jefferson into and out of her own phrasing.
The poem's italicized passages come either directly or with slight
changes from Jefferson's own correspondence with John Adams, his
early friend, great rival, and then eventual friend again. Allbery's
own words capture not only the diction but also the cadence and
other sound effects of Jefferson's own style, especially in the heavy
alliteration, the balanced clauses ("of the feeder" / "of the fighter"),
and the way both alliteration and repetition reinforce and even mimic
sense ("*to beat and beat / the beaten track*"). Allbery ventriloquizes
not only Jefferson but a whole eighteenth-century state of mind. For
these reasons and others, the decision to place her poem first in the
book, although dictated by the fact that her last name begins with an
"A," was a happy coincidence.

A later poem, by Gabrielle Calvocoressi, mimics not the sound
of Jefferson's writings but instead the sound of his slaves' voices.
Entitled "Monticello Smokehouse Festivity" (4), the poem is
preceded by the instruction that it is "*To be sung at high volume, by*
a large group, in rounds, so the house shakes." This poem's opening
stanza differs significantly from Allbery's first stanza (already
quoted):

> Every house has a room the guests don't know. Yes.
> Every house has a room the guests don't know. Belly

Deep beneath the shoes with their red leather soles.
Every house has a room the guests don't know.

This poem, in this stanza and in four more of equal length and similar style, pretty clearly alludes to the secrets of Monticello, Jefferson's magnificent, self-designed Palladian mansion. Intended as a physical embodiment of Jefferson's highest ideals of order, reason, and decorum, Monticello—both the house itself and the surrounding estate—was largely built by slaves. Calvocoressi's poem lets us hear the kinds of songs those slaves may have sung, but the poem also suggests how much was hidden at Monticello— not meant to be seen. The slavery there was, of course, obvious. But the likelihood that Jefferson maintained a decades-long relationship with Sally Hemings, a slave who was his dead wife's half-sister, was something Jefferson tried to hide, just as he hid his likely paternity of Sally's many children. Calvocoressi's poem suggests these hidden aspects of life at Monticello, but it does so in a way that is impressively artful.

A later text, by the distinguished poet Lucille Clifton (9), refers much more explicitly to the Jefferson-Hemings relationship, and it does so in just a few short but stinging lines. Here is the entire poem:

monticello

(*history: sally hemmings* [sic]*, slave at Monticello,
bore several children with bright red hair*)

God declares no independence.
here come sons
from this black sally
branded with Jefferson hair.

Clifton's cleverness here unites irony, sarcasm, stinging humor, and even a touch of anger. Jefferson, she implies, may have declared independence from Britain, but he could not achieve freedom from the simple facts of biology: sex with a slave, in his day, was almost sure to produce children—and not *only* children but children who resembled their father in ways that would then have been considered embarrassing. Jefferson himself was "branded," by God and like a slave, with a distinctive sign—in this case red hair. If his hair had been black, the fact that he had fathered Sally's children might have been less obvious. God, in that sense, played a trick on Jefferson, ensuring that Jefferson could not deceive his contemporaries about his relationship with Sally, just as he could not deceive God. Sally's children were "branded" with Jefferson's red hair just as other slaves might be branded by having their flesh burned. And Clifton even (perhaps) manages to allude, ironically, in line 2, to the famous Beatles song "Here comes the sun." At the very least, it is almost impossible for a reader today to read line 2 and not think of one of the most cheerful little ditties ever written. The irony is potent, to say the least.

Spaar's Volume: II

Other especially well-written poems in Spaar's volume include Michael Collier's "Jefferson's Bees" (10–11); Stephen Cushman's "Cut and Paste" (12–13); and Kate Daniels's "Reading a Biography of Thomas Jefferson in the Months of My Son's Recovery" (14–18). Daniels's long poem, in several passages, manages to capture Jefferson's complexity. On the one hand she pays complicated tribute to his status as a political philosopher and practical statesman:

> Before we *were*
> Ourselves he knew us. Explained us
> To ourselves. Gave us a language whereby
> We understood the restless grandiosities of our forebears,
> And set us off on our well-trod path of personal
> Liberty and greedy freedom-seeking. Minted the metaphors
> We go on living by and misinterpreting, and clobbering
> Over the heads of the rest of the world—Still,
> His language stirs me up. Still, I believe
> He was a great man, and seek in the painful
> Contradictions of his personal life and public
> Service, ongoing signs of how to live
> In *this* strange era. (16)

Although Daniels's poem, with its long lines and plain language, sometimes risks sounding prosaic, it is full of paradoxes that help enhance its interest. How can someone know "us" (perhaps a pun on "United States"?) before we "*were* / Ourselves"? This phrasing implies that Jefferson knew fundamental traits of the American people before there was a separate America with separate Americans. But perhaps the phrasing also alludes to Jeremiah 1:5: "Before I formed you in the womb I knew you, before you were born I set you apart; I appointed you as a prophet to the nations" (New International Version). If so, then the speaker is suggesting that Jefferson was not merely a Founder but almost a kind of Creator. And if such an allusion *is* meant to be heard, then lines 7–8 of the quoted passage from the poem take on an ironic tinge: the country "appointed" to be a "prophet to the nations" clobbers "the rest of the world" with its Jeffersonian doctrines. Similarly complex is the speaker's suggestion that Jefferson's promotion of liberty has led to "greedy freedom-seeking."

Later in the poem, toward its end, the speaker deals with other complexities of Jefferson's life. She imagines him

Tying shut the bed curtains of a lover he inventoried
Among his personal property. With whom he made
Six children. Though he owned her.
And then owned them. His own Sons
And Daughters . . . [ellipses in original] (18)

Here the phrasing is also subtly complicated. Note how Jefferson ties shut the bed curtains. Does he do this just to achieve greater personal intimacy with Sally, or in order not to run any chance of discovery? Note how the noun "lover" conflicts with the verb "inventoried"— the noun suggesting true affection and the verb suggesting mere ownership. Note how the ensuing three sentences are fragments, as if the speaker cannot quite bring herself to say what she is saying— as if her shocked mind can only speak in broken sentences. Daniels's poem, like the others already cited, has a distinctive style of its own. And, in fact, it is partly this mixture of styles and perspectives that helps make Spaar's volume so worthwhile.

Rita Dove, in the next poem ("What Doesn't Happen") imagines a young, apparently black violinist, brought in Paris to play for a group of wealthy citizens (19–20). Jefferson is there, in his role as U. S. ambassador, and when the youth looks out from the stage and into the crowd, he sees a

> tall man on the aisle, with hair
> the orange of fading leaves; and the two girls beside him—
> one a younger composition of snow and embers,
> but the other—oh, the other dark, dark yet warm
> as the violin's nut-brown sheen . . . miraculous creature
> who fastens her solemn black gaze on the boy as if to say
> *you are what I am, what I yearn to be—*
>
> so that he plays only for her and not her keepers;
> and when he is finally free to stare back,
> applause rippling over the ramparts—even then
> she does not smile. (20)

Little does the black youth know that the dark-colored girl is, or soon will be, the mistress of the older man, whose daughter she has accompanied from America. Her thought—"*you are what I am, what I yearn to be*"—has an effective double meaning: he is "dark," as he she is; but he, in France, is free in a way that she is not and can probably never hope to be. And what do we make of that final phrase, "she does not smile"? Is she not smiling because she feels sad and anguished about being a slave? Or is she not smiling because she dare not show any romantic interest in him, especially in her owner's presence? Like many effective poems, Dove's ends on a note of tantalizing ambiguity and uncertainty.

Spaar's collection contains many rich poems—some *too* rich, too brimming with effective language, to be analyzed very fully here. One such poem ("Jefferson's Daughters" [44–46]) is by Jennifer Key. It memorably describes the humdrum lives of Mary and Martha Jefferson, who have been to Paris, know what an active social life is like, but are now shut up behind the glass windows of their father's rural Virginia mansion. Equally impressive is

"Daddy Hemmings Was Good with Curves," by Yusef Komunyakaa (47–48), which is as skillfully constructed as the well-crafted woodworks it describes. Another effective poem ("Epiphanies" [49–50]) is by Maurice Manning, and still another ("Symmetry" [53]) is by Elizabeth Seydel Morgan, who provides an especially memorable final line. "Monticello," by Carol Muske-Dukes (54), is full of memorable images and striking sounds as well as sly ironies and a neatly symmetrical design.

Various later poems in Spaar's collection reward both reading and rereading, but one of the best, by Chet'la Sebree, is entitled "Asylum from Grief, September 1795" (67). Here the speaker is Sally Hemings talking, either directly to Jefferson or imagining what she might say if she could, in fact, speak freely. The poem's first line seems to allude to its title: "You found it in my bosom—", with the "it" here presumably meaning "Asylum from Grief." Jefferson, who had deeply loved his dead wife, Martha, had promised her that he would not remarry. Unwilling to break this promise and court white women, he instead turned to Hemings for solace, love, and sexual satisfaction. Hemings was actually his wife's half-sister and thus strongly resembled her in physical appearance. As Hemings puts it in the poem, with effective alliteration, Jefferson "fancied her father's features in my face." He "retraced the whole series of [his] fondness / on my two-shades too brown skin"—another pair of well-written lines in which "traced" echoes "face" and foreshadows "shades" and in which "too" plays with the preceding "two." Sebree isn't content merely to make her points blandly; instead, she makes genuine poetry out of the situation she imagines. Her words are worth reading not only for what they say but for how they sound and interact.

More examples of Sebree's poetic skill appear in the following stanza. Hemings there tells Jefferson "You were a diplomat of bedroom politics"—a clever metaphor that at first might suggest his relationship with Hemings but which in the next line seems to refer to his relationship with his wife: he "kept [his] promise to never wed again." By structuring this sentence as she does, Sebree suggests *both* meanings, implying that Jefferson was a diplomat both with Sally *and* with Martha. But even now the implications of the sentence are not exhausted, because we realize that while he *had* to be diplomatic with his wife, nothing *required* him to be diplomatic with his slave. Sebree has created a poem worth reading (and remembering) *as* a poem, not simply as a set of ideas. One last example of her skill appears in the very next few words: "Still / flesh you hungered—flesh you found." "Still" here can imply "nevertheless" (in spite of your promise) and also, momentarily, "still, you are your flesh." Jefferson, still a relatively young man when his wife died, was still a man of flesh and blood. He "hungered" for "flesh"—and he "found" it, conveniently, in the form of a young slave who would have had little real say in the matter.

Sebree's poem is full of this sort of linguistic richness, this sort of subtle play with words, sounds, punctuation, and syntax. In the text's final lines, Sally reveals that she is now pregnant with Jefferson's child: she is now "bearing a body // one shade closer to the one you mourned, / one shade closer to a world that is yours." Here again Sebree shows a subtle effectiveness in her music, especially in the alliteration of "**b**earing a **b**ody," in the repetition of "one shade closer," and in the understated echo of "mourned" and "yours." Indeed, that final word—"yours"—seems especially poignant: it implies the distance between Jefferson and Sally: she is *in* his world but not fully *of* it. She is a possession in his world just like any other possession that is his, that he owns. The child to whom she will give birth will be, technically and racially, superior to his or her own mother. The child, in one sense embodying the closest kind of union that can exist between two people, will also forever be a reminder to its mother that she is a slave, one shade darker than her child and, therefore, one degree less important in Jefferson's "world."

Sebree's poem is one of the most effective poems—*as a poem*—in the whole of Spaar's collection. Various other texts in that anthology are very much worth discussing, but as space is limited, it seems best to end now by remarking that Spaar's volume—which might have seemed unlikely to succeed (how can fifty poems on an American statesman succeed, except occasionally, as poems?)

prospers quite well indeed. This is a book well worth reading, and then reading again.

Mary Jo Salter's "The Hand of Thomas Jefferson"

If a collection of fifty separate poems on Jefferson might initially seem unlikely to succeed as a collection *of poetry*, what about a very long poem on Jefferson by one individual poet? For that is precisely what Mary Jo Salter has offered in her nearly twenty-page, multi-stanza poem "The Hand of Thomas Jefferson" (*A Phone Call* 124–38). To make things even more challenging for herself, Salter uses a complicated system of rhymes, half rhymes, and near rhymes but does so in a way that rarely sounds contrived or artificial. Salter, after all, is a talented poet and is up for the challenge. She has published seven collections of poetry, co-edited the *Norton Anthology of Poetry*, long taught at Mount Holyoke College and at Johns Hopkins, and for more than two decades was vice president of the Poetry Society of America. These kinds of qualifications, however, are far less important than her poems themselves. Anyone who has read them knows that Salter not only sets ambitious goals but usually achieves them.

"The Hand of Thomas Jefferson" is no exception. The risks of writing a poem on a figure as well known and controversial as Jefferson are obvious. How does one say anything worth reading? How does one avoid platitudes? How does one avoid creating or— even worse—merely repeating propaganda of one sort or another? How does one neither avoid controversy nor become mired in it. In short, how does one avoid creating what might have better been an essay instead of a poem? Only a fairly "close" reading of Salter's poem can answer these kinds of questions.

The first section of Salter's text is labeled *"Philadelphia, 1776,"* a subtitle that might already suggest all sorts of clichés, as if we were about to begin reading a filmscript for a tedious historical documentary. But note how skillfully Salter begins:

> War had begun. And one could hear its drums
> in the psalm of scorn he ranted at the tyrant.

"He has refused . . . He has forbidden . . .
He has plundered our seas . . .": so the verses went
from the hand of Jefferson, at thirty-three
the youngest of the committee whose assignment
was to authorize a nation. [. . .]. . . .(124)

There is much to admire here, including the abruptness and brevity of the first sentence; the effective half-echoes in "one," "begun," and "drums"; the alliteration and irony of "psalm of scorn" (one doesn't normally think of psalms as scornful); the unexpected verb "ranting"; and the clever echo of "*rant*ing" and "ty*rant*." Salter next quotes three examples of anaphora (phrases with similar beginnings) from the Declaration of Independence, calling them "verses" and thereby implying that Jefferson himself was a kind of poet. (This suggestion sets up something coming later.) Meanwhile, "went" not only looks back, in a kind of rhyme, to "tyrant" but also looks forward to "assignment." And if the final three lines here run the risk of sounding prosaic, Salter pulls back from that danger through her clever pun on "authorize": Jefferson created a nation as an author might create a poem. And Jefferson also "authorize[d]" a nation by giving it, through the Declaration, both legal and moral authority. This opening stanza is an auspicious beginning to the entire poem, which is full of such subtle and satisfying phrasing.

In the poem's second stanza (124), Salter at first plays repeatedly with the "ent" sound ("arguments"; dependent"; "independence"; "sense"; "wrenched"; and "invention"); puns when referring to "the common sense of Paine"; uses both alliteration and assonance when mentioning the "logic of Locke"; and then cleverly enacts the very process she refers to when she says that in Jefferson's Declaration "reason" was "wrenched from treason." This, in other words, is a poet who is less interested in making points than in making words memorable—that is, in creating literature with the same kind of attention to stylistic detail that Jefferson displayed. Meanwhile, in lines from the third stanza Salter shows not only this talent for phrasing but also a nice sense of historical irony. Although John Adams and Benjamin Franklin let Jefferson's first draft pass, in the subsequent debate the delegates

struck out much more: his outcry at the "market
where MEN should be bought & sold." Foiled, he learned
firsthand, at least, a government by consent.
He bowed to the majority, and was governed. (124)

The first four words of the first quoted line—"struck out much more"—are all heavily accented. The words' sound thus reinforces the forcefulness of their meaning. But what the delegates "struck out" were precisely words objecting to slavery—the sin Jefferson despised but never himself rejected and thus the sin for which he is, ironically, best known today. Jefferson "bowed to the majority, and was governed" (a nice echo of "learned" from earlier), but he was never governed by a minority, at least after independence, as his slaves and all slaves were. As Salter's poem tells it (and as there is much evidence to verify), Jefferson opposed slavery and wanted to abolish it but was continually defeated whenever he proposed its abolition. Ironically, "government by consent" meant that only white, wealthy males had the consent to govern. White women did not have the power to consent; poor white men did not; and black slaves most certainly did not. Jefferson, an eloquent opponent of slavery in theory, never quite freed himself from that awful tar baby in actual practice. And, what's worse, he *could* have freed himself, but chose not to.

As the quoted passages already suggest, Salter knows how to work effectively with words, and each new section of her poem displays her various talents. Section II, for instance——subtitled "*Paris, 1876*"—is much longer than Section I (sixteen stanzas instead of five). The stanzas' designs also differ from those of the first section. In that section, each stanza had consisted of seven lines, with each line flush with the left-hand margin. In section II, each stanza consists of nine lines, only two of which are flush with the left-hand margin. Here, for instance, is this section's second stanza, which describes Jefferson's reaction to the premature death of his beloved wife:

For days, weeks, the knife of grief
pinned him to his room; he paced

as if movement alone proved him still alive;
then, hour upon hour, he rode
on horseback with his daughter Patsy past
the checkered plot of gravestones under
which more children lay, to the forest
where no calling could reach his hearing. Or
so he believed at first. (125)

Once more Salter effectively plays with sounds and meanings: "the knife of grief"; the emphatic emphasis on the monosyllabic "pinned"'; the alliteration of "pinned" and "paced" and "proved"; the subtle echo of "**move**ment" in "**prove**d"; the clever play of "**Patsy past**"; the "checkered plot" (which echoes a reference in the preceding stanza to the couple's "Unchequered / happiness"); the skillfully delayed reference to the dead children surrounding their now-dead mother; the balanced verbs "calling" and "hearing." And then, to his surprise and ours, the subtle touch of suspense ("Or / so he believed at first"), where "first" subtlY echoes "forest."

Almost every stanza of Salter's poem reveals such riches when read closely. She is a talented poet, and this is an accomplished poem. The rest of section II deals with Jefferson's time in Paris as the American ambassador to a government threatened with revolution partly inspired by the revolution he had helped lead. But most of section II deals with the ambassador's intense attraction to a married woman named Maria Cosway, the Italian wife of an English painter. Their love never had a chance to really develop: Maria had to leave France when her husband left. But his affection for her was an important event in his life as a man, not merely a statesman.

The poem's third and final section—subtitled "*Monticello, 1826*"—takes us down to the year of Jefferson's death, half a century to the day after he signed the Declaration of Independence. (Miraculously, John Adams, his old friend, rival, and then friend again, died on that very same day.) Section III employs relatively short and simple stanza forms: four lines each, with each second and fourth line indented. Here are the section's first two stanzas:

> Long ago, when he was President,
>   he'd open up the White House door
> to the public on two weighty days a year,
>   each with two meanings. Reticent
>
> at any cost about his private life,
>   he chose the first of January
> to note general renewal. (Who knew but he
>   when Martha had become his wife?)   (130)

These lines underscore a theme important to the work as a whole: the intersection and overlapping of public and private matters both in Jefferson's life and in the poem itself. The other day when Jefferson opened the White House to the public was, of course, July Fourth, with its shared public and private meanings, but January 1 was not only a day of "general renewal" but also the anniversary of his marriage to Martha, the woman he deeply loved and who loved him deeply in return. Of course, Martha's death led, ultimately, to his involvement with two other women. Maria Cosway has already been mentioned; it remains to be seen, however, how Salter will deal with Sally Hemings.

The answer—a bit surprising today—is that mostly she *doesn't* deal with Hemings. Salter was writing at a time when the relationship between Jefferson and Sally had not yet been generally accepted or essentially proved by studies of DNA. Surely, if she had written her poem in the early 2000s, she would have dealt (or had to deal) in greater detail with this issue. As it is, writing before even the Jefferson Foundation had to admit that the Jefferson / Hemings relationship seemed certain, Salter dealt with the matter—and with slavery in general—in just a few lines. Writing mainly about Jefferson's old age, she reports that

> . . . Once he seemed ready
> to free the slaves in a flash; but his sense
>
> of impotence has deepened, along with debt,
>   and unable to compute a way

to free his own, he has no more to say.
    Unable to conceive a blanket

emancipation, nor a society
    where black and white are knit as one,
he wraps himself in a "mantle of resignation"
    and wishes, above all, to be free

forever of the subject. His time is over.
    He'll take the answer to his grave
whether he fathered children with his slave,
    Sally Hemings. . . .   (133–34)

Some modern readers may find this an overly charitable treatment of the issue: Jefferson, they might say, was a notorious overspender and might well have been able to free his slaves if he had spent less money on himself, his estate, and his own family. Would he really have been consigning himself, his children, and his grandchildren to abject poverty if he had chosen to emancipate the human beings he owned? It *is* true that he had several times proposed complete abolition of legal slavery and had each time been defeated in the attempt, but for many persons living today his "sense / of impotence" will not seem an acceptable excuse for failing to act on his own. (The African American mayor of Charlottesville, the town most tightly linked to Jefferson's name and legacy, recently proclaimed his belief that Jefferson is now literally burning in hell; see Kangadis.)

However, one responds to this matter, the quoted lines reveal once more Salter's genuine gifts as a poet. The noun "flash" almost mimics, in sound, the very quickness it describes. The skillfully developed metaphor, almost a metaphysical conceit because of its length (involving a "blanket," knitting, wrapping, and a "mantle") is skillfully sustained only several lines but is never too insistent. Especially interesting, although perhaps disappointing to some readers, is the clever use of sentence structure in these two lines: "He'll take the answer to his grave // whether he fathered children with his slave." At first we might assume that the "answer" Jefferson will take to his grave involves a general "answer" or solution to the problem of slavery. But Salter very effectively uses enjambment here: she runs the sense of the sentence not only into an ensuing line but in fact into a new stanza, using no punctuation to slow down or interrupt the reading process. She thereby catches us by surprise when we discover that the "answer" Jefferson takes to his grave is not any answer to the issue of slavery, in general, but any answer about his relationship with Sally Hemings, in particular. And then the matter is dropped, suddenly and somewhat inexplicably, so that the poem leaves us feeling the very sense of disappointment, of wanting an explanation or at least further words of some sort, than either Jefferson or Salter provides.

Instead, the poem concludes with stanzas that take us back to Jefferson himself, especially Jefferson in his final years, with death approaching. If anything, the ensuing stanzas remind us just how extravagantly Jefferson spent, in his final years, to build Monticello and may thus, inadvertently, enhance our contemporary uneasiness about his failure to free his slaves. But the poem, almost in its very last lines, returns once more to the issue of slavery—an issue that bedeviled Jefferson during his life and, if anything, has bedeviled his reputation even more in his death. Salter describes how, after that death,

> … Monticello tumbles into ruin,
>   Patsy [his beloved daughter] penniless, the hammer
>
> that built her house now traded for the gavel
>   of the auctioneer who splits
> whole families her father owned to bits,
>   unfreed by law or his good will,
>
> and the country's shifting house still barely stands
>   undivided. (137–38)

These are ominous, almost final words. They seem to foreshadow the Civil War, the almost inevitable result of the problem of slavery, a problem neither Jefferson nor his countrymen could ever seem to resolve simply or by peaceful means. Salter's words remind us that at least Jefferson kept his families of slaves together while he lived, but her words also inadvertently remind us (who know more now than she did when she wrote) that among those families were Jefferson's own long-time lover and the children he sired with her. Raising this particular issue at the end of her poem was almost surely not Salter's intention. But historical knowledge has advanced in the years since she wrote, and so it is now almost impossible to read the poem's final lines without feeling queasy. Ironically, the reputation of Jefferson, the only president who might also justly be called a scientist, now seems forever likely to be tainted by the kind of scientific evidence—DNA—he could probably never imagine in his own time. Surely, if Salter were to rewrite her poem today, she would feel obliged to treat the Hemings issue more fully than she did when she originally wrote "The Hand of Thomas Jefferson."

Jefferson as a Subject for Literature

Of all the so-called "Founding Fathers," Jefferson may be the one most likely either to inspire or to intimidate literary artists. He may inspire some of them because he seems so complex, and creators of literature—poets, novelists, dramatists, scriptwriters, and writers of short fiction—tend to love complexity, both in their subjects and in their texts. On the other hand, he may intimidate some literary artists, who may feel uncomfortable dealing with precisely the kinds of complexities Jefferson raises: Was he a racist? Was he a rapist? Should he be judged by the "standards of a later time," or are those simply the standards of fundamental humanity? Perhaps writers will gravitate, as apparently they have long tended to do, toward "safer" subjects, more "respectable" founding fathers. There are, for instance, significantly more listings, in the Library of Congress catalog, for "Franklin, Benjamin—Fiction" than there are for works of fiction about Thomas Jefferson, and there are *many* more such listings for George Washington. (Jefferson, on the other hand, has a few more listings than John Adams.) Franklin and especially Washington seem less controversial subjects than Jefferson. Perhaps, for that reason, they will continue to attract more attention from literary artists, especially from writers writing for children. But as

Salter's poem and Spaar's collection suggest, Jefferson is likely to be a founding father who especially attracts the attention of writers willing to tackle particularly complicated subjects.

Works Cited

Kangadis, Nick. "Too Much? Charlottesville Mayor Said Despite Removing Jefferson's Birthday, 'He's Still Able to Celebrate His Birthday in Hell.'" 2 Aug. 2019, www.mrctv.org/blog/charlottesville-mayor-said-despite-removing-jeffersons-birthday-hes-still-able-celebrate-his.

Salter, Mary Jo. *A Phone Call to the Future*. Knopf, 2008.

Spaar, Lisa Russ. *Monticello in Mind: Fifty Contemporary Poems on Jefferson*. U of Virginia P, 2016.

Ken Burns's Documentary Film *Thomas Jefferson*: A Survey of Responses_____

Kyla Free

Ken Burns is certainly the most acclaimed U. S. maker of documentary films of the past forty years, and perhaps ever. His popular televised programs—usually aired on the Public Broadcasting System (PBS)—have almost always dealt with important topics in American history and culture, including *Brooklyn Bridge* (1981); *The Shakers: Hands to Work, Hearts to God* (1984); and *The Statue of Liberty* (1985). Later projects included *The Civil War* (1990), *Baseball* (1994), *Jazz* (2001), *The War* (2007), *The National Parks: America's Best Idea* (2009), *Prohibition* (2011), *The Roosevelts* (2014), *The Vietnam War* (2017), and *Country Music* (2019). These long-form efforts have usually appeared over several weeks, but Burns has also made a number of shorter films, including biographies of *Thomas Hart Benton* (1988), *Mark Twain* (2001), and *Thomas Jefferson* (1997). Burns had long wanted to make a film about Jefferson but has said he is glad other projects intervened. By the time he did get around to Jefferson, he had become the unrivalled American master of directing documentary films. He brought to the Jefferson undertaking close to twenty years of experience and expertise.

Like most of Burns's documentaries, his film on Jefferson received extremely positive reviews. Wholly negative reactions were almost nonexistent; and although the film did elicit a few mixed responses, most assessments were glowing. The documentary remains readily available on DVD and is probably the one film that most teachers of Jefferson use most often and that most non-professionals interested in Jefferson are most likely to view. How, precisely, was the film received when it was first broadcast? Which features most bothered its few critics? Which aspects most impressed its many admirers? How, precisely, did Burns deal with the man who is, today, probably the most controversial of all the founding fathers? In particular, how did Burns treat Jefferson's ideas and practices concerning slavery? What final, overall picture of Thomas Jefferson emerged from *Thomas Jefferson: A Film by Ken Burns* (the project's full title)? These are a few of the questions this essay will try to answer.

Negative and Mixed Reviews

One of the few fairly negative reactions to Burns's *Jefferson* was originally published—anonymously—in California's *Orange County Register*. Under a headline reading "Ken Burns' 'Jefferson' Shallow," the unnamed critic began by claiming that this documentary "feels much like a warm glass of milk. It makes a gentle, nourishing but nonexciting TV view, in good, old PBS fashion" (2B). Even this writer, however, briefly conceded that the film qualified "as another worthy TV poem by Burns" and called it "a provocative and thoughtful view of a legendary U.S. president." Later, however, a more negative tone returned, especially when the reviewer asserted that the "repeated plaintive music . . . eventually becomes a tad much," although the critic did admit that "the film features many articulate interviews with Jefferson scholars, from Clay Jenkinson to Gore Vidal and George Will. Still," the writer continued, *Thomas Jefferson* is not visual enough to make a riveting TV ride. . . . Visual gaps are filled with recurring images of Jefferson's beloved home Monticello from endless angles, including silvery photographs made in the platinum process of the 1850s by contemporary photographer Robert C. Lautman. Sadly," the reviewer thought, "the lush texture of platinum is lost on TV." This commentator ended, however, by writing that "[a]s always, Burns does not shy [away] from probing all facets of his subject, from Jefferson's admirable intelligence to what was morally corrupt." But the writer felt that "in the end, Jefferson the man is left largely unresolved, as Burns searches for the larger cultural ramifications of Jefferson's life, resonating today in our conflict over personal liberty, big government and race" (2B).

A slightly more positive response to the documentary was offered by Walt Belcher in a piece under the unpromising headline "Ken Burns Follows His Formula on 'Thomas Jefferson.'" Like many reviewers, Belcher began by emphasizing the contrast between Jefferson the proponent of human freedom and Jefferson the life-long slave owner. "That contradiction between the ideal and the reality," Belcher wrote, lay "at the heart" of Burns's film:

> Because race relations and personal freedoms still divide America, Burns says a look back at Jefferson is important today. "The arrogance of the present is that it assumes that the past is not as good," Burns said in a recent interview. "An investigation of the past tells us who we were and what we have become." (47)

Belcher advised his readers that if

> you have seen Burns' "Civil War" or "Baseball," then you know the routine: A Burns film blends folk music, observations from historians, passages read by famous people, new footage of historic sites, and vintage photographs. Because Jefferson (1773–1826) predates photography, Burns was handicapped by a shortage of visuals. He had to rely on a handful of paintings.

Belcher wrote that this film, like previous Burns documentaries, "moves at a languid pace, offering a bittersweet portrait of our third president. It is flawed by its length. Burns," he abruptly concluded, "should have put a cork in some of the pontificating historians" (47).

In another somewhat mixed response—that began positively but ended by emphasizing problems—Tom Jicha of the Florida *Sun-Sentinel* prefaced his review with an ominous contrast, insisting that no "historical documentary will ever be more acclaimed than *The Civil War*," a 1990 Ken Burns production, which was "the highest rated in the history of PBS." Yet Jicha quoted Burns, "the executive producer-director-co-writer-chief cinematographer-music director of the landmark series," as saying that *Thomas Jefferson* is the work he [had] really been looking forward to doing." According to Jicha, this fact alone should have been "reason enough for viewers to anticipate the two-part series." He noted that along with traditional references to family and political achievements, a common "thread" running through the film is attention to Jefferson's "views on slavery and race," including words "used to both condemn and support slavery." Jicha thought that by blending mysteries, contradictions, and achievements in his presentation of the life of this Founding Father, Burns had incorporated "historical and storytelling perspectives" with "asides and anecdotes" in a way that made the investment of "four years" in production "well spent." He acknowledged that Burns had tackled "the near impossible" in daring "to craft a multinight TV show about a man who predated photography." And he also pointed to the ways this film echoed familiar patterns from Burns's previous productions, including "tinkling piano and mournful violin [music] behind grave recitations of letters and anecdotes." These traits, he thought, "invit[ed] parody." Because Burns could not include substantial visual supports, he had to rely heavily on audio features to distract audiences from "the absurd irrelevance of most of the video," which Jicha considered "dominated by still lifes and landscapes." Citing examples of details he considered absurd, Jicha gibed at the imagery of "trees and roads" to illustrate details of "Jefferson's youth," a "chair" to represent a "friend's death," and a "window" to picture the "passing of Jefferson's father." Sarcastically, he added, "Burns must be a frustrated glazier." Emphasizing the failures of what he regarded as hackneyed efforts, Jicha closed by suggesting that "[i]f PBS had a dollar for every story told [that involved] looking either into or out of a window," then "there would be no need for a government subsidy next year."

Positive Reviews

Like Jicha, Walter Goodman of the *New York Times* commented that "problems linger in this three-hour biography" but asserted that "'Thomas Jefferson' is a considerable accomplishment, a thoughtful and affecting portrait." Goodman pointed out that Burns, although "[l]acking photographs" to include, "fills the screen with the architectural details and furniture of Monticello." In fact, he suggested that audiences "may feel [they've] tuned into a commercial for Colonial interiors or an on-line flower show." He found the imagery "tasteful" and "even at times beautiful" but thought that *Thomas Jefferson* lacked the "immediacy and action" provided by the photography of Burns's *The Civil War*, instead presenting "static" and "distancing" illustrations. Goodman even quipped, "Was Monticello always foggy?" However, he thought these problems did "not detract much from Mr. Burns's achievement in bringing out Jefferson's continuing influence on the idea of America." Goodman stated that the "narration, though delivered somnolently . . . is up to the usual standards," that "the [Jefferson] quotations [voiced by Sam Waterston] are apropos," and that "the period music sounds right." He considered the "work as a whole . . . evidence of television's ability, in the hands of serious producers, to be serious about our history."

Tony Scott of *Variety* applauded "Geoffrey C. Ward's lucid script," which was "jammed into . . . three tight hours," as a "worthy, step-by-step appreciation" of Jefferson. Scott noted that "with no photos . . . and little word from intimates," Burns's "lovely appraisal" had to rely "for visuals on portraits, paintings of landscapes, contemporary shots of nostalgic places and items, [and] silhouettes of a horseman or carriage passing against a crimson sky." At "no time," he said, "does the great man stroll down a Virginia lane, walk across a parquet Paris floor, or effectively rise to call out in his soft tones his wondrous words." Scott credited Sam Waterston, who "voic[es] Jefferson's graceful prose" with "giv[ing] history its proper pauses," but he regretted that the film does not explore "how the gentleman spoke at informal occasions and about what." However, Scott wrote that "Burns' expert report does a cunning job of boiling down early presidential politics." He expressed admiration for the "camerawork and editing," particularly the "still camerawork at Monticello," which "creates an eerie sense of historical perspective, as though the great man himself might stride into view." Scott also touched on Jefferson's complexity, noting that in this "glowing account, facts of Jefferson's life are ticked off fairly enough, but the human Jefferson remains elusive": Burns did not examine "dark areas" in Jefferson's life but merely those unexplored. Scott wondered why Jefferson never "set his slaves free," unlike "many of his fellow patriots," but he insisted that "such a man" would have a "reasonable answer." On the whole, Scott credited "Burns and co-producer Camilla Rockwell" with exploring Jefferson's life "in a respectable, responsible fashion" and praised writer Ward for serving up a "slice of history valuable to schools and to anyone familiar with the elusive, magnificent intellect who planned the republic."

Steve Johnson, of the *Chicago Tribune*, wrote that the film warranted "creating the title National Documentarian and naming Burns" to that position. He noted the "comparative brevity" of the "relatively perfunctory three hours" of *Jefferson*, in contrast to Burns's more "sprawling" works, such as *Baseball* and *The Civil War*. He thought that while this film did not "explain the man whom historians have long struggled to fathom," it succeeded in "at least lay[ing] out why [Jefferson] causes so much learned head-scratching." Burns's production, he wrote, created "a stirring reaffirmation of the American founding ideal" and reminded viewers that "a man can be heroic in one realm of life and a scoundrel in another." Johnson observed various "techniques that Burns perfected and popularized," which "have almost become clichés of documentary making: the slow, probing pans over paintings and period photographs, [and] the mixture of eloquent narrative . . . and contemporary source material read by actors," although Johnson pointed out that Sam Waterston's vocals contrasted with the voice of the real Jefferson, "who was said to have an unimpressive" style of speaking. Johnson also praised the input of famed "talking-head historians," including George Will and Gore Vidal, whose "comments are kept relevant and eloquent." Johnson was more impressed, however, with a man he called the "surprise star of the picture," Clay Jenkinson, "a historian at the University of Nevada at Reno who travels the country portraying Jefferson" and who "provides a resonant coda, or a dollop of enlightenment, in virtually every section." The film as a whole, Johnson wrote, is "not a mediocre middle ground" depiction but rather a "passionate" work "where at the end Jefferson comes out smelling like a rose after having stunk" in many preceding sections. Johnson focused on the issue of "Jefferson's slaveholding" and on the film's success in "shooting down the standard defense" that Jefferson "was just a man of his times." He said that the answer to a key question—"whether Jefferson fathered children by his

slave Sally Hemings," which "has fascinated recent interpreters"—
"is unknowable." He reported that Burns himself, however, had
cautioned against "getting distracted by the sexuality of it" and had
pointed to the greater issue: "He owned her. He could do anything
with her, and we forget that."

Ed Bark, of *The Dallas Morning News*, also praised Burns
emphatically, writing, "We hold this truth to be self-evident:
Ken Burns' 'Thomas Jefferson' again shows he has no peer as a
historical filmmaker" (5A). Bark wrote that while this film is
"barely a sketch compared with previous sweeping landscapes such
as 'The Civil War,' 'Baseball' and 'The West,'" its "[t]hree hours
is enough" to allow Burns "to dissect a complex founding father
who preached life, liberty and the pursuit of happiness while at the
same time holding slaves until his death. Was he," Bark asked, "a
contemptible hypocrite or merely a man of his times and of puzzling
inconsistencies? Burns," he continued, "wrestles with that elemental
question without ever pinning it down. Bark quoted Burns as saying,

> "I would rather look at him as a hero in a classical sense. . . . To
> tolerate the ambiguities and the contradictions. That's the kind
> of history I tried to do in 'The Civil War.' It wasn't enough to say
> the 'right side' won. I . . . still felt it was important to know what a
> Southern mother felt when she lost a son on the battlefield. So, too,
> to get inside Jefferson was not to find an easy categorization that he's
> good or bad. But to see something much larger. . . . He is a kind of
> Rosetta Stone of the American experience.. . . A massive tectonic
> intelligence that has formed and rattled the faultlines of our history,
> our present moment and, I hope, if we are lucky, our future." (5A)

Bark expressed thanks that the film "understands the virtue of quieter
understatement. Stylistically, it mimics the filmmaker's previous
works. The requisite Burns hypnosis," Bark wrote, "is achieved via
soft piano and guitar music, interviews with well-spoken scholars,
voice-overs by prominent actors and a collection of evocative
images." But Bark also noted that unlike Burns's "other acclaimed
works, *Jefferson* is set entirely in pre-photographic times. Burns,"
he wrote, "compensates by using paintings, drawings and a variety

of filmed impressions. Perhaps he shoots through windows more than he should. But as the mood takes hold, we're not inclined to quibble" (5A).

Equally enthusiastic was George F. Will, the well-known conservative columnist. He called the film "a timely corrective, a visually sumptuous and intellectually judicious appraisal of Jefferson" (12A). By including "various analysts," Will wrote, Burns had managed "to be admiring without being enthralled." He thought that Burns recognized "that heroism is not saintliness" and that "a cool appraising eye need not be a jaundiced one." In particular, Will observed Burns's "agnostic" examination of the "theory that Jefferson" had "had a long sexual relationship, and children, with a slave, Sally Hemings." According to Wills, Burns's production underscored that while Jefferson "proclaimed equality, . . . one-fifth of all Americans were owned by other Americans." He added that the film "unsparingly" noted that although Washington and "Jefferson's cousin John Randolph and Jefferson's neighbor Edward Cotes" freed their slaves, "Jefferson never did, even as Virginia's population of free blacks was rising in a 30-year period from 2,000 to 30,000." Will also thought that Burns's work "puncture[d] Jefferson's pose of ambitionless-ness" by examining his keen competition with his political rivals. But despite admitting the complications and even the flaws of Jefferson's character, Will strongly championed Burns's careful examination of Jefferson and contrasted it with the work of other students of the third President:

> Many historians and others, in their intellectual crudity, immaturity and mean-mindedness, respond to complexity with contempt and to excellence with envy. They pander to the democratic spirit gone rancid in resentment of excellence, and they leave our national memory parched. Ken Burns, an irrigator, causes our capacity for political admiration for love of greatness in public people to bloom anew. (12A)

Howard Rosenberg, of *The Los Angeles Times*, another admirer of the film, called the documentary "a smasher." Burns's "smart credo," said Rosenberg, is that documentaries "must be not only provocative, illuminating, comprehensive and accurate but also presented in ways that make them widely appealing as well as suitable for framing." He added that Burns's well-deserved reputation for excellence allowed him to "command big budgets," resulting in films that are "simply gorgeous" (F1). Rosenberg did concede a sense of "sameness to parts of Burns' films (this one's familiar single, soulful violin as background for a chunk of narration, for example), as if these traits were indelible and Burns their slave" (F13). He even wrote, "Enough already." Yet Rosenberg, in general, described Burns's "blend of scholarship and technique" as "stunning." Burns, he thought, used effective "language to engage masses on the airwaves without compromising quality or the U.S. history he's telling." He also applauded the film's "visual texture," observing that it was created "almost entirely from paintings, documents and historic rooms and buildings. Or, as in the opening, from chess pieces on a board." He praised two scenes, in particular. One showed pages of the Declaration of Independence with a piano playing "*My Country 'Tis of Thee*" in the background. Another offered "a deeply moving depiction of Jefferson's wife, Patsy, on her deathbed, with him at her side." Rosenberg called this "masterful scene-crafting . . . vintage Burns" because it conveyed strong emotions "almost entirely through footage of writings on a page." But Rosenberg also praised Burns in other respects, saying that the filmmaker did not "obscure [Jefferson] behind platitudes," especially when depicting Jefferson's role as a slaveholder. Ultimately, Rosenberg praised Burns for his ability to leave the "fascinating enigma" of Jefferson the slave owner intact so that we depart his film still puzzled by "the notorious mystery of Jefferson's sexual life," especially his relationship with Sally Hemings. Rosenberg ended by extolling the honestly enigmatic aspects of the documentary, commenting that "mystery is often what makes history such an adventure" (F13).

Yet another admirer of Burns's efforts was Robert Strauss of *The Philadelphia Inquirer*, who wrote that he was even more impressed with *Thomas Jefferson* than the "admirable [and] massive *The Civil War* and *Baseball*" (C1). He believed, in fact, that Burns was "best in the shorter films," in which he was "forced to winnow out the extraneous and concentrate on the pith." Strauss called *Thomas Jefferson* "by most standards a long-piece" but felt that "the three hours fly by as Burns manages just the right tone, combining deference and criticism of that Redheaded Guy on the Nickel." He praised Burns's use of drawings and paintings in the absence of photographs, commenting that the film "relies more on the story of Jefferson's life than on the scenery, and is thus a bit talky. That's OK," he added, "for the usual PBS crowd, but the rug rats who watch *Rugrats* will find it a difficult go." Strauss added that while Burns's "*Baseball* was criticized for being endless and, despite its length, essentially pointless," Burns "resurrects himself with *Thomas Jefferson*, peeling back layer after layer as he searches for the core of this enigmatic man" (C1).

Bill Mann, in a special piece for *The San Francisco Examiner*, also generally praised Burns's complex presentation of the third President, although he felt that the film failed to give viewers "a firm grasp on" the "multifaceted author" of the Declaration of Independence (B3). This reviewer emphasized that Jefferson "was a complex man, both statesman and scientist (among his inventions was the first dictating machine)," but he felt that this complexity was only "sketched in this exhaustively researched film." All in all, however, Mann was impressed. He wrote that the "more Burns shows us about this supremely multitalented man of contradictions, the more one appreciates Jefferson as a human being." Mann noted that Burns, impressively, had made a worthwhile film "without the aid of photographs, which propelled his *Civil War* and *Baseball*." He believed that even "when Burns is forced to use, as he often does, 'beauty shots' of Jefferson's never-completed Virginia estate, Monticello, as a visual backdrop, the passages still have enough vibrance and lucidity to advance the story." Mann especially praised Burns for revealing "so much of Jefferson's life without offering simple conclusions." He concluded that although television "is a notoriously shallow medium," *Thomas Jefferson* "is anything but" (B3).

Renée Graham, of the *Boston Globe*, offered much briefer but still very positive opinions. She said Burns had tackled a "difficult subject" in a "fascinating film" and suggested that although he had pointed out unattractive aspects of Jefferson's life, he had never resorted to "character assassination." And although she regretted that he had been unable to use actual photographs (since photography did not exist during Jefferson's day), she called this regret a "minor quibble" about a genuinely "compelling film" (E8). Also offering relatively brief assessments of the documentary was Gail Pennington of the St. Louis *Post-Dispatch*. Pennington called the film "a masterly portrait of our very complicated third president" and said that by the time Burns had finished with Jefferson, "we still may not feel that we completely know the man John Adams called a shadow, but we certainly see him a lot more clearly" (6D). She thought that even though Burns could not use photographs, he had compensated "in fine style" by "blending drawings and paintings of Jefferson and other key players in his story with lovely, often soft-focus pictures of places mentioned, especially the famous Monticello. Burns also," she continued, "effectively zeroes in on bits and pieces of the Declaration of Independence in Jefferson's own handwriting, complete with strikeouts and blots. Talking-head historians," she added, "appear frequently but are blessedly succinct and short-winded" (6D). Finally, another fairly brief assessment was offered by Jim Schembri in the Australian newspaper *The Age*, who called Burns's film an "exhaustive, critical, loving, gorgeous-looking portrait of Jefferson"—a man who was, "according to Burns, . . . that rarest of all things: a modest political hero. And, like the best heroes, he was deeply flawed" (2). Schembri felt that sometimes in Burns's film a "love of American history often drifts into outright infatuation and, on-screen, that love can sometimes get a tad laborious. Points are not just made and developed, they are strip mined for every last detail." Schembri concluded that at his "best, however, Burns does powerfully evoke some intensely personal passages about Jefferson's troubled personal life" (2).

Much lengthier than the comments by Pennington, Graham, and Schembri was an assessment by Dave Drury in the Hartford *Courant*, who wrote that "Ken Burns has created a coherent, accessible portrait of America's most enigmatic and fascinating Founding Father." Drury predicted that viewers would "recognize the Burns narrative touch: His effective use of voice-overs drawn from the words of Jefferson and his contemporaries; a soundtrack developed from music of the era; [and] an array of historians and commentators weighing in with anecdotes, interpretations and insights" (E1). According to Drury, "Burns shows Jefferson's appealing genius without ignoring his shortcomings." In this reviewer's opinion, the documentary moved "crisply. Sometimes too crisply, given the magnitude and longevity of the subject." Drury thought that "Jefferson's split with Alexander Hamilton, which led to the formation of the two-party system, is treated cursorily. So, too, is Jefferson's presidency." Turning to other matters, Drury suggested that in this film none "of the on-camera historians and authors—who include familiar faces such as [George] Will and Gore Vidal—exhibit the charisma and story-telling talent of Shelby Foote, whom Burns used so effectively in 'The Civil War.'" Drury thought that a "black historian, John Hope Franklin, has the best moments." But he concluded by asserting that despite having expressed a few "minor quibbles," he thought that overall the documentary provided "a balanced, elegant, often moving look at this most indispensable figure in American and world history" (E7).

Even more positive was a lengthy assessment of the film by Eugene Marino in the Rochester *Democrat and Chronicle*. Marino's main assessment seems worth quoting in full. He wrote that Burns had made

> Monticello a living, breathing symbol of Jefferson. There's gorgeous film of the mansion in the morning mist, in the snow and in the bright summer sun, and Burns lovingly weaves his camera throughout the rooms or lets it linger on an architectural detail. He also gives us close-ups of a quill pen on parchment, of period eyeglasses on a tablecloth, of drafts of the Declaration in Jefferson's handwriting, with his corrections. And there are the usual ambient sounds of birds or gunfire or crowds. These all help greatly, of course. And the on-camera historians and writers—among them George Will, Gore Vidal and Garry Wills—speak articulately and often with awe about Jefferson and his contradictions. They, especially, eloquently breathe

life into his ideals and ideas, and the film gives us a clear sense of the themes and mysteries of his life. That the man himself remains just beyond the film's grasp is an inevitability, not a failure. Never afraid of sentiment, Burns lapses only once into sentimentality: "America (My Country, 'Tis of Thee)" plays, too loudly, underneath an actor s reading of the Declaration, as if Jefferson's deathless words need help. It would have been helpful for the film to dwell longer on Jefferson's and Alexander Hamilton's competing visions of the nation, and how they stubbornly remain at the center of American political culture. But, as Vidal says, "Jefferson is American scripture." And to a film as good as *Thomas Jefferson*, the only response is, amen. (4C)

Steve Hall of the *Indianapolis News*, in a generally positive review of the film, found the frequent views of Jefferson's mansion less appealing and appropriate than they seemed to Marino. Hall wrote that viewers "are treated to lovingly crafted shots of: Monticello shrouded in the mists of morning. Monticello caressed by a soft rain. Monticello in the fiery ochre of sunset. Is this," Hall jokingly asked, "a documentary, or a three-hour commercial for the Virginia Department of Tourism?" (D7). He concluded, however, that the "gorgeous photography fits the reverential tone of *Thomas Jefferson*" and said the film "flows with the sweet, unhurried pace of molasses," portraying "its subject sympathetically while noting the contradictions inherent in his life." Burns, Hall wrote, "returns again and again to the theme that tragedy often intersected with [Jefferson's] greatest achievements." According to Hall, the director had managed to "mix the personal and professional in a winning way." He concluded that despite "Jefferson's 'do as I say, not as I do' approach to slavery, it is hard to dislike this redheaded man with the superior intellect" (D7).

Conclusion

Ken Burns's film *Thomas Jefferson* remains, more than twenty years after it first aired, the most widely watched and most widely praised documentary about the third President. It is still often used in high school and university classrooms and/or assigned for home viewing. Anyone seeking a respected film about Jefferson is still today likely to turn first to Burns's documentary. These are just a few reasons that it has seemed worth recording, conveniently and in one place, the kinds of reactions the film first evoked when it was initially broadcast in 1997.

Works Cited

Bark, Ed. "'Jefferson' a Study in Complexity." Review of *Thomas Jefferson*, directed by Ken Burns. Eau Claire WI *Leader-Telegram*, 18 Feb. 1997, p. 5A. www.newspapers.com/clip/35337502/leadertelegram/.

Belcher, Walt. "Ken Burns Follows His Formula." Review of *Thomas Jefferson*, directed by Ken Burns. *The Tampa Tribune* 16 Feb. 1997, p. 47. www.newspapers.com/clip/35349174/the_tampa_tribune/.

Drury, Dave. "Portrait of an Enigmatic Jefferson." Review of *Thomas Jefferson*, directed by Ken Burns. The *Hartford Courant*, 15 Feb. 1997, pp. E1, E7. www.newspapers.com/clip/35348210/hartford_courant/.

Goodman, Walter. "Jefferson, Still a Force in the Idea of America." Review of *Thomas Jefferson*, directed by Ken Burns. *The New York Times* 18 Feb. 1997, www.nytimes.com/1997/02/18/arts/jefferson-still-a-force-in-the-idea-of-america.html.

Graham, Renée. "Burns Sheds Light on Jefferson's Shadows." Review of *Thomas Jefferson*, directed by Ken Burns. *The Boston Globe*, 18 Feb. 1997, p. E8. www.newspapers.com/clip/35347932/the_boston_globe/.

Hall, Steve. "Documentary on Jefferson Shows 2 Sides." Review of *Thomas Jefferson*, directed by Ken Burns. *The Indianapolis News*, 18 Feb. 1997, p. D7. www.newspapers.com/clip/35350139/the_indianapolis_news/.

Jicha, Tom. "Jefferson: A Man of Contradictions." Review of *Thomas Jefferson*, directed by Ken Burns. South Florida *Sun Sentinel*, 18 Feb. 1997. www.sun-sentinel.com/news/fl-xpm-1997-02-18-9702140394-story.html.

Johnson, Steve. "Ken Burns' New Film Sheds Light on the Enigma That Was Our 3rd President." Review of *Thomas Jefferson*, directed by Ken Burns. *Chicago Tribune*, 2 Feb. 1997. www.chicagotribune.com/news/ct-xpm-1997-02-17-9702170094-story.html.

"Ken Burns' 'Jefferson' Shallow." Review of *Thomas Jefferson*, directed by Ken Burns. *Tampa Bay Times*, 18 Feb. 2019, p. 2B. www. newspapers.com/clip/35337737/tampa_bay_times/.

Mann, Bill. "Ken Burns Brings Jefferson to TV." Review of *Thomas Jefferson*, directed by Ken Burns. *The San Francisco Examiner*, 18 Feb. 1997, p. B3. www.newspapers.com/clip/35340353/the_san_ francisco_examiner/.

Marino, Eugene. "A Monumental Thomas Jefferson Is Captured Well in 3-Hour Epic." Review of *Thomas Jefferson*, directed by Ken Burns. The Rochester *Democrat and Chronicle*, 18 Feb. 1997, pp. 4A, 4C. www.newspapers.com/clip/35349551/democrat_and_chronicle/.

Pennington, Gail. "Ken Burns Turns to Great Americans." Review of *Thomas Jefferson*, directed by Ken Burns. *The St. Louis Post-Dispatch*, 18 Feb. 1997, p. 6D. www.newspapers.com/clip/35349971/ st_louis_postdispatch/.

Rosenberg, Howard. "A Triumph of Life, Liberty and Pursuit of 'Jefferson.'" Review of *Thomas Jefferson*, directed by Ken Burns. *The Los Angeles Times*, 17 Feb. 1997, pp. F1, F13.

Schembri, Jim. "*Thomas Jefferson*." Review of *Thomas Jefferson*, directed by Ken Burns. The Melbourne *Age*, 3 July 1997, Green Previews Guide, p. 2. www.newspapers.com/clip/35349283/the_age/.

Scott, Tony. "*Thomas Jefferson*." Review of *Thomas Jefferson*, directed by Ken Burns. *Variety*, 17 Feb. 1997. variety.com/1997/tv/reviews/ thomas-jefferson-2-1200448765/.

Strauss, Robert. "Filming the Contradictions of Jefferson." Review of *Thomas Jefferson*, directed by Ken Burns. *The Philadelphia Inquirer*, 18 Feb. 1997, p. C1. www.newspapers.com/clip/35340124/ the_philadelphia_inquirer/.

Will, George. "Ken Burns' PBS Portrayal of Thomas Jefferson Worth Watching This Week." Review of *Thomas Jefferson*, directed by Ken Burns. Longview, TX *News-Journal* 18 Feb. 1997, p. 12A. www. newspapers.com/clip/35338268/longview_newsjournal/.

Sally Hemings: An American Scandal: A Survey of Reactions to the 2000 CBS Miniseries___

Suzanne Strength

In 1998, DNA evidence more or less established that Thomas Jefferson had not only had a 38-year relationship with Sally Hemings, one of his slaves, but that he had also fathered her children. In 2000, the CBS Television network broadcast a four-hour miniseries about the Jefferson-Hemings relationship. The film, entitled *Sally Hemings: An American Scandal*, which starred Sam Neill as Jefferson and Carmen Ejogo as Hemings, provoked varied and widespread reactions. It was one of the top ten programs that week in the television ratings, and it received some positive, some mixed, and some very negative reviews from various critics. It attracted mostly positive reactions from Jefferson's African American descendants, who were glad that the story they had known about for more than two centuries had now become very public knowledge. Some other African Americans, however, were disgusted by the series. They thought it had turned what was essentially child-abuse and an on-going series of rapes into a cheap soap opera, with Hemings herself as a main instigator of a long-term "romantic affair."

The idea for the miniseries had come from Tina Andrews, a black actress and screenwriter who had written the script and worked for years to get the program made. When Jefferson's involvement with Hemings was finally admitted even by numerous Jefferson scholars and institutions, CBS approved the project and advertised it extensively. The company's investment paid off: not only was the $15 million series (broadcast over two nights) widely watched and much discussed, but it also earned numerous awards and nominations for awards. These included nominations as Best Mini-Series for the 2001 Golden Satellite Awards; a National Association for the Advancement of Colored People (NAACP) Image Award for Outstanding Television Movie; the Minority in Business (MIB) Award for Outstanding Television Achievement; the 2002 MIB/

Prism Award for Outstanding Television Miniseries; and a Writers Guild of America Award for an Original Long Form production. In addition, Tina Andrews's book-length account of her efforts to bring the miniseries to TV (which included her script) won an NAACP Image Award for Outstanding Achievement in Literary Nonfiction (see Andrews).

Interestingly, Andrews's film was much better received than the major 1995 Hollywood film *Jefferson in Paris*, which had been made by Merchant Ivory Productions, one of the most successful production companies of the late twentieth century. *Jefferson in Paris*—which starred Hollywood A-listers Nick Nolte and Greta Scacchi—had mostly been a critical and financial disaster. Compared to this earlier film and the negative reception it received, *Sally Hemings: An American Scandal* had been a real success. It is still easily available online and on DVD and still remains probably the only successful "dramatic" (as opposed to documentary) film about Thomas Jefferson.

The purpose of this essay is to survey Andrews's explanations of why she conceived the Jefferson-Hemings relationship as she did; to report reactions to the film (negative, mixed, and positive) by various critics; and, finally, to report how the film was received in the African American community, some of whom loved it, and some of whom despised it.

Andrews's Intentions in Making the Film

In the book Andrews published after her film was broadcast, she discussed the dilemmas she faced, saying that she had discovered "there was no 'right' way to present such taboo subject matter without offending someone's sensibilities." She continued:

> Had I written it as 38 years of the rape of mother Africa, white Americans would have dismissed it as conjecture, racism and the continued demoralization of Virginia's "favorite son." . . . And if I presented a love story, there would have been those to say "impossible" because it was morally reprehensible to even suggest that Jefferson could have a deep and abiding affection for a black woman because, to them, white men cannot possibly love black women. It also had

the potential of alienating African Americans for whom the subject of slavery has as an inviolable component numerous scenarios of the heinous abuse of black females. For most African Americans the "master / slave" relationship is inherently coercive and the question of miscegenation will always be the absolute and painful result of rape. Consequently, no rendition of the story other than abuse and sexual depravity will be tolerated. So where was the politically correct middle? I was damned if I did, and damned if I didn't. (Andrews 5–6)

In the many interviews Andrews gave both before and after her film was made, she carefully explained why she thought the relationship between Jefferson and Hemings did, in fact, involve some genuine affection. "You can't be benign with this material," Andrews told Kinney Littlefield. "It must be represented as either a love story or abuse. And anyone looking at the historical record will not see abuse. . . . And I'm only telling one story not slavery in America everywhere." Andrews said that her research had turned up no other relationship between Hemings and another man: "this is a woman who only had children nine months after Jefferson would come back and stay on the plantation. She never had a slave husband. And when he died, she took care of his grave for the last nine years of her life" (qtd in Littlefield). Patricia Brennan also reported that Andrews had claimed that

"everything that's in the movie is based on a true incident or the principals themselves. It was a 38-year relationship. . . . There was some sort of emotion and monogamy between these two people. If he could have, I believe in my heart of hearts he would have married Sally Hemings. [Her film] tells the story we wanted to tell. . . .We think there really was a love relationship. He never married, never dated anyone seriously; it's the story that's told by the relatives. It may not have been as romantic as ours." (qtd in Brennan)

But some sort of romance, she continually maintained, almost had to be involved.

When interviewed by Laura Graeber for *The New York Times*, Andrews stressed her desire to tell the story "from the African-

American woman's point of view." Meanwhile, Craig Anderson, the film's executive producer, declared the relationship between Hemings and Jefferson a love story and argued that history supported that view. Anderson and Andrews claimed that Jefferson had had Sally "educated as thoroughly as his own daughters" and that he had "granted her children their freedom when he was destitute." They said that Hemings had "remained devoted even after Jefferson's death in 1826" and had "tended his grave until she died." While Andrews and Anderson admitted that they took the known facts and "connected the dots," they maintained that they "took pains to ensure [the film's] historical accuracy." Anderson said that because using only the few known facts would have resulted in a very dull story, the production did "update" the relationship between Jefferson and Hemings, and she admitted that she used Hemings's character to "voice her [own] concerns over Jefferson's hypocrisy."

Another article, by Valerie Kuklenski, though commenting briefly on the production itself, was mainly a background piece. It described the miniseries as "a romantic tale of forbidden love, 19th-century politics and the protection of a national hero's image and legacy." Kuklenski said that while the film might be "enjoyed or criticized for its soap-opera story elements and the romance-novel look of its publicity photos," it was, in fact, based on "a 200-year-old debate centered on conflicting 'truths' about this very under-documented aspect of Jefferson's life." She noted Tina Andrews's statement that she was very happy for the Hemings family, because they had long waited to have their story told.

Another background piece, this one by Bob Thomas for the Associated Press, mainly reflected Sam Neill's perspective on the miniseries. Neill, a New Zealander, admitted that at first he had had only a very basic knowledge of Jefferson, but he thought that this fact actually aided him in playing Jefferson the man. He could "explore [Jefferson's life] at his leisure, without much preconception" and certainly with "no iconic preconceptions," so that he could "bring a fresh eye to the man." Neill found "some sad aspects" in the third president, partly "because he was rather hopeless at finance and his dream for Monticello [his famous estate] crumbled. He was a somewhat neglected figure toward the end of his life." All in all, Neill considered Jefferson a man "with foibles and weaknesses. As well as greatness."

Finally, Frances Grandy Taylor, taking a slightly different approach, talked to the more than six hundred Hemings descendants who came to Columbus, Ohio, for a special screening of the miniseries. She reported a difference of opinion among family members as to whether the Jefferson-Hemings relationship could have involved love.

Reviewers, meanwhile, as is often the case, expressed a wide range of views. Their responses ranged from negative to mixed to positive.

Negative Reviews

Ed Bark, in a review originally published in the *Dallas Morning News*, quickly and immediately dismissed the film. Calling it based on fact "but bubbling with soapy melodrama," he wrote that the program "ends up taking more liberties than our founding fathers ever fought for." Bark attacked the program for suffering from "allegedly transparent fiction, a mediocre script, and ham-handed direction" (YT–3). Likewise, Caryn James's mostly negative review in the *New York Times* argued that all the film's "heavy-handed historical references" could not "disguise" its "soap-opera soul." James did find the miniseries "[s]olidly directed and prettily shot" and praised its "stunning re-creations of Monticello in its various stages of building." She also thought Ejogo "beautiful and dignified" and even conceded that on "the level of banal romantic storytelling, the film asserts an undeniable pull." But James maintained that "Tina Andrews's mawkish script" reduced "the characters to anachronistic clichés." She asserted that only a "few glimmers of thoughtfulness hint at what a more substantial script could have done." Ultimately James argued that the film's

> flaws have nothing to do with the fusty issue of fiction distorting fact; drama can invent whatever it likes, as long as the invention makes sense. But this film ends with a howler. After Jefferson's death, Sally waves a piece of paper at Martha and says she was freed years before.

She chose to stay with him. This will be news to historians and is an even bigger problem dramatically, as "Sally Hemings" brings the concept of smart women, foolish choices, to an entirely new level. (James, 2000)

Rob Owen, of *The Pittsburgh Post-Gazette*, was also unimpressed. He did praise some good performances, mentioning Carmen Ejogo in particular, but he also noted that neither main actor was American. Owen argued that the film departed from traditional TV presentations of history because the precise nature of the Jefferson-Hemings relationship remains a mystery. He called the production "light on history, heavy on fiction," with "a hearty dollop of romance novel dialogue." He considered its lack of surprises a failing and suggested that although the film might interest some "who pine for tales of forbidden romance," viewers serious about history should "tune elsewhere."

Another particularly bad review came from Robert Bianco, of *USA Today*. He called the miniseries "addlebrained" and said it turned Sally Hemings into a "romance-novel ninny." He condemned Andrews for "see[ing] the story in soap terms" and found "no connection" between this film and the real world. Bianco argued that Andrews had not only entirely "invented" Sally's personality but had also removed all personality from Jefferson, turning him into a "lovesick goof, bereft of political cunning, will, or intellect." He did praise Ejogo but said she was "mired" in a badly written role. He concluded by especially attacking the film's ending. (Bianco, 2000)

Megan Rosenfeld of *The Washington Post* likewise had very little good to say about the film. Although she began by calling it "glamorous, nicely acted, and beautifully photographed," she later mostly rejected it as "bunk," saying it was "so fundamentally silly in concept that it trivializes the legacy of both central characters." She advised viewers to pretend it had nothing to do with reality if they planned to watch it. She especially faulted it as a piece of history, observing that although we know much about Jefferson we know almost nothing about Hemings or their relationship. Rosenfeld objected to the film's presentation of love between them, commenting that although love "is strange and all that, . . . there is probably another word for what went on between these two." She did like a subplot about Henry, a slave who supposedly wanted to marry Sally, and she praised "a delightful scene near the beginning where the king and queen of France arrive at their party in Versailles preceded by a squad of costumed tykes carrying sparklers." Moreover, after having found so many flaws, she did concede that "many of the elements are excellent" and that "the production looks as though no expense has been spared. The only problem," she concluded, "is the basic premise."

Phil Kloer, of *The Atlanta Journal-Constitution*, also disliked *Sally Hemings*. Commenting on the script, he wrote that when Jefferson tells Sally "'You belong to me,' [this phrase] has a queasy double meaning. What is normally a sweet endearment is literal here, as Sally is his slave." Kloer argued that CBS had "made this important part of American history into a pulpy melodrama," and he also questioned the film's historical accuracy. Assessing the performances, he said that Neill "plays Jefferson as if constantly wondering if he left the iron turned on in his dressing room." Kloer's only positive comments, concerning Carmen Ejogo's performance, were very positive indeed: "The best thing about 'Sally Hemings' is Sally, or at least the actress who plays her: Carmen Ejogo, a British actress who is half-black . . . and all grace." Like several other critics, Kloer found the program's second half was particularly dull. Although commending CBS for devoting four hours to a movie about an interracial romance, he wrote that in the final analysis "what matters is whether [such a work] is done well" and concluded that in this case "mostly, it isn't."

Tom Jicha, of the Florida *Sun Sentinel*, was also disappointed by the film, but his disappointment differed from that of many other critics. Jicha felt the miniseries negated the scope and value of Jefferson's contribution to the nation. He compared the program to the act of "smearing elephant dung on an image of the Virgin Mary and calling it art." Although conceding that Jefferson was "guilty of one of history's great contradictions," Jicha reminded readers that

Jefferson lived in a time when slavery was still accepted and widely practiced. Jicha wrote that "the only defense that can be mounted is that Jefferson was a man of his time and it is unfair to apply contemporary standards to figures of another era. . . . In less civilized nations," he continued, "dissidents throw ropes around statues of national heroes and topple them. In America, we make tell-all TV movies." Although Jicha noted the liberties taken by the script, he did like Sam Neill's performance, calling Neill "a smart choice as Jefferson" because he played the third president "as a low-keyed and flawed man, not a statue come to life." Ultimately, however, the best that Jicha was able to say was to call the miniseries "mildly entertaining."

Another unfavorable review was published as an opinion piece by Steve L. Belton in the Minneapolis *Star Tribune*. Belton called the program a "concocted love story about a man's relationship with his property." He felt it portrayed Hemings as a "contented concubine who was troubled only by Jefferson's hypocritical support of slavery." Although Belton thought the exact nature of the historical relationship between Jefferson and Hemings was unclear, CBS had chosen to "make the salacious speculation that slave Hemings and master Jefferson were deeply, passionately and eternally in love." Belton considered this approach a "sensational parody of known facts" and argued that, in light of the film's pervasive romantic undertones, it could have been sponsored by the company that published Harlequin romance novels. Belton asserted that because Sally was a slave and lacked the right to refuse Jefferson, the possibility of a truly loving relationship was highly unlikely. He called CBS's decision to broadcast the film during Black History Month a poor choice and dismissed the miniseries as an "odious offering."

Also negative was a review by R. D. Heldenfels of the Akron *Beacon Journal*. Although attacking the film's "cheap melodrama and historical trickery," Heldenfels considered the story itself appealing. He called it a timeless story of "a complicated relationship involving power and race, as well as sexual attraction" but said these traits could not negate dramatic flaws that turned the program into "romantic pulp, with a fundamentally modern woman let loose in the historical past." Heldenfels called the film a "blatant rewriting of history" and thought it "descends into wacky land" when Hemings uses magic to kill a malicious character. Heldenfels claimed there is no evidence of a letter from Jefferson freeing Sally, although the miniseries claims Jefferson wrote one. This critic was troubled by the presentation of Sally as Jefferson's equal, rather than someone bound by slavery, and in general he considered the film dramatically weak, even expressing pity for the actors.

A particularly negative review, an unsigned editorial in *The Philadelphia Tribune*, expressed considerable offense that the film presented the Jefferson-Hemings relationship as a love story, calling this approach "a fraud . . . perpetrated against the American television audience" and condemning the film for turning history into cheap entertainment. The result, this editorial claimed,

> is not history. This is Hollywood, and not even very good Hollywood. It is a blasphemy to the memories of both Hemings and Jefferson for the sake of a politically correct, 21st century view of who some people would like for them to have been.

The writer considered it

> doubtful that we will ever truly know or understand the motivations of Thomas Jefferson. But movies such as this will never advance that understanding. History is always being rewritten. But we should never accept history where scholarship is virtually nonexistent and where the motivations are purely financial. However, that is what Hollywood does best.

Finally, various other negative responses to the film appeared in an article by Milton McGriff in the *Philadelphia Tribune*. McGriff quoted Maisha Sullivan, who had organized a protest of the film, as saying that Jefferson "was not only a rapist, he was a pedophile and an enslaver." Sullivan considered the miniseries "a mockery of our ancestors" and took particular exception to the portrayal of Hemings seducing Jefferson, saying that "I was sick to my stomach."

McGriff also talked to Joyce A. Joyce, chairwoman of the African American Studies Department at Temple University, who said that she found part one painful to watch: "Both black people and white people have been seriously scarred by slavery and we read and interpret everything from the perspective of those scars." McGriff quoted another Temple scholar, Charles Blockson, as saying that the Jefferson-Hemings relationship was "glorified rape" and that the miniseries was "another rip-off." Blockson said that the relationship was not a love story and that Jefferson "was a hypocrite." According to McGriff, the local station had received assurances from CBS that "they had taken great care" in shooting the series and that the network had acknowledged that this film provided only one version of events. McGriff reported that a spokeswoman had suggested that people watch it and "make up their own minds."

Mixed Reviews

Howard Rosenberg, of the *Los Angeles Times*, was one of many critics who had mixed opinions about the miniseries. He questioned its factual value but called it "enjoyable as middle-brow embellished history featuring that ravishing Brit, Carmen Ejogo, as Hemings" (D12). In this film, he wrote,

> careful scholarship and informed analysis have been air-pumped into a tumultuous CBS ratings-sweeps event that the producers acknowledge is not something you'd want to engrave in stone. It does rub some shine off Jefferson, not necessarily because he slept with Hemings and likely fathered her children—many white plantation owners indulged similarly with black slaves—but because the private man depicted here conflicts in many ways with the one-dimensional gleaming icon of numerous histories. (D12)

Rosenberg concluded abruptly and comically: "You want history, read a book" (D12).

Similarly, Steve Johnson of the *Chicago Tribune* saw both strengths and weaknesses in *Sally Hemings*. Johnson wrote that the film provoked, in him, a certain amount of "irritated . . . head-scratching" (5.3). He said that because so few facts about Jefferson and Hemings were really known,

> writer Tina Andrews was free to invent. Her invention just feels a little shaky, however, like a bridge that will get you across the river without ever inspiring complete confidence in its soundness. "Sally Hemings" falls into the trap of many historical films, intermittently losing the audience to musings on what is and isn't true. . . .
>
> Andrews, who first explored the topic in the 1985 Chicago play "The Mistress of Monticello," never loses sight of the symbolic significance of the relationship, never gets caught up in the temptation to make this about heaving chests, one fair, one a little darker. (To the contrary, the love scenes are almost all shot in the near-dark, which could be either a suggestion that skin tone shouldn't matter or a sop to racist sensibilities.)
>
> Her movie's central concern is with the specific idea of calling Jefferson to task, and there are individual moments that do so powerfully The production is tasteful, even a little languid. Sam Neill as Jefferson and British actress Carmen Ejogo as Sally do fine work. The question, however, is whether material this volatile, and this resonant in American life, simply isn't better served by a documentary. (5.3)

Matthew Gilbert, of the *Boston Globe*, also had ambivalent views about *Sally*. While he called it a "bold envisioning of history," he also thought it felt "more like a torrid romance novel than a glimpse of one of the country's most controversial alliances." He said many of the movie's images could "provide covers for trashy paperbacks" and that its dialogue "lapses into bloated melodrama," but he thought the movie became better as it moved along. Gilbert felt that "while none of the supporting actors, including [Diahann] Carroll," had "a chance to shine," Ejogo and Neill did a nice job of portraying their characters. He finished by calling *Sally Hemings* "a slight improvement on the tedious *Jefferson in Paris*" and hoped it would be only "one in an ongoing series of glimpses at one of the most important relationships in American history."

Lisa Lipman, of the Charleston, South Carolina *Post and Courier*, offered a mixed but mostly favorable review. She noted that the miniseries took some liberties with the truth but felt it stuck "with the truth enough to give viewers a basic idea of what happened" and that it added enough drama to "keep the average romance-novel reader entranced for all four hours." Lipman thought the movie's only "weak moment" occurred when Jefferson stressed Sally's resemblance to his deceased wife—a comment Lipman considered unnecessary. In fact, in general she was not impressed with Neill's performance, but she thought Ejogo conveyed "Hemings' frustrations and joys so convincingly that it's hard for a viewer to take her eyes off her." Lipman concluded that although those who prefer documentaries might disdain *Sally Hemings*, for those who prefer historical dramas the film was "a fun way to spend a couple of evenings while learning about the sexier side of our country's heritage."

David Kronke, of the New York *Daily News*, feeling that *Sally* had potential, made both positive and negative comments about the miniseries. He felt that the depth and complexity of emotions and issues involved in this film were so much a part of it that to refer to it as a "sweeping love story seems something of a cop-out" but argued that there were good points to the project. While he felt that "even the opening lines sound like a romance novel," the film "finds its footing as it conjoins Hemings and Thomas Jefferson smoothly and credibly." Kronke found contradictions in Sally's situation: she loved Jefferson and accepted the privileges she enjoyed while still remaining a slave and still loving her people. Kronke suggested that although, in the film, Jefferson had only to tell Sally that she loved him in order to temporarily settle their disagreements, those tensions weren't really or finally settled. According to Kronke, Andrews, rather than treating the couple's problems seriously, provided distractions in the form of "external villains," including "Jefferson's prudish daughter Martha" and "a ludicrously foppish journalist who hounds Jefferson about his mistress." Kronke accused the director, Charles Haid, of contributing to this kind of distraction by "staging a lot of ornate party sequences" that gave the film "a sense of spectacle without contributing to the real drama at hand." This critic considered the miniseries too long and, like many other critics, complained about the poor makeup job done on the aging characters. Although he also thought that the film's efforts to make Ejogo "glamorous" were excessive, he did think that Neill's skill as an actor helped him salvage certain scenes. Kronke concluded by calling *Sally Hemings* adequate but argued if "had it aspired for a little more, it could've been a true TV event."

Positive Reviews

One very positive review, by Catherine Clinton, appeared in the *Journal of American History*. Clinton briefly praised the main actors' performances but focused chiefly on the film's historical aspects. Unlike other reviewers, Clinton conceded the need for invented scenes. Initially she had worried "that the historical inaccuracies might . . . drive [her] to distraction" but ultimately, to her surprise, she found the film "both thought provoking and absorbing." She particularly praised "Diahann Carroll's impressive portrait of Betty Hemings" for offering "insight into the complexities of antebellum slavery and life at Monticello" and was also "pleasantly surprised" that the film acknowledged that "Sally Hemings was the half-sister of Jefferson's deceased wife." Clinton found it "amazing to see for the first time on network television white actors portraying bondsmen and—women," noting that historical "evidence suggests many individuals held in bondage were so light skinned that they appeared to be "white." She also argued that the "portrait of Jefferson's nephews, the Carr brothers, as despicable yet respectable exemplars of white southern manhood rang all too true." And she even found the depiction of Patsy ultimately "stirring" as an authentic "portrait of a white southern woman."

Clinton noted that historians had long debated Jefferson's relationship with Sally and asked,

> If distinguished scholars ignore compelling coincidences, why shouldn't the television industry weigh in with its own interpretation? All televised dramas take liberties, and this one is no exception. . . . I was on the edge of my seat, wondering how the film would resolve the conflict I had heard historians heatedly debate at conferences across the country for the past two years: If Hemings and Jefferson

did have the intimate connection DNA evidence suggested, what was the nature of that relationship?

Clinton did criticize some of the "shopworn dialogue, . . . melodramatic romantic tantrums," and flawed final make-up. But she concluded that despite "hyped-up plot twists"—such as

> Sally helping fugitive slaves, Sally being whipped by a vengeful overseer, etc., etc. . . . this fictionalized portrait of famed and infamous [persons] caught in slavery's skein allowed millions of American viewers to ponder, if only for a night or two, the ambivalence slavery created for all Americans and its legacy for us today. The Hemings project, however flawed, was an all-too-rare moment of historical reflection on network television—one that raised questions about slavery, about sex, about race, and, finally, about history's responsibility to those intersecting issues. Historians may demand more from purported docudramas, but . . . we must be grateful for the respite this historical film affords. (Clinton, 2000)

Barbara Phillips of *The Wall Street Journal* praised both the acting and the plot, saying Ejogo made "Sally utterly believable" and that Neill managed "to capture the contradictory nature of the great man, the intriguing mystery at his core." She called the production a "class act" and noted the extensive research that went into its every facet. Phillips quoted Jefferson biographer Joe Ellis as saying that even though the story contained unverifiable elements, it also offered "little nuggets of authentic detail littered throughout." She also mentioned another Jefferson biographer's assertion that known facts substantiated the program's suggestion that there was more to the Hemings-Jefferson relationship than just sex, and she quoted Ellis's opinion that the miniseries was "an extraordinarily powerful historical dramatization, almost certain to have a strong impact on its viewers."

Diane Holloway, of *The Austin American-Statesman*, also reacted favorably to the miniseries. She called it a "compelling saga despite its tawdry title" and thought the relationship between Jefferson and Hemings was "tastefully depicted." She praised the performances by both Ejogo and Neill, saying that the only times they weren't believable were in the scenes before the affair begins. Holloway called the movie "pretty to look at" even though its plot was "not a pretty story despite its romantic core." She also noted that the movie depicted "how commonplace interracial sex was on plantations—and that most of it was rape, not love." But she observed that in this film the feelings between Jefferson and Hemings were clearly mutual. Holloway did mention a few minor flaws but concluded by calling the miniseries "an intriguing look at what might have been . . . and probably was."

Another positive review came from A. M. Jamison of *The Dayton Daily News*. He thought the miniseries posed "intriguing questions" about the Hemings-Jefferson relationship and noted that when facts were unknown the film tried "to fill in the gaps." He felt it did "a good job of outlining the harsh realities of slavery," called the first three hours "suspenseful and dramatic," but thought the fourth hour was lacking. He highly complimented the performances by Ejogo and Neill, calling the acting "nuanced" and saying that the two leads conveyed "the complexities of such a union." Jamison also complimented Carroll and Mare Winningham (who played Jefferson daughter Martha) but not Mario Van Peebles (who played Sally's brother). He concluded that we

> may never know who Hemings really was. But we can infer that she was a resourceful woman who made the most of her resources to ensure her children's freedom. We come to appreciate Jefferson as a flawed but accessible hero, rather than as a two-dimensional icon.

Linda Stasi, of *The New York Post*, considered *Sally Hemings* definitely worth watching. She described the story as involving a plotline as "old as Caesar and Cleopatra and as right-this-minute as Monica and Bill." She was particularly enthusiastic about Carmen Ejogo and Sam Neill as the main characters and listed several other traits: "It's got scandal, good acting, an overlong script, and something like 5,000 new costumes. In other words, if you're a miniseries freak, this one's for you." She concluded by calling it "worth the watch just to learn things like the fact that Jefferson, an author of the Declaration of Independence and founder of the University of Virginia, died without a dime to his name."

Conclusion

Although *Sally Hemings: An American Scandal* was itself viewed as somewhat scandalous by some early reviewers, commentators, and academics, the miniseries also attracted a fair share of positive reactions. Many members of the Hemings family themselves were glad to see their long-standing claims of descent from Jefferson affirmed on national television; and although a few reviewers disliked nearly every aspect of the production, others defended the miniseries for various reasons. It is still easily and inexpensively available online and on DVD and has received remarkably positive reviews from "real people" on Amazon.com, where (as of September 24, 2019) 194 different persons had given it nearly a perfect five-star rating. Of course, as always with any film, new viewers will ultimately need to make up their own minds, but enough people have already endorsed the film to make it seem worth watching and thinking about.

Works Cited

Andrews, Tina. *Sally Hemings: An American Scandal: The Struggle to Tell the Controversial True Story*. Malibu, 2001.

Bark, Ed. "History as Bodice-Ripper: These 'Truths' Far from Self-Evident." Review of *Sally Hemings: An American Scandal*, directed by Charles Haid. Hackensack, NJ *Record*, 13 Feb. 2000, YT–3. www.newspapers.com/clip/34881895/the_record/.

Belton, Steven L. "CBS Concocted a Love Story about a Man's Relationship with His Property." Review of *Sally Hemings: An American Scandal*, directed by Charles Haid. The Minneapolis *Star-Tribune* 27 Feb. 2000, p. A25. www.newspapers.com/clip/34881808/star_tribune/.

Bianco, Robert. "Soaped-up 'Sally' Plays a Founding Father for a Fool." Review of *Sally Hemings: An American Scandal*, directed by Charles Haid. *USA Today*, 11 February 2000: 1E.

Brennan, Patricia. "A President's Love Story." Review of *Sally Hemings: An American Scandal*, directed by Charles Haid. *Washington Post*,13 Feb. 2000: Y06. www.washingtonpost.com/archive/lifestyle/tv/2000/02/13/a-presidents-love-story/83134858-d0b4-4a11-8bfd-f4b20dadc512/

Clinton, Catherine. "Sally Hemings: An American Scandal." Review of *Sally Hemings: An American Scandal*, directed by Charles Haid. *Journal of American History, vol.* 87, no. 3, Dec. 2000, pp. 1151–52. doi.org/10.2307/2675447.

Gilbert, Matthew. "'Sally Hemings' A Step above Soap Opera." *Boston Globe*, 12 Feb. 2000, p. F3. www.newspapers.com/image/4286646 45/?terms=%22%27Sally%2BHemings%27%2Ba%2BStep%2Babo ve%2BSoap%2BOpera.%22.

Graeber, Laurel. "Some Truths Are Not So Self-Evident." *New York Times*, 13 Feb. 2000, www.nytimes.com/2000/02/13/tv/spotlight-some-truths-are-not-so-self-evident.html.

Heldenfels, R. D. "More Bunk Than History: Jefferson-Hemings Drama is Dramatically and Factually Lame." Akron *Beacon-Journal*, 7 Feb. 2000, pp. B6, B10. www.newspapers.com/clip/34881578/the_akron_beacon_journal/.

Holloway, Diane. "'American Scandal' Tells an Ugly Story." Review of *Sally Hemings: An American Scandal*, directed by Charles Haid. *Austin American Statesman*, 13 Feb. 2000, p. K3.

James, Caryn. "TV WEEKEND; A Founding Father and Perhaps the Mother." Review of *Sally Hemings: An American Scandal*, directed by Charles Haid. *The New York Times*,11 Feb. 2000, www.nytimes. com/2000/02/11/movies/tv-weekend-a-founding-father-and-perhaps-the-mother.html.

Jamison, A. M. "Jefferson and Hemings: A Love Story." Review of *Sally Hemings: An American Scandal*, directed by Charles Haid. *Dayton Daily News*, 13 Feb. 2000, p. 1C.

Jicha, Tom. "Scandalmongers: The Relationship between Thomas Jefferson and Sally Hemings is Explored and Sensationalism in New CBS Telefilm." Review of *Sally Hemings: An American Scandal*, directed by Charles Haid. *Fort Lauderdale Sun Sentinel*, 12 Feb. 2000, p. 3D.

Johnson, Steve. "By Lumping Black Shows, TV Reveals It Still Doesn't Get It." Review of *Sally Hemings: An American Scandal*, directed by Charles Haid. *Chicago Tribune*, 11 Feb. 2000, pp. 5.1, 5.3. www.newspapers.com/image/170537663.

Kloer, Phil. "Fanciful Look at Hemings Romance." Review of *Sally Hemings: An American Scandal*, directed by Charles Haid. *The Atlanta Constitution*, 11 Feb. 2000, p. E1. www.newspapers.com/image/403236716/.

Kronke, David. "Jefferson's Not-So-Little Secret Presidential Romance Not Without Conflicts." Review of *Sally Hemings: An American Scandal*, directed by Charles Haid. *Los Angeles Daily News*, 13 Feb. 2000, p. L3.

Kuklenski, Valerie. "A President's Declaration of Love." CBS Miniseries Explores Bond between Jefferson, His Slave." Review of *Sally Hemings: An American Scandal*, directed by Charles Haid. Marshall, TX *Longview News-Journal TV Week*, Feb. 13–19, 2000, Page 7A. https://www.newspapers.com/image/221650233/. Accessed 20 Sep. 2019.

_____. "Tale of Forbidden Love American Hero." Review of *Sally Hemings: An American Scandal*, directed by Charles Haid. *The Gazette* [Montreal] 13 Feb. 2000: C6.

Lipman, Lisa. "'Sally Hemings' Gives Racy Look at Jefferson's Life." Review of *Sally Hemings: An American Scandal*, directed by Charles Haid. Charleston, SC *Post and Courier*, 13 Feb. 2000. p. 1.

Littlefield, Kinney. "CBS Miniseries Puts Romantic Spin on Relationship with Slave." Review of *Sally Hemings: An American Scandal*, directed by Charles Haid. Jackson, MS *Clarion Ledger*, 12 Feb. 2000, p. 6E. www.newspapers.com/clip/34882190/clarionledger/.

McGriff, Milton. "Sally Hemings Movie Ripped." Review of *Sally Hemings: An American Scandal*, directed by Charles Haid. *Philadelphia Tribune*, 15 Feb. 2000, p. 1A.

Owen, Rob. "Producers of CBS Miniseries 'Sally Hemings' Were No Slaves to the Facts." Review of *Sally Hemings: An American Scandal*, directed by Charles Haid. Pittsburgh *Post-Gazette*, 11 Feb. 2000, old.post-gazette.com/tv/20000211owen3.asp.

Philadelphia Tribune Editorial. "Sally Hemings Movie: A Mockery of History." Review of *Sally Hemings: An American Scandal*, directed by Charles Haid. *Philadelphia Tribune*, 15 Feb. 2000, p. 6A.

Phillips, Barbara D. "A Surfer's Guide to TV: 'An American Scandal.'" Review of *Sally Hemings: An American Scandal*, directed by Charles Haid. *Wall Street Journal*, 11 Feb. 2000, p. W4. www.wsj.com/articles/SB950225740999794107.

Rosenfeld, Megan. "CBS's 'Scandal': Taking Liberties." Review of *Sally Hemings: An American Scandal*, directed by Charles Haid. *Washington Post* 12 Feb. 2000: C04. www.washingtonpost.com/archive/lifestyle/2000/02/12/cbss-scandal-taking-liberties/7fe77ae4-3357-49a1-81eb-18c6717dd7c4/.

Stasi, Linda. "'Sally' An Affair to Remember." Review of *Sally Hemings: An American Scandal*, directed by Charles Haid. *New York Post*, 11 Feb. 2000, p. 117. nypost.com/2000/02/11/sally-an-affair-to-remember/.

Rosenberg, Howard. "Embellish History? Hey, It's Television." Review of *Sally Hemings: An American Scandal*, directed by Charles Haid. *The Los Angeles Times*, 15 Feb. 2000, pp. D1, D12. www.newspapers.com/clip/34882158/the_los_angeles_times/.

Taylor, Frances Grandy. "The Hemings Affair." Review of *Sally Hemings: An American Scandal*, directed by Charles Haid. Hartfort, CT *Courant*, 8 Feb. 2000, p. D1. www.courant.com/news/connecticut/hc-xpm-2000-02-08-0002081220-story.html.

Thomas, Bob. "Jefferson's Scandal Dramatized." Review of *Sally Hemings: An American Scandal*, directed by Charles Haid. Oklahoma City *Daily Oklahoman TV This Week*, 13 Feb. 2000, p. 9. www.newspapers.com/clip/34881679/the_daily_oklahoman/.

Jefferson and Me: A View from Abroad_____

Hannah Spahn

1. How and why did you first become interested in Jefferson?

I never really heard of a man called Thomas Jefferson from elementary to high school. It was only as an undergraduate at the University of Freiburg when I decided to major in Amerikanistik (American Studies) that I began to learn anything substantial about the events and people associated with the American Enlightenment and the American Revolution. What first drew me into the field and has continued to fascinate me ever since is the complex sense of continuity with the past that characterizes so many popular and scholarly approaches to American history and that I found to be particularly striking in the context of the founding period. When I began to follow the heated academic and public discussions about the so-called "founding fathers" or "founders," my first impression was that someone still needed to break the news that these people were actually no longer with us. It seemed to me that they were being treated almost like living elder statesmen, who were detached enough from political life to float somewhere above the controversies of the day, but whose advice still counted and who continued to be invited to public ceremonies. (The person coming closest to their transcendent status in recent German politics, to my knowledge, was our former Federal Chancellor Helmut Schmidt, who evolved from a politician known for his contentiousness to a white-haired oracle of the republic—but he left this world, not in 1799 or 1826, but in 2015, and the dense fog through which he conveyed eternal truths to the nation was not owing to the mists of time, but merely to his chain-smoking.)

This peculiar "presence" of the eighteenth-century founders in American culture struck me as especially prominent in Thomas Jefferson's case. Just before John Adams managed to make the fiftieth anniversary of American independence the occasion of his own apotheosis (like Jefferson, passing away with great precision on July 4, 1826), he is reported to have sighed, "Thomas Jefferson survives." Whether or not that sigh was historical, countless Jefferson admirers and critics appear to have understood it literally, to conclude from the intensity of their reactions of either deeply-felt enthusiasm or profound disgust. When I began to study Jefferson in the late 1990s, I was astonished by the vitriolic as well as strangely heroic language of some of his critics, who treated their subject not only as if he were still around to suffer personally from their negative judgment, but also as if they were taking great personal risks because he was still alive and powerful enough to judge *them*. Meanwhile, I was equally puzzled by a question habitually asked by his admirers: What would Jefferson say or do if he were alive today? What, indeed? As a young student just beginning to learn about the American Revolution, I thought that the question was utterly nonsensical—and the fact that it was asked so predictably by well-educated people in America, absolutely intriguing. What on earth could they be thinking?

What completely won me over to these questions as a topic of research was the observation that Jefferson himself appeared to have thought along similar lines. For instance, he anticipated his bipolar twentieth-century reception—the "defense-attack paradigm," as it is often called in Jefferson studies—when he expressed his fear that there would be a "tribunal of posterity" to morally judge the actions (or lack of them) of his generation, while in his more optimistic moments, he modestly described members of the same generation as an "assembly of demigods." As I would eventually argue in my first book in English, *Thomas Jefferson, Time, and History*, one of the reasons for this seemingly split perspective had to do with a concept of history premised on exemplarity and analogy, which came into crisis in Jefferson's lifetime, but which he tried his best to consolidate, and successfully so in regard to the American founding generation. In Jefferson's intellectual world, the assumption that personal example was able to transcend time and history was crucial. At one end of the spectrum, there was a secularized *exemplum exemplorum*—his obsession with a historical

Jesus, about whom Jefferson only regretted that he had already died at thirty-three (the same age at which he had drafted the Declaration of Independence)—while at the other end of the spectrum, there were the Caesars of this world, perpetually lurking around the next historical corner to usurp political power and destroy the republic.

My experiences with European history had been entirely different. Instead of continuity, similarity, and exemplarity, I had grown up to expect rupture, fragmentation, and strangeness from history. In the Germany of my childhood, of course, there were compelling reasons to emphasize that the past was, indeed, a "foreign country." I was born thirty years after the end of World War II, at a time when the greatest imaginable historical catastrophe was still very much present in the conversations of the older people. Given Germany's role in bringing about this catastrophe, however, in everyday-life this presence of the past mainly served the paradoxical function of emphasizing its absence. Unlike in America, the past was supposed to be, most of all, one thing: thank goodness, over. This psychological need for the categorical difference and past-ness of the past in my native culture (in contrast to William Faulkner's oft-quoted insistence that the past is neither dead nor past) was not only the result of the great political upheavals and enormous moral barbarities of the first half of the twentieth century. Somewhat uncannily, a "romantic" emphasis on the heterogeneity, contingency, irrationality, and unpredictability of history had been around much longer and significantly shaped the understanding of other historical periods as well.

Thus, my European eighteenth century was at once closer and much farther away than the American eighteenth century I began to study at the university. On one level, it seemed not all that long ago: Many of my family members (unlike myself) had still learned ancient Greek in high school, which resulted in a worldview in which even the ancient Romans could be viewed as rather annoyingly modern and superficial people. Moreover, the eighteenth century was a concrete part of life because of the buildings from that time scattered through the land- and cityscapes, because of the random piece of dysfunctional period furniture in the living room, and not least because of the practice of classical music, with which I spent a considerable and arguably exaggerated amount of time at the cello and piano as a teenager (and whose continuity with the past was condensed in my piano teacher's memorable observation that if Mozart hadn't died young and Beethoven turned deaf long ago, they would immediately do so now if they had to listen to me play). However, in many other ways, the European eighteenth century was much further removed from the present than the Jeffersonian America I encountered at the university. While my piano teacher might ironically ponder the reactions by classical composers to my apocalyptic rendering of a D-major rondo, it would be very difficult on this side of the water to find anyone seriously interested in the question of what eighteenth-century figures such as Frederick of Prussia or Catherine of Russia would do or say if they were suddenly brought back to life today. And although these monarchs sent so many of their hapless subjects to die cruel deaths in the European battlefields, very few of the victims' descendants today would ever dream of writing or reading such vitriolic criticism as has become prominent in Jefferson's case to bring that fact back to public attention. With rare exceptions such as Barbara Stollberg-Rilinger's much-acclaimed recent biography of Maria Theresa, books about European political or literary figures from the period simply cannot expect to garner any amount of wide-spread public interest or emotional investment comparable to that received by studies of the American eighteenth century.

This cultural difference has made me ask how far the current course of accelerated globalization is transforming our approaches to the Enlightenment and the eighteenth century. It seems clear that the "presence" of Jefferson and the founding generation is coming under pressure from various directions. While Jefferson and many of his peers have been under severe criticism in academic circles at least from the 1960s onwards, they may now be running the danger of losing their public status in civil religion as well, to conclude, for example, from their striking absence in the current American president's inaugural address. Meanwhile, in recent Americanist scholarship as well as in contemporary literary explorations of the past, the moral center of American history appears to gravitate away from the Enlightenment beginnings of the nation to problems associated with American slavery and its aftermath. Indeed, claims about the *longue durée* of slavery might become the true inheritors of the curious phenomenon of the founders' "presence" in American culture, while also incorporating aspects of the contingency and fragmentation more characteristic of European approaches to the past. However, it is possible that Jefferson scholarship may not suffer all that much from this shift in perspective. More than other slaveholding presidents such as George Washington, James Madison, or James Monroe, Jefferson has always been at the center of American cultural discourses about slavery as well.

2. What are your thoughts on Jefferson and slavery and particularly on the matter of Sally Hemings?

I took Sally Hemings to be a central figure of American history long before I knew anything about Thomas Jefferson. The reason was that as a young girl—it must have been before we moved to Berlin when I was fourteen—I read all the historical novels that I could find in the public library of the small town in Eastern Westphalia where I grew up. Among them happened to be a German translation of Barbara Chase-Riboud's *Sally Hemings* (*Die Frau aus Virginia*) [The Woman from Virginia]. From this book, I retained a vivid impression of Hemings, but must confess that somehow, I seem to have barely noticed Jefferson. (Truth be told, with early American history forming no part whatsoever of my curriculum at school, it is also likely that it took me the first hundred pages or so to realize that the period I was reading about was *not* the one I knew from watching *North and South* with my grandmother.) However, my conviction that Jefferson's relationship to slavery cannot be understood without Sally Hemings does not simply result from the early bias of my blissfully uninformed reading of Chase-Riboud's work. When I began to learn more about Jefferson's life and writings and followed the "American controversy" about the Jefferson-Hemings relationship, I found the excited style of the controversy itself almost more interesting than the details of its subject matter. As a historian or biographer dealing with an historical person's intimate life, one is ultimately left with probabilities. And what are the odds that a countryside widower who was too much in debt for it to be wise to marry again and have more legal heirs, but who had hundreds of people including attractive women such as Hemings under his unquestioned control, would resist the opportunity of a sexual relationship for several decades, especially in a social environment in which the sexual exploitation of the enslaved was wide-spread and usually went unsanctioned? The fact that so many people clung so tenaciously to the notion of Jefferson's uniquely blameless private life, even though Hemings had been a publicly discussed figure since James Callender's campaign during Jefferson's presidency, seemed to me the historical phenomenon more in need of explanation than the exact nature of the relationship itself. That so much energy should be invested in denying the more likely alternative, even by professional historians trained to rationally weigh different degrees of probability, testifies to the deep cultural significance of the idea of a Hemings-Jefferson family at the origins of the American nation.

To be sure, assessing the concrete personal dimension of this family remains a great challenge. In particular, I have found the problem that someone who was proud of his concept of generational sovereignty would keep several of his own children enslaved during his lifetime—the American equivalent, as it were, to the author of *Émile* placing his own children in an orphanage—even more difficult to grasp than the question of how precisely to imagine the relationship between the parents. Path-breaking work on the psychological and cultural plausibility of this half-free, half-enslaved family has been done by Annette Gordon-Reed in *The Hemingses of Monticello* and her recent collaboration with Peter Onuf, *"Most Blessed of the Patriarchs": Thomas Jefferson and the Empire of the Imagination*. Also as a result of works such as these, today studying Jefferson at Monticello is no longer possible without acknowledging the importance of Sally Hemings.

What is more, Sally Hemings plays a crucial role on a symbolic level. Part of a development long prefigured and paralleled by African American literary history, from the first preserved African

American novel in the nineteenth century, William Wells Brown's *Clotel* presenting a fictionalized Hemings and her descendants to, most recently, Ta-Nehisi Coates's *The Water Dancer*, the slave plantation on the five-cent coin has become a cultural icon that has come to stand less for Jefferson's architectural talents or his cultivated style of living than for his life-long dependence on slavery and his enslaved family with Sally Hemings. It was not only the combination of Jefferson's draftsmanship of the Declaration of Independence and his slave ownership in general, but in particular the longstanding public discussion of Sally Hemings that has made him, more than any of his slaveholding peers, an "American synecdoche," that is, the most prominent personification of the dialectics of the American Enlightenment or the embodiment of the "American dilemma" of the persistence of slavery in a modern democracy. Ironically, it may be Sally Hemings as well who will make Jefferson survive, yet again. At the present moment at least, it seems as if only Hemings and all that she stands for has the cultural capital necessary for easing his transition in the cultural shift, as sketched above, from the presence of the founding to the presence of slavery at the moral center of American history.

Apart from its material, personal, social, symbolic and literary aspects, of course, slavery was also a complex conceptual problem in Jefferson's political philosophy. There has been much brilliant scholarship on this issue in the past decades, and there is always more, so it seems to me (at least, I hope) that my thought in the field has been constantly evolving over the past twenty years. I began at a point where most people probably begin to approach the topic. The occasion was a seminar on the Early Republic in my studies for the master's degree at the John F. Kennedy Institute for North American Studies at Freie Universität Berlin, where I happened to give an oral presentation on Jefferson and slavery. As my perspective had already been somewhat Americanized by then, not least due to a year spent at an American college, I was very upset with Jefferson and gave what must have been rather an inflammatory talk on the scandalous slaveholder who was also the author of the Declaration of Independence. Many of my sentences started with "How could he" and "Why did he not," I bitterly complained about his racism and sexism, made great use of the classical contrast between his words and actions, and it is quite likely that I repeatedly used the word *hypocritical*.

The talk went well enough insofar as the audience seemed pleased, and I received a good grade for my performance. However, I succinctly remember that I went home quite dissatisfied with myself, as I couldn't get rid of the impression that I may have accurately described my own sentiments or those of the majority of the people in the room, but hadn't come up with any historical explanation for Jefferson's attitude to slavery. Hypocrisy, really? How could a single personal or even supposedly collective character trait account for a historical problem of such enormous proportions? And what precisely did I mean by Jefferson's racism? Colloquially, the term is used for such vastly different phenomena—ranging from, for example, the intended or supposed condescension involved in asking someone where he or she is "really" from to the systematic slaughter of millions of people within a mere dozen years of twentieth-century history—that without further information it is almost meaningless and, therefore, always needs to be carefully specified in scholarly discourse. For instance, did Jefferson's racism evolve during his lifetime, was he conscious of it as a problem or not, whom did it involve, how exactly did it manifest itself in his writings, personal interactions, economy, politics, architecture, or psychology, to what or whom should it be compared, how precisely could it be aligned with a universalist Enlightenment philosophy, was it a feeling or opinion, belief or conviction, tactics or strategy, was it a cause, a correlation, or an outcome of his attitude to slavery, hypocritical or not, when and where: slavery on his own plantations, slavery in the colonies, in the state of Virginia, in the United States, in the Atlantic world, or in the abstract?

3. In what ways do you think that Jefferson is relevant today?

These and many other questions about Jefferson's relationship to slavery only seemed to produce more questions. The more time I spent trying to answer them, the more I became convinced that studying Jefferson's relationship to slavery offered a unique window into core problems of modern American culture and perhaps of transatlantic modernity in general. Before I knew it, I was writing my Magister thesis on the topic (which, in the old German system, was a lengthy affair, so it became the little book, *Jefferson und die Sklaverei: Verrat an der Aufklärung?* [Jefferson and Slavery: Betrayal of the Enlightenment?]) and afterwards continued for the PhD to ask about the relationship between slavery and Jefferson's view of American history. The beauty of studying Jefferson at the Kennedy Institute at that point was that I had the large early American section of the best Americanist library in the country all to myself since no one else thought of studying such a temporally remote topic, and I could almost determine by the level of dust that had accumulated on a book whether or not I had already read it. (Nevertheless, today I would strongly recommend using *Founders Online* for quotable sources as well.) In this environment, I was always a little on the defense for being crazy enough to study this "dead white male" *par excellence*, even in his worst moral dilemma. From what I have said above, however, it has probably already become apparent that I am of the unbiased opinion that Jefferson, or rather the study of Jefferson's life and thought, is hugely relevant today.

To be sure, *relevance* itself has become a tricky issue in our changing academic landscape. Confronted with the social "relevance" section in writing and reading grant applications, project proposals, and the like, I am trying to hold a torch for the not immediately relevant topics, especially since one can or should, by definition, never know the outcome of a research project before it is finished. Yet, it is of course important to reflect on the reasons why one is drawn to a topic at a particular moment, and which problems one is hoping that this topic may help illuminate.

In a nutshell, as I see it, the study of Jefferson is relevant in today's world in two major respects. First, Jefferson and his generation contributed significantly to the shaping of an era whose late phases we may be witnessing today and about which, it now often seems, we may have been taking too many things for granted.

While their writings certainly cannot be expected to offer immediate answers to contemporary political questions, they already discussed problems whose long-term effects still concern us today. Among them, Jefferson's involvement with slavery and the evolution of modern American racism are only the most obvious. He also reflected intensely on other problems that appear to be still, or again, unresolved in our present historical moment: questions of how to ensure political participation in a large democracy, how to regulate relations between the states and with the rest of the world, how to deal with the natural environment, how to understand the rights and duties of different generations, how to imagine the relationship between truth and politics, how to organize public education, how to overcome political polarization, and so on.

Secondly, and related to the goal of better understanding the Enlightenment origins of modern democracies with all their problems, Jefferson is relevant today precisely in his identity as a "dead white male" who played a prominent part in a postcolonial conflict that ushered in new forms of colonialism. Also as a result of the ongoing specialization of the humanities over the past half-century, however, postcolonial scholars in particular have been rather disinclined to study Jefferson in any detail, as if afraid they might otherwise "give him a platform" that would enable his arguments to continue exerting what they tend to see as their destructive influence. However, as Frank Cogliano has recently pointed out, the more closely Jefferson has been studied, the more scholars have found to criticize in him. Especially from the perspective of scholars in search of an alternative to the worldviews originating in the Jeffersonian Enlightenment, it might, therefore, be useful to become closely acquainted with Jefferson's thought, lest they be running the danger either of barking up the wrong trees, or of inadvertently repeating arguments he and other Enlightenment figures developed long ago.

4. What traits do you most admire about Jefferson *as a writer*?

Jefferson is still relevant today also because he is such good reading. I have not always entertained this view, however. In his own time,

Jefferson was known for his "masterly pen." It was the reputation of his literary mastery that led to his draftsmanship—or, as he later wished it to be remembered on his tombstone—authorship of the Declaration of Independence. Although indisputably the Declaration was not only a great political and philosophical accomplishment, but also a great literary one, I used to find it quite difficult to apply this assessment to his other writings. Jefferson's imagery can be rather off-putting, for instance, his predilection for sanguinary metaphors such as the "tree of liberty" that had to be "refreshed from time to time with the blood of patriots & tyrants" as its "natural manure," or the Virgilian "rivers of blood" that he thought had yet to flow before European countries would become republican. Moreover, Jefferson's syntax initially struck me as excessively elaborate on some occasions, such as in the *Summary View of the Rights of British America*, but needlessly austere and abrupt on others, such as in his *Autobiography*. And although I thought that Jefferson's personal correspondence fulfilled the function of making him seem approachable and personable at least better than did his autobiographical writings (the *Autobiography* and the *Anas*), it still came across as rather stilted and detached in tone, even, for example, in his supposedly light-hearted and entertaining love letters to Maria Cosway. In general, I used to think of Jefferson as too one-dimensionally serious to be a really good writer—at least until the moment when someone asked me whether, as a German, I was not secretly attracted to his mile long sentences and his dramatic lack of a sense of humor. Good point. (To be fair, there are rumors that Jefferson's sense of humor actually existed. Even if true, of course, as a German I probably wouldn't notice. So I can only testify to Jefferson's truly Germanic temperament in this regard. No doubt this is what comes from spending too much time, as Jefferson did, with King Alfred and the Anglo-Saxons!)

The famous question of Jefferson's sense of humor aside, my critical attitude to the above points has changed over the years. In part this may result from gradually becoming better at historicizing his language, in part from having too often made the depressing experience of giving papers in which my quotations from Jefferson's language, with its sophisticated sense of rhythm and flow, rolled off the tongue much more easily than did my own sentences. According to Henry Adams's thin-lipped appreciation of Jefferson's writings, they "often betrayed subtile feeling for artistic form"—possibly too subtile, Adams seemed to be saying. However, while the question of form continues to be debated, especially concerning *Notes on the State of Virginia*, I have come to regard it as one of Jefferson's most interesting literary qualities that he was beginning to experiment with different artistic forms and styles. Ultimately, it may be this combination of literary and political experimentalism that is making me go back to Jefferson again and again: in his writings as in his architecture, and within a worldview in which originality was just beginning to matter, he was always in search of finding the best possible expression of the American experiment.

RESOURCES

1743	Thomas Jefferson is born on April 13, 1743, at Shadwell (an estate owned by his father, Peter Jefferson), in what is now Albemarle County, Virginia. He is tutored on the estate.
1752	He begins studying at a local school headed by the Reverend William Douglas.
1760–1762	He attends the College of William and Mary, where he is especially influenced by Professor William Small.
1762–67	He studies law under George Wythe, a prominent and much-respected Virginia lawyer.
1767	He begins practicing law and soon establishes a reputation as a successful lawyer.
1769	Fulfilling a youthful dream, he oversees the start of construction of Monticello, an imposing neo-classical home set atop a hill outside of Charlottesville, Virginia. He continues adding to and altering the home throughout the rest of his life.
1769–76	He serves in the Virginia House of Burgesses.
1772	Jefferson weds Martha Wayles Skelton, with whom he is very happily married until her death a decade later, during which time she gives birth to six children, not all of whom survive.
1775–76	Jefferson, having long objected to perceived mistreatment by Britain of its American colonies, attends the Continental Congress in Philadelphia, where he is given the task of preparing the Declaration

of Independence. War now begins between the colonies and Great Britain.

1776–79	Jefferson serves in the Virginia House of Delegates, where he champions the separation of church and state.
1779–81	Jefferson serves two terms as Governor of Virginia and in 1781 narrowly escapes being captured by the British.
1782	Jefferson's beloved wife Martha dies, but not before asking Jefferson to promise that he will never remarry—a promise he makes. Jefferson is devasted by his wife's death.
1783-84	He serves in the colonial congress.
1785	He becomes the American Minister to France. It is around this time that he apparently becomes sexually involved with Sally Hemings, one of his slaves who is also the half-sister of his dead wife, Martha.
1789	After Jefferson returns from France, President George Washington appoints him as the new nation's first Secretary of State, a position he holds until the end of 1793.
1796	Jefferson, a Republican in favor of a limited Federal government, runs for President against John Adams, a Federalist who favors greater power for the national government. When Adams wins, Jefferson automatically becomes Vice President.
1800	Jefferson is very narrowly elected the third President of the United States.

1803	He authorizes the Louisiana Purchase, in which the United States buys from France a huge territory stretching all the way from the Mississippi River to the Pacific Ocean.
1804	Jefferson sends Meriwether Lewis and William Clark to explore and map the new territories and report their findings. He is reelected to a second term as President.
1809	Jefferson retires from public office and returns to Monticello.
1819	He establishes the University of Virginia, an effort he considers one of his major achievements.
1826	Jefferson dies at Monticello on July 4, 1826, exactly fifty years after the signing of the Declaration of Independence and on precisely the same day as the death of his old friend and sometimes-rival John Adams.

Works by Thomas Jefferson_____

Jefferson wrote so very much during his lifetime that full editions of his writings can run to scores of volumes. The selections below are derived from the excellent edition of the *Writings* of Jefferson prepared by Merrill D. Peterson and published in one volume in 1984 by the Library of America. Even the works listed below do not include Peterson's generous selection of Jefferson's most important letters.

Major Works

A Summary View of the Rights of British America (written in 1774)

Declaration of Independence (1776)

Notes on the State of Virginia (published 1785)

Autobiography (begun in 1821; unpublished in Jefferson's lifetime)

Public Papers

Resolutions of Congress on Lord North's Conciliatory Proposal (1775)

Draft Constitution for Virginia (1776)

Revisal of the Laws: Drafts of Legislation

> *A Bill for Establishing Religious Freedom* (1777, 1779)
>
> *A Bill for Proportioning Crimes and Punishments* (1778, 1779)
>
> *A Bill for the More General Diffusion of Knowledge* (1778)
>
> *A Bill Declaring Who Shall Be Deemed Citizens of this Commonwealth* (1779)

Report on Government for Western Territory (1784)

Observations on the Whale-Fishery (1788)

Plan for Establishing Uniformity in the Coinage, Weights, and Measures (1790)

Opinion on the Constitutionality of a National Bank (1791)

Opinion on the French Treaties (1793)

Report on the Privileges and Restrictions on the Commerce of the United States in Foreign Countries (1793)

Draft of the Kentucky Resolutions (1798)

Report of the Commissioners for the University of Virginia (1818)

Memorial on the Book Duty (1821)

From the Minutes of the Board of Visitors, University of Virginia (1822-1825)

Draft Declaration and Protest of the Commonwealth of Virginia, on the Principles of the Constitution of the United States of America, and on the Violations of them (1825)

Addresses, Messages, and Replies

Response to the Citizens of Albemarle (February 12, 1790)

First Inaugural Address as President (March 4, 1801)

To Elias Shipman and Others, A Committee of the Merchants of New Haven (July 12, 1801)

First Annual Message as President (December 8, 1801)

To Messrs. Nehemiah Dodge and Others, A Committee of the Danbury Baptist Association, in the State of Connecticut (January 1, 1802)

Second Annual Message (December 15, 1802)

Special Message (January 28, 1802)

Special Message (February 24, 1803)

Third Annual Message (October 17, 1803)

Special Message (October 21, 1803)

Special Message (November 4, 1803)

Special Message (November 25, 1803)

Special Message (December 5, 1803)

Special Message (January 16, 1804)

Special Message (March 20, 1804)

Fourth Annual Message (November 8, 1804)

Second Inaugural Address (March 4, 1805)

Fifth Annual Message (December 3, 1805)

Special Message (January 13, 1806)

Special Message (January 17, 1806)

Special Message (February 3, 1806)

Special Message (February 19, 1806)

Special Message (March 20, 1806)

Special Message (April 14, 1806)

Sixth Annual Message (December 2, 1806)

Special Message (December 3, 1806)

Special Message (January 22, 1807)

Special Message (January 28, 1807)

Special Message (January 31, 1807)

Special Message (February 10, 1807)

Seventh Annual Message (October 27, 1807)

Special Message (November 23, 1807)

Special Message (December 18, 1807)

Special Message (January 20, 1808)

Special Message (January 30, 1808)

Special Message (January 30, 1808)

Special Message (February 2, 1808)

Special Message (February 4, 1808)

Special Message (February 9, 1808)

Special Message (February 15, 1808)

Special Message (February 19, 1808)

Special Message (February 25, 1808)

Special Message (March 7, 1808)

Special Message (March 17, 1808)

Special Message (March 18, 1808)

Special Message (March 22, 1808)

Eighth Annual Message (November 8, 1808)

Special Message (December 30, 1808)

Special Message (January 6, 1809)

To the Inhabitants of Albemarle County, in Virginia (April 3, 1809)

Indian Addresses

To Brother John Baptist de Coigne (June 1781)

To Brother Handsome Lake (November 3, 1802)

To the Brothers of the Choctaw Nation (December 17, 1803)

To the Chiefs of the Cherokee Nation (January 10, 1806)

To the Wolf and People of the Mandan Nation (December 30, 1806)

Miscellany

Reply to the Representations of Affairs in America by British Newspapers (1784)

Answers and Observations for Démeunier's Article on the United States in the Encyclopédie Methodique (1786)

    1. *From Answers To Démeunier's First Queries* (January 24, 1786)

        The Confederation

        Broils among the States

    2. From *Observations on Démeunier's Manuscript, June 22, 1786*

        Indented [sic] *Servants*

        Crimes and Punishments

        The Society of the Cincinnati

        Populating the Continent

    3. *To Jean Nicolas Démeunier, June 26, 1786*

Thoughts on English Prosody (1786)

Travel Journals

    A Tour to Some of the Gardens of England (1786)

    Memorandums on a Tour from Paris to Amsterdam, Strasburg, and back to Paris (1788)

    Travelling Notes for Mr. Rutledge and Mr. Shippen (1788)

The Anas (1791–1806)

Notes on Professor Ebeling's Letter of July 30, 1795

A Memorandum (Services to My Country) [c. 1800]

A Memorandum (Rules of Etiquette; c. November, 1803)

Bibliography

Appleby, Joyce. *Without Resolution: The Jeffersonian Tension in American Nationalism: An Inaugural Lecture Delivered before the University of Oxford on 25 April 1991*. Oxford U P, 1991.

Berman, Eleanor D. *Thomas Jefferson among the Arts: An Essay in Early American Esthetics*. Philosophical Library, 1947.

Bowman, Rex, and Carlos Santos. *Rot, Riot, and Rebellion: Mr. Jefferson's Struggle to Save the University that Changed America*. U of Virginia P, 2013.

Browne, Stephen H. *Jefferson's Call for Nationhood: The First Inaugural Address*. Texas A&M U P, 2003.

Burstein, Andrew. *Democracy's Muse: How Thomas Jefferson Became an FDR Liberal, A Reagan Republican, and a Tea Party Fanatic, All the While Being Dead*. U of Virginia P, 2015.

_____. *Jefferson's Secrets: Death and Desire at Monticello*. Basic Books, 2005.

Cogliano, Francis D. *Thomas Jefferson: Reputation and Legacy*. U of Virginia P, 2006.

DeMille, Oliver Van. *A Thomas Jefferson Education: Teaching a Generation of Leaders for the Twenty-first Century*. George Wythe College P, 2000.

Dowling, William C. *Literary Federalism in the Age of Jefferson: Joseph Dennie and the Portfolio, 1801–1812*. U of South Carolina P, 1999.

Fliegelman, Jay. *Declaring Independence: Jefferson, Natural Language and the Culture of Performance*. Stanford U P, 1993.

Golden, James L., and Alan L. Golden. *Thomas Jefferson and the Rhetoric of Virtue*. Rowman & Littlefield, 2002.

Hayes, Kevin J. *The Road to Monticello: The Life and Mind of Thomas Jefferson*. Oxford U P, 2008.

Hayes, Kevin J., editor. *Jefferson in His Own Time: A Biographical Chronicle of His Life, Drawn from Recollections, Interviews, and Memoirs by Family, Friends, and Associates*. U of Iowa P, 2012.

Heller, Caroline. *Appropriating Thomas Jefferson, 1929–1945: We Are All Jeffersonians Now*. Peter Lang, 2019.

Howard, Donald E. *The Role of Reading in Nine Famous Lives*. McFarland & Co., 2005.

Jackson, Donald. *Thomas Jefferson and the Stony Mountains: Exploring the West from Monticello*. U of Oklahoma P, 1993.

Jefferson, Thomas. *Jefferson's Literary Commonplace Book*, edited by Douglas L. Wilson. Princeton U P, 1989.

_____. *The Literary Bible of Thomas Jefferson: His Commonplace Book of Philosophers and Poets*. Greenwood P, 1969.

_____. *Thomas Jefferson's Scrapbooks: Poems of Nation, Family, and Romantic Love Collected by America's Third President*, edited and introduced by Jonathan Gross. Steerforth P, 2006.

Jenkinson, Clay. *Becoming Jefferson's People: Re-inventing the American Republic in the Twenty-first Century*. Marmarth P, 2004.

Jones, Howard Mumford. *Jeffersonianism and the American Novel*. Teachers College P, 1966.

Kelsall, M. M. *Jefferson and the Iconography of Romanticism: Folk, Land, Culture, and the Romantic Nation*. St. Martin's P, 1999.

Lemire, Elise Virginia. *"Miscegenation": Making Race in America*. U of Pennsylvania P, 2002.

Marsh, Alec. *Money and Modernity: Pound, Williams, and the Spirit of Jefferson*. U of Alabama P, 1998.

Maybury, Rick. *Evaluating Books: What Would Thomas Jefferson Think about This?: Guidelines for Selecting Books Consistent with the Principles of America's Founders*. Bluestocking P, 2004.

McDonald, Robert M. S. *Confounding Father: Thomas Jefferson's Image in His Own Time*. U of Virginia P, 2016.

_____, editor. *Light and Liberty: Thomas Jefferson and the Power of Knowledge*. U of Virginia P, 2012.

Miller, Charles A. *Ship of State: The Nautical Metaphors of Thomas Jefferson: with Numerous Examples by Other Writers from Classical Antiquity to the Present*. U P of America, 2003.

Moses, Wilson Jeremiah. *Thomas Jefferson, A Modern Prometheus*. Cambridge U P, 2019.

Onuf, Peter S. *The Mind of Thomas Jefferson*. U of Virginia P, 2007.

Pederson, William D., and Frank J. Williams, editors. *A Great Presidential Triumvirate at Home and Abroad: Washington, Jefferson, and Lincoln*. Nova Science Publishers, 2006.

Peterson, Merrill D. *The Jefferson Image in the American Mind*. 1960; 1985. U P of Virginia, 1998.

Rizer, Arthur L. *Jefferson's Pen: The Art of Persuasion*. American Bar Association, 2016.

Sanford, Charles B. *Thomas Jefferson and His Library: A Study of His Literary Interests and of the Religious Attitudes Revealed by Relevant Titles in His Library*. Archon Books, 1977.

Three Presidents and Their Books: The Reading of Jefferson [by] Arthur Bestor; Lincoln [by] David C. Mearns; Franklin D. Roosevelt [by] Jonathan Daniels. U of Illinois P, 1955.

Wagoner, Jennings L. *Jefferson and Education*. U of North Carolina P, 2004.

About the Editor

Robert C. Evans is I. B. Young Professor of English at Auburn University at Montgomery, where he has taught since 1982. In 1984, he received his PhD from Princeton University, where he held Weaver and Whiting fellowships as well as a University fellowship. In later years his research was supported by fellowships from the Newberry Library (twice), the American Council of Learned Societies, the Folger Shakespeare Library (twice), the Mellon Foundation, the Huntington Library, the National Endowment for the Humanities, the American Philosophical Society, and the UCLA Center for Medieval and Renaissance Studies.

In 1982, he was awarded the G. E. Bentley Prize and in 1989 was selected Professor of the Year for Alabama by the Council for the Advancement and Support of Education. At AUM he has received the Faculty Excellence Award and has been named Distinguished Research Professor, Distinguished Teaching Professor, and University Alumni Professor. Most recently he was named Professor of the Year by the South Atlantic Association of Departments of English. In 2020 he won the Eugene Current-Garcia Distinguished Scholar Award presented annually by the Alabama College English Teachers Association.

He is a contributing editor to the John Donne *Variorum Edition*, senior editor of *The Ben Jonson Journal*, and is the author or editor of over fifty books (on such topics as Ben Jonson, Martha Moulsworth, Kate Chopin, John Donne, Frank O'Connor, Brian Friel, Ambrose Bierce, Amy Tan, early modern women writers, pluralist literary theory, literary criticism, twentieth-century American writers, American novelists, Shakespeare, and seventeenth-century English literature). He is also the author of roughly four hundred published or forthcoming essays or notes (in print and online) on a variety of topics, especially dealing with Renaissance literature, critical theory, women writers, short fiction, and literature of the nineteenth and twentieth centuries.

Contributors

John B. Boles is the William P. Hobby Professor of History at Rice University and former editor (1983–2013) of the *Journal of Southern History*. He has held the Robert Foster Cherry Visiting Professorship for Distinguished Teaching at Baylor University (2001) and the Fulbright Distinguished Professorship (2005) and the Leibnitz Visiting Professorship (2009) at the University of Leipzig. He has written numerous books and articles, including *The Great Revival, 1787–1805: The Origins of the Southern Evangelical Mind* (1972); *Black Southerners, 1619–1869* (1983); *The South Through Time: A History of an American Region* (3 editions, 1995, 1999, 2004); *University Builder: Edgar Odell Lovett and the Founding of the Rice Institute* (2 editions, 2007, 2012); and, most recently, *Jefferson: Architect of American Liberty* (2017). He had the privilege of directing the dissertations of over sixty doctoral students. In 2017, he served as president of the Southern Historical Association.

Steven D. Ealy is a senior fellow at Liberty Fund, an education foundation. He received a BA from Furman University and a PhD in political science from the University of Georgia. Before joining Liberty Fund, he taught political science at Armstrong State University in Savannah, Georgia. He has written on Robert Penn Warren, Ralph Ellison, Edmund Burke, Eric Voegelin, The *Federalist Papers* and Constitutional interpretation, the history and philosophy of American philanthropy, and reading the *Qur'an*.

Kyla Free is an independent scholar with a strong interest in English and American literature. She taught for two years at the Hubei Institute of Education in Wuhan, China. More recently, she has taught for thirteen years at Brewbaker Technology Magnet High School in Montgomery, Alabama, where she presently teaches AP Literature and Composition and English 12.

Kevin J. Hayes, Emeritus Professor of English at the University of Central Oklahoma, now lives and writes in Toledo, Ohio. He is the author of several books concerning early American intellectual life, including *The Library of William Byrd of Westover* (1997), the winner of the Virginia

Library History Award; *The Road to Monticello: The Life and Mind of Thomas Jefferson* (2008); *The Mind of a Patriot: Patrick Henry and the World of Ideas* (2008); and *George Washington, A Life in Books* (2017), the winner of the George Washington Book Prize. He is currently completing a new work, *Shakespeare and the Making of America.*

John A. Ragosta, a historian at the Robert H. Smith International Center for Jefferson Studies at Monticello, has taught law and history at the University of Virginia, George Washington University, and Oberlin, Hamilton, and Randolph Colleges. A fellow at Virginia Humanities, Dr. Ragosta has also held fellowships through the Jack Miller Center at Colonial Williamsburg and Monticello. He is author of *Religious Freedom: Jefferson's Legacy, America's Creed* (University of Virginia Press, 2013) and *Wellspring of Liberty: How Virginia's Religious Dissenters Helped to Win the American Revolution & Secured Religious Liberty* (Oxford, 2010). His most recent book, *Patrick Henry: Proclaiming a Revolution*, was released by Routledge (2016). He is also co-editor of *The Founding of Thomas Jefferson's University* (UVA, 2019). Before returning to academia, Ragosta practiced international trade law. An award-winning author, Ragosta holds a PhD (early American history) and a JD from the University of Virginia.

Daniel R. Roeber is a historian of American religious and intellectual history specializing in the intersection of religion and politics. Previous work includes entries in the *Encyclopedia of Christianity in the United States* and the forthcoming *American Religious History: Belief and Society through Time*, which includes a long-form essay on political life in colonial America and the early republic. He is currently revising his first monograph, tentatively entitled *Establishing Disestablishment: Federal Support of Religion in the Early Republic.*

Brandon Schneeberger is a Visiting Assistant Professor at Oklahoma State University. He has published articles on Thomas Jefferson and Samuel Johnson and is the author of the Ben Jonson page for *Oxford Bibliographies*. He serves as Managing Editor for the *Ben Jonson Journal.*

Hannah Spahn is currently principal investigator (German Research Foundation) of the project "Character and Cosmopolitanism in Nineteenth-Century African American Literature" at the Department of English and American Studies, University of Potsdam, Germany. Before joining the faculty at Potsdam, she has been Wissenschaftliche Mitarbeiterin, Department of Culture, at the John F. Kennedy Institute for North American Studies, Freie Universität Berlin, Postdoctoral Fellow at the Institute for Advanced Studies, University of Edinburgh, and Gilder Lehrman Junior Research Fellow at the International Center for Jefferson Studies, Charlottesville, Virginia. She is author of *Thomas Jefferson, Time, and History* (University of Virginia Press, 2011) and *Thomas Jefferson: Verrat an der Aufklärung?* (Berliner Beiträge zur Amerikanistik, 2002) and co-editor, with Peter Nicolaisen, of *Cosmopolitanism and Nationhood in the Age of Jefferson* (Universitätsverlag Winter, 2013).

Suzanne Strength is an independent scholar with a strong interest in the relationships between literature and film.

Nicolas Tredell has published 20 books and around 400 essays and articles on authors ranging from Shakespeare to Zadie Smith and on key literary and cultural topics. Recent books include *Anatomy of Amis* (Paupers' Press, 2017), a comprehensive account of Martin Amis's work; *Conversations with Critics* (Verbivoracious Press, 2015), a collection of his interviews with leading writers of fiction, poetry and criticism; *Novels to Some Purpose: The Fiction of Colin Wilson* (Paupers' Press, 2015); *Shakespeare: The Tragedies* (Red Globe Press, 2012); *C. P. Snow: The Dynamics of Hope* (Palgrave, 2012); and *A Midsummer Night's Dream: A Reader's Guide to Essential Criticism* (Palgrave, 2010). He is Consultant Editor of Red Globe's Essential Criticism series, which now numbers 88 volumes, eight of which he has produced. His latest published essay, "Declaration and Dream: American Literature 1776–2018", features in *The Literature Reader: Key Thinkers on Key Topics* (English and Media Centre, 2019).

Index

abolition xlv, 79, 180, 183

Act of Establishing Religious Freedom 4

Adam & Eve xxii

Adams, Henry xxii, 232

Adams, John xvi, xxii, xxxix, xlii, xlvi, xlvii, 9, 22, 26, 29, 34, 89, 140, 148, 166, 171, 179, 181, 185, 197, 221

Adams, John Quincy 8, 12, 14, 17

Adams, Samuel xxi

"Address to the Delaware Nation" 140

Adventures of Capt. Neville Frowde 146

Aeneid 56

aesthetic 90, 93, 94, 95, 96, 97

African Americans xiii, xxxi, xxxii, xxxviii, 33, 41, 42, 92, 202, 204

Age, The 197

Akenside, Mark 27

Alien & Sedition Acts of 1798 xxvii

Allbery, Debra 171

allegiance 6

alliteration 38, 56, 65, 105, 106, 112, 114, 171, 176, 177, 179, 181

All the King's Men 166, 168

allusion 93, 122, 174

ambassador xviii, xxi, xxii, 21, 103, 175, 181

American culture 89, 221, 225, 229

American Dream, the 39

American Enlightenment 221, 227

American exceptionalism xix

American history xiii, xiv, xvi, 38, 85, 87, 143, 152, 153, 159, 187, 197, 208, 212, 221, 225, 227, 229

American imagination xl

American patriotism 7

American Revolution 31, 51, 79, 87, 99, 119, 221, 222

American West 162

Anacreon 26

anaphora 36, 38, 67, 68, 179

anarchy xxi, xxvi, 128

Anderson, Craig 205

Andrews, Kieran 141

Andrews, Tina xiii, 202, 203, 205, 206, 212

Anglo-Saxon 23, 28, 30, 31

Annals of Congress 9, 17

antithesis 56, 68, 138

apologia 35

Apostle of Liberty xxvi

aristocracy xix, xx, xxx, 165

Aristotle 22, 39, 47, 153

Articles of Confederation 79

Associated Press 205

Atlanta Journal-Constitution, The 208

Austin American-Statesman, The 215

Austin, David 9

Autobiography ix, 34, 43, 46, 47, 88, 100, 101, 231

Bailyn, Bernard xx

barbarism 37, 41

Barbary pirates 21

Monticello xii, xv, xvi, xvii, xviii, xxv, xxxvii, xliv, xlv, xlvi, xlvii, 80, 81, 82, 83, 84, 86, 112, 123, 127, 149, 170, 171, 172, 176, 181, 184, 186, 188, 190, 191, 196, 197, 198, 199, 205, 206, 212, 214, 226
"*Monticello, 1826*" 181
Monticello in Mind: Fifty Contemporary Poems on Jefferson xii, 170, 186
morality xxv, 52, 117
Morgan, Edmund xxix, xxxvi
Morgan, Elizabeth Seydel 176
Morgenthau, Hans 152
Moriarty, Dean 38
Morton, Thomas 136
Mount Rushmore xxxvii, 76
Muske-Dukes, Carol 176
mystery 195, 207, 215

National Association for the Advancement of Colored People (NAACP) 202
national identity viii, ix, 4, 6, 33, 34, 38
nationalism 6
Native American diplomacy 139, 140
Native Americans 33, 41, 42, 43, 158
Native culture 162, 163, 223
Neill, Sam xiii, 202, 205, 209, 212, 216
neologism 140
New Deal 151
New England xx, xxxviii, 6, 7, 16
New English Canaan 136, 149

New Testament 85
New York Post, The 216, 220
New York Times, The 190, 200, 204, 206, 218
Nez Perce War of 1877 158
Niebuhr, Reinhold 151
Nobel Prize 33, 48
Nolte, Nick 203
nomadic 160
Norbeck, Edward 74
Norton Anthology of Poetry 178
Notes on the State of Virginia ix, xli, xlv, 34, 44, 48, 78, 84, 88, 92, 98, 102, 157, 158, 160, 166, 232

O'Brien, Conor Cruise xv, xxiv, xxvi
O'Gorman, Frank 87
Old Testament 41, 98
onomatopoeia 63
Onuf, Peter xvii, xli, 226
opposition x, xxii, xxiii, xxxiii, 30, 80, 165
oppression viii, xxxix, 4, 47, 101
optimism 156
oral tradition 138, 140
Orange County Register 188
orthodox 85
O'Shaughnessy, Andrew xl
Ossian 27, 28, 29
Otway, Thomas 27
Owen, Rob 207

Page, John 135, 148
Paradise Lost 27, 35, 60
Paradise, Sal 38
paradox 67, 78, 155, 164